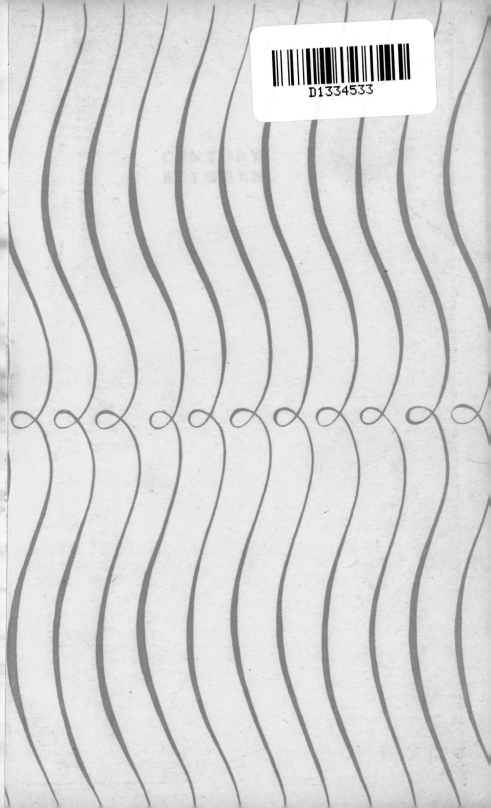

N.M.ROTHSCHILD.ESQ.

EUROPE'S GREATEST BANKER.

As a youth he came to England in a sailing boat and travelled to Manchester where he worked in the office of a cotton broker. He founded
the London House in New Court at the age of twenty-six and shortly
afterwards was able to finance the war against Napoleon.

A CENTURY BETWEEN

by Robert Henrey

WILLIAM HEINEMANN LTD. LONDON AND TORONTO

FIRST PUBLISHED 1937

PRINTED IN GREAT BRITAIN AT THE WINDMILL PRESS
KINGSWOOD, SURREY

TO
MY MOTHER

ILLUSTRATIONS

CHAPTER ONE

ONE summer afternoon in 1834, Nathan Rothschild, founder of the London house, drove from New Court, his office in St. Swithin's Lane, to his home in Piccadilly. He was at this time short but rather well proportioned. He had an almost round face, a slightly Judaically pouting lower lip, laughing eyes, and tufts of curly hair on either side of his otherwise bald head. His home was pointed out to strangers because he was nearly as famous a personage as the Iron Duke. All people knew, or thought they knew, how he had sent carrier pigeons to England with advance information about the result of the Battle of Waterloo.

Nathan was now fifty-six years of age. He was the third of those five brothers who had established kindred Banking Houses in Europe. It was in '98 that he had left Frankfort-on-the-Main to make his first journey to England. His father Mayer Amschel and his mother Gudule (or Frau Rothschild, as she was known in the family) had stood on the threshold of their home in the Jews' street to bid him farewell. He had crossed the Channel in a small sailing craft and travelled by coach to Manchester, where one morning he walked into the office of Mr. Behrens, the cotton broker. Nathan did not then speak a word of English, but he pulled from his pocket a letter from his father and was set to work to learn the language and master the business. He wrote his letters home in the small Hebrew characters of his native tongue. Five years later the young German spoke English fairly fluently though with a strong accent, and he decided to travel to London, where he might set up business of his own and marry a wife. The Banking House soon became the mightiest in the country and Nathan worked closely with his brothers abroad.

Mayer Amschel was now dead but his widow, Frau Rothschild,

I

a tiny, frail lady of eighty-one, still clung to the modest home that her sons had left as young men. The Frankfort business was in the hands of Nathan's eldest brother Amschel Mayer. Solomon was in Vienna, Charles in Naples and James in Paris. All these had been made Austrian noblemen and took the title of 'Baron,' but Nathan preferred to be known quite simply as Mr. N. M. Rothschild.

Nathan's wife was a tall woman with a rather oval face and dark hair that fell in little curls over her forehead. She was authoritative and even masterful, but was held in great affection by her seven children, four of whom were sons.

Lionel, the eldest, was now twenty-six and beginning to relieve his father of some of his work at New Court. Anthony and Nathaniel were also partners. The youngest was called Mayer Amschel (after his grandfather) and was sixteen.

Nathan was fond of telling his sons the story of the man with the bundle of sticks. He meant them to understand that unity may be reached not only by getting together in business but also by marrying within the family.

Already the houses of London and Vienna had been brought together in this way. Charlotte, Nathan's eldest daughter, was married to Anselm Solomon, whose father had founded the Viennese branch.

When Nathan reached home that summer's day he called his second daughter, Hannah Mayer, into the study and told her that he planned to send her on a visit to his brother James in Paris. Hannah was a beautiful girl of nineteen with a fair skin, blue eyes and a small but graceful figure. Not quite so obvious, behind those delicate features, were a good deal of determination and an easily ruffled temper.

Hannah's childhood had shown her to be singularly gifted. She had a sweet singing voice and under expert tuition had learnt to play the harp exquisitely. Mendelssohn, Rossini and Moscheles were frequent visitors to the Rothschild home and Rossini, in particular, had contributed to her musical education. He played

2

HANNAH MAYER DE ROTHSCHILD.

A beautiful girl of nineteen with fair skin and blue eyes. Mendelssohn and Rossini taught her music and her father, of the Battle of Waterloo fame, gave her a harp of pure gold.

over fragments of his operas to the young girl and taught her to memorise them in such a way that she might later play the airs without the script. Nathan was proud of his daughter's accomplishments and when she was five years old had given her a tiny harp made of real gold. Hannah treasured this gift. Once, much carried away by her love of music and beautiful thoughts, she imagined herself, like King David, inspired. Suddenly the dentist was announced and she ran to hide under the table.

During the troubled years of Hannah's childhood, most of Europe's most famous figures had called at the house in Piccadilly. She caught many glimpses of the Duke of Wellington and of the great Frenchman, Talleyrand, Ambassador at the Court of St. James since 1830, whose eccentricity it was to make salt cellars out of lumps of bread at table. Once a week, she had an old Hebrew master who would arrive tired after a long and dusty walk. He spent most of the hour which should have been devoted to teaching, peacefully consuming a large basin of bread and milk.

Hannah was delighted at this chance to visit her uncle in Paris. Baron James had married Betty, the daughter of his brother Solomon of Vienna, in the 'twenties. Baroness James had arrived as a married woman in Paris when she was scarcely out of the school-room, but she quickly used her gifts to start a salon and to do the honours of her house. She had a generous heart and a gift for brilliant conversation and succeeded in bringing together men who were famous in politics and literature.

Paris was then passing through a period of reconstruction. Louis Philippe was king of the French. Republicans and Bonapartists growled in the provinces and sometimes clashed in the streets of the capital, but their efforts were in the smouldering stage not yet ready to burst into flame. Abroad, the campaign in Algeria was about to give France a rich and wealthy colony. At home free education had come at last whilst the bankers had been given every opportunity to expand their houses.

Baroness James had two children—a daughter, Charlotte, aged

nine and a son, Alphonse, two years younger. Though she gave valuable help to her husband by entertaining on an almost royal scale, she watched over her children's education with great care, teaching them the German and Hebrew tongues and rigorously directing their religious upbringing.

There was at that time a close understanding between the French branch of the Rothschilds and the Royal House. Baron James strove to show his gratitude to Louis Philippe for the excellent way in which Jews were then treated in France, while Queen Marie Amélie and Baroness James became almost devoted friends.

Already James had found time to turn to other things than banking. He had purchased an estate in the department of the Seine and Marne, known as Ferrières, where he was busy developing both the château and its grounds.

Hannah was received with much affection. Her youthful beauty, her fair complexion and her waist, so narrow that a man could span it with his two hands, made an instant impression on Ary Scheffer, the great French painter, who was a constant visitor to the Rothschild home. The attention was flattering. Scheffer begged for permission to paint a portrait of her and this was granted.

Meanwhile there were day dresses to be inspected with masses of coloured organdie and folds of muslin; bonnets of *paille de riz* and ostrich feathers, carriage dresses of figured muslin, public promenade dresses and others for evening wear made of black velvet, with fichus and mittens of black lace. Baroness James arranged to give a ball in honour of her visiting niece. The entire household showed signs of excitement for several days in advance.

The dress that Hannah was to wear at the ball was of white satin cut narrow in the skirt with a trimming of small red roses. The sleeves were tight at the elbows, increasing in width until they were gathered in at the wristbands. Over this dress she wore a small pelerine trimmed with lace.

From early childhood Hannah had been taught to dance. There was the shawl dance that was extremely graceful and the gavotte that was considered even more difficult than the minuet. Hannah's dancing master had been in the habit of pulling a kit out of his pocket and scraping upon its strings as he made his pupil do a double *entrechat* in the steps of the gavotte. This consisted of crossing and recrossing her feet twice whilst taking a slight leap in the air.

The ball was graced by the King and the Queen of the French. Hannah, in her white satin dress and with the flowers in her hair, appeared like a figure of Dresden china. Through the salons of the Rothschild home there moved leaders in politics, in the diplomatic world and in literature. The setting was gorgeous. From St. Petersburg, from Vienna and from Naples had come visiting statesmen and bankers.

During the evening Baroness James introduced Hannah to Prince Edmond de Clary, the wealthy young scion of a noble Viennese family whose father had travelled to Paris on an official mission from the Austrian court at the time of the Emperor Napoleon's marriage to Marie-Louise. De Clary was in his twenty-first year and had a high forehead, a firm mouth and the proud look of his Florentine ancestors. He had no sooner set eyes on Nathan's younger daughter than he fell desperately in love with her. They danced together twice and the Prince doubtless spoke softly to his companion under the chandeliers, paying her compliments and questioning her with a thousand artifices. Late in the evening Prince Clary scanned the guests to discover some person who might be a close friend of Nathan's. It was then that his eyes fell on Prince Pal Antal d'Esterhazy, a Hungarian diplomat whose ancestry could be traced to the thirteenth century. Prince Esterhazy, who had been appointed ambassador to London shortly after the Battle of Waterloo, knew Nathan intimately. He was generally reputed to be the most extravagant diplomat in Europe and had scandalised Englishmen by his habit of shaking his Hungarian jacket on the parquet floor of a ballroom for the pleasure of seeing women scramble for the pearls and diamonds that fell from it.

Prince Clary hurried towards Prince Esterhazy and, taking him aside, told him that he had danced twice with Hannah and was infatuated. He begged him to go with all speed to London and plead with Nathan for the hand of his daughter. Prince Esterhazy hesitated but finally agreed. He left Paris the next morning.

Nathan stormed when he heard the news. Doubtless at that moment there came to his mind the full significance of his legendary bundle of sticks. The request was flatly and vehemently refused. Prince Esterhazy's eloquence could obtain no better answer than: "I will never allow my daughter to marry a Christian."

Hannah was summoned home. Three carriages were packed with gifts from Baron James for his brother's family in London. There were boxes of fruit and chocolate, then a rarity in England, and coloured satins. But the trip had ended sooner than Hannah anticipated and Ary Scheffer was unable to finish his drawing.

CHAPTER TWO

ON July 30, 1836, about one hour after the London Stock Exchange had been open, the market turned suddenly weak. Funds had opened idly at round about the overnight closing levels and most members were content to discuss the news from Spain and the excessive heat. Quite unexpectedly prices began to fall and the volume increased as selling orders poured in for both English and foreign stock. Market operators were at first inclined to believe that this action was due to the bears.

It was supposed that the bear party, after putting the account for the settlement into a satisfactory train, had begun to throw stock on the market in the hope of bringing out sellers. There was nothing unusual in this. News from Spain and Portugal had not been encouraging and it was noticeable that the stocks of these two countries were falling faster than the rest of the market.

Then a messenger from New Court happened to mention that an express had arrived in town from Frankfort. Mr. Nathan Mayer de Rothschild, founder of the London house of that name, was known to have left some weeks before for Frankfort to attend the wedding of his eldest son. It was rumoured that Nathan had caught a chill on the journey and was seriously ill.

The house in New Court was besieged by members making anxious enquiries about his health. Towards the lunch hour not only was the rumour of his illness confirmed but it also became known that one of his younger sons had left suddenly for Frankfort. This news spread and the market broke wide open.

On Monday, August 1, traders were at their posts earlier than usual. The illness of the great banker monopolised conversation, and it was learnt that another express had arrived from Frankfort with news of July 27, at which period no change of importance had taken place.

7

It was difficult to exaggerate the holdings of Nathan not only for his own account, but for others in the national securities of various states, and it was obvious that his death might cause a serious slump, but market commentators pointed out that when an event is foreseen or apprehended it is generally found in Stock Exchange transactions that all its work is done, or even more than all, before it takes place. In modern times this is known as discounting the news. Moreover, Nathan was only one member of a firm whose name for prudence was already well established. Some of the bears began quietly covering during the afternoon and there followed a rally in English funds that caused them to remain almost unchanged on the day.

The next morning the volume of business dried up altogether except in foreign funds in which Nathan had specialised. No express reached New Court from Frankfort that day, but towards evening there were rumours that the famous banker was dead. Carrier pigeons, it was said, had brought the news by way of Paris.

On Wednesday the news was out. Mr. Nathan de Rothschild had died at Frankfort on the evening of Thursday, July 28. It had taken the London market exactly six days to know the facts. Prices opened strong and closed at the best of the day. Some traders who had thrown their funds overboard earlier in the week now started to buy them back on the grounds that Nathan's death was a bull point. They argued that many old and wealthy firms that had feared to enter competition with the all-powerful house of Rothschild because of Nathan's immense personal influence and command of capital, would now be willing to come back into business. Members made a rush for the Frankfort newspapers that had been brought into the Stock Exchange by a courier. They took note that Nathan's four brothers still held their houses securely on their shoulders, with Amschel Mayer at Frankfort, Solomon at Vienna, Charles at Naples and James in Paris. They read that Nathan would be succeeded in the manage-ment of the London house by his eldest son, Lionel, whose marriage at Frankfort had so unwittingly caused the death of his father.

The bride Lionel had gone to claim was Charlotte, the seventeen-years-old daughter of Baron Charles at Naples. The idea of this wedding had given much satisfaction to Nathan, for it was the second time that one of his children married within the family. The chill that sent him to his bed was sudden, but exactly twenty hours before his death he called a notary and dictated his last will and testament.

This will was afterwards taken as a model of Rothschild policy. If Mayer Amschel had actually laid the foundations of the house in Frankfort a generation ago, it was his third son Nathan who did most to consolidate its fortunes and cause the name to become legendary. In these last hours of his life, Nathan laid down the strict law of unity that was to keep the business in the hands of the brothers, their sons and their sons' sons. With his head propped on the high pillows, the chief of the London house spoke in the guttural tones of his native German tongue and the notary's quill pen flew over the parchment.

Whatever Hannah may have thought about Prince Clary's failure to obtain her hand in marriage, she was never greatly in sympathy with the members of her own community, and there must have been passages in her father's will that gave her cause for serious thought.

"Inasmuch," Nathan had stated, "as it has pleased all-gracious God, in His inscrutable disposition, to visit me with sickness at this place, of which indeed through Him, the Almighty, I hope to recover, still, as the lives of all mankind stand in His hand and as I cannot know in what manner it will be His will to call me from this world, so I have thought it proper, now, while I possess my full mental faculties, to make, after due consideration, my testament and therein state what my will is."

It was a dramatic opening because of its clarity. The great financier who had beaten the rest of the world with the result of the Battle of Waterloo, was dictating the most important contract in his life with only a few hours to go. He gave this picture of what was passing through his mind in that darkened Frankfort room. The terms of the will, its precise laws, are historic. That opening sentence shows the man as he was.

Methodically he expounded the theme song of the bundle of sticks. He tells, with the authority that money gives, his fervent desire that his four sons should always act together in union and peace, and, as if to make the partnership more binding, the woman who had aided him in prosperity and been affectionate in adversity was to co-operate with her sons on all important occasions. She was to have a voice in every deliberation. Her sons might never engage in a transaction of moment without having previously sought the maternal advice.

Nathan made specific mention of Hannah and of her young sister Louisa.

"Their marriage can only take place with the sanction of their mother or brothers, and in the event, which is not to be supposed, that in such a respect they shall not be able materially to agree, or their mother or their brothers should refuse their consent, then shall my brothers decide thereon and their decision is to be complied with unconditionally by all parties."

It is reasonable to suppose that, in drafting this clause in the will, Nathan remembered the episode in Paris.

LOUISA DE ROTHSCHILD.

She was Hannah's youngest sister. Charles de Rothschild arrived in London to claim her as his bride and he took her to live in the old town of Frankfort-on-the-Main. Seven daughters were born to them —no son.

CHAPTER THREE

DURING the spring of 1838 there came into the Rothschild home in Piccadilly a young man called Henry FitzRoy, who was already being singled out for political promotion.

FitzRoy was now thirty. He was the younger son of the second Baron Southampton, who died when he was a child. His brother, who now bore the title, and he, had been brought up by an austerely Calvinistic mother. She punished her sons severely, whipping them herself and allowing them few pleasures. She would weigh their food, carefully reserving what was left over for the following meal. Once FitzRoy asked her for a horse. She refused the horse but sent him a tract by return.

As the boys grew to manhood they passed out of the maternal influence. Lord Southampton, the elder, was married to a fine but haughty woman who was accustomed to say that there was nothing like blood. She was a striking figure and moved with an intentional yet graceful dignity, giving careful consideration to such actions as getting in and out of a carriage. She was accustomed to great luxury, and when taking her afternoon drive in the country round her estate at Whittlebury, would appear in a barouche drawn by four grey horses with outriders.

The Dowager Lady Southampton was now growing old, and this spring she had taken to her bed. Nevertheless, until recently she had been active, going from place to place in a black poke bonnet, preaching and discoursing from the top of a barrel.

This strange upbringing had left a certain timidity in FitzRoy's character. He worked hard and took life seriously, too seriously sometimes. He was a man of ardent feelings and deep convictions. But when he came into a room every woman looked up. He stood well over six feet, with thick black hair, bright blue eyes, and a ready smile. He wore curly side-whiskers, not up on the cheek-bones but level with the corners of his mouth. He was a tower of strength and rode a horse to perfection.

Hannah saw him and fell desperately in love. During the spring and early summer they had many opportunities to meet. They went several times to the opera.

Their outlook on life must have been fundamentally different. Hannah had been petted and spoilt by Europe's wealthiest banker. FitzRoy may have been temporarily driven away from religion by an unhappy childhood, but there were moments that remained deep and vivid. The most persistent memory was that of his younger sister, Laura, who had died at the age of thirteen. This little girl had gone through an operation, long before the discovery of anæsthetics, with incredible courage. Laura had been attacked by a white swelling on her knee while the family was staying at Clifton. After every known remedy had proved useless a surgeon was finally sent for from London, who declared that only amputation could save the girl's life. Lady Southampton was overwhelmed. The amputation of a limb at that time was almost barbarous. Several days passed before she could summon up courage to break the news to her daughter, but Laura listened without the least agitation and answered: "God demands my limb but not my life."

"Do you think me unkind, my love, to have made such a decision?" asked her mother.

"Oh, no, Mamma!" answered Laura. "What else could you have done? You know you have tried everything."

"If you had it in your choice, would you prefer to die, as you must do, if this operation is not performed?"

"Oh! to die, to be sure, Mamma; for then I am certain I should be happy; but then, you know, that would be taking my life into my own hands, and I could not expect God to support me on my death-bed, nor could I think that, when suffering this, I might be made to glorify God by being of use to Mr. Baynton, my surgeon. I like always to have you, and I should like to have you in the room with me at the time of the operation. But then, Mamma, you must not, for it would do you harm; I would like to have Bird, the housekeeper, with me if it will not hurt her."

The surgeons arrived the following morning at eleven, and Lady Southampton went to acquaint Laura that the operation was to take place. On hearing that it was so near, tears rolled down her cheeks, and she said: "Oh! Mamma, pray for me!" She was taken out of bed like a lamb. When they wished to put a bandage on her eyes she said: "Oh, no. You needn't. I'll shut my eyes; but if you wish it, you may do it," and they put on the handkerchief. She held a nosegay between her finger and thumb when taken out of bed and it remained so until the end of the operation. She never uttered a scream. Towards the close the surgeon praised her and she answered: "Don't praise me, there should not even have been that 'oh!'" The operation had taken place on Thursday in Passion Week. A week later she sat propped up in her bed eating an orange and remarked: "I am so happy in bed. I would not for the world have my leg back again, for, you know, it is better to enter life half maimed than, having two legs, to enter into hell fire."

Laura died a few months later.

Hannah must have listened to these things with strange emotion. As the weeks passed and FitzRoy came more frequently to the house in Piccadilly the question of marriage preoccupied him. He was generally considered to be heir to the title because his brother was childless, but he was not wealthy. He decided to make no definite move until the end of the summer. Just now a particularly busy session in Parliament was drawing to a close. Europe had changed greatly since the death of Nathan in 1836. At home King William the Fourth had died and a new Queen, in all the freshness of youth, had mounted the throne. The country had passed through the uncertainties that follow the death of a sovereign and had taken part in the excitement of an accession. Popular opinion was still trying to appraise the young Queen's merits.

There had been no dearth of critics at the time of her accession. Hardly had King William drawn his last breath than men looked back on a sorry procession of English monarchs and found them wanting. It had been said that the institution of monarchy was fading from the esteem and veneration of mankind and that kingly government was no longer compatible with an advanced and enlightened state of society. The French unrest had already sown seeds of discontent beyond its frontiers. The future of English monarchy depended on Queen Victoria. By her conduct she would either accelerate its downfall or prolong its existence, and it was fortunate that her very youth exemplified the end of an old era and the beginning of a new one. She was to set the nation on a new course.

Of late there had been some touching proofs of loyalty.

One morning as the Lincoln mail coach reached Falkingham, a small wicker basket, mounted for convenience on a broom, had been hoisted to the coachman by an old woman who had come out of a wayside cottage. On top of the basket was sewn a piece of paper on which had been written neatly with a crow quill: "To her Majesty, Queen Victoria, Defender of England, Ireland and Elsewhere." Passengers who, out of curiosity, lifted the lid, found a small tortoiseshell kitten sitting on a wad of muslin. A piece of bread had been placed beside it in case it should feel hungry before reaching London.

The stage coach was still the normal way of travelling just as the candle was still the common means of lighting. The railroad had already made its appearance, but as yet it performed no very important service in transport. Locomotives exploded with the sound of a cannon. The London to Birmingham railroad company was willing to pay a reward of ten pounds to any person giving information that would lead to the arrest of people found guilty of obstructing the passage of trains, and doctors were urging their clients not to travel in tunnels.

In the clubs men talked about the scene at the Guildhall when Mr. Walter Hancock, accompanied by three friends, had driven all the way from Stratford in a steam-gig. They discussed the new coinage that many criticised on the grounds that the effigy of the young Queen was without any emblem of sovereignty. It was said to lack intellectual character.

Travelling was a rather risky business. It was not unusual for a diligence to be stopped by men armed with muskets who would make the passengers alight and give up their money and jewels. In the streets of London omnibus owners advised their passengers to keep their hands in front of them to avoid the unpleasant occurrences that were reported each day, and from a spot not far from Lord Holland's park in Kensington came reports of frequent highway robberies in broad daylight.

It was possible to meet with every stage of development— the country yokel in his smock using the ultra-modern metal plough, the top-hatted railroad prospector, who would occasion-ally get stoned, and the runaway couple driving their post-chaise to Gretna Green. Romance clung to the road. Only a short time ago a post-chaise and four had driven towards Ealing at a rapid rate, changing horses at the "White Hart" Inn. A youth and a girl who stepped down from this equipage clammered loudly for fresh horses, but, before these could be procured, the sound of wheels was heard and the girl, white with terror, darted across the road into the "Oxford Arms" public-house and ran upstairs. The Oxford coach clattered into the courtyard and an infuriated father knocked down the young man who was eloping with his daughter. He declared that the girl was nineteen and had an income of £45,000.

These were the things that happened in real life.

From the sea came stories of mutiny and piracy. The brig *Hebden* of Scarborough brought to Greenock three passengers and two members of the crew of an American brig *Braganza*. These people had been picked up at sea three hundred and fifty miles from the coast of Portugal after being exposed for twenty-five hours.

It had been a case of mutiny. The captain and second mate of the *Braganza* did their best to ward off the mutineers, but they only had one cutlass between them. In less than an hour the sailors were in control of the ship. As a concession the passengers and two of the crew had been allowed to take off in a long-boat.

While the first locomotives steamed gently up hills and the steam-jig was a sort of prelude to the motor-car on our roads, the balloon figured as an after-dinner amusement. At the Royal Gardens at Vauxhall there was actually a double ascent. These were the Royal Nassau balloon and the Coronation balloon, and the idea was that both should leave the ground at precisely the same moment.

Children still played at fighting Bonaparte, whether on the sands at Brighton or across a table full of toy soldiers, and the campaigns of the great Frenchman remained for the grown-ups the most topical subject of the big show. At Astley there was a spectacle known as Bonaparte's Invasion of Russia or the Conflagration of Moscow, and this was followed by feats of living lions, tigers and leopards.

The bill at the Haymarket theatre was shared on alternate nights by the American comedian Hill and by Charles Surface and Walter Lacey playing in the *School for Scandal*. People were showing interest in the first experiments by men of science. They crowded the Royal Gallery of Practical Science to see what were described as Gymnotus Electricus or living specimens of the electric eel.

FitzRoy was hearing a great clamour go up in Parliament for an increase in armaments. People claimed that England was defenceless and prostrate. Some argued that even twelve months of arming would hardly put the country in a solid condition against exterior contingencies. There was a definite feeling against meddling in foreign politics. Isolationists claimed that for more than a century we had been perpetually engaged in wars abroad in which we had no interest, and that it was now the time to adopt the American policy and attend to our own business.

16

The Continent was full of kings in fine uniforms taking the salute on crowded parade grounds.

The King of Hanover was said to be making trouble. It had not been possible for Queen Victoria, being a woman, to extend her sovereignty over Hanover as four kings of England had done before. The Duke of Cumberland, son of George III, therefore, listened to the heralds proclaiming the death of King William and, crossing the water, claimed the throne of Hanover, thus taking his place among the monarchs of Europe.

Whatever the British public may have thought about the link that had snapped between England and Hanover after a century and a quarter, there was gossip for idle tongues. Prince George of Cumberland, the King's only son, was blind. He had lost one eye recently and the other as a child when playing with a string of beads in a shop at Kew. There had been frequent rumours of his marriage and indeed one of these was now coupling his name with that of a daughter of the Emperor Nicholas of Russia. The diplomats shook their heads and there were hurried meetings in the chancelleries of Europe. This suggested a deliberate transfer of the kingdom of Hanover to the Russian Crown, because the blindness of the young prince would make it necessary that, on his accession, some regency should be appointed. A feminine Russian hand would guide a blind Hanoverian's pen at the bottom of every state document. The kingdom of Hanover would go over and join the territory of the Poles, as another Russian province, and it looked as if King Ernest was biting the English hand that for so long had fed him.

The news from Russia was confined to bloodshed and oppression. While the Emperor Nicholas, who had spent his childhood 'partly in dreaming, partly in drawing all sorts of nonsense,' was parading in uniform with his friend the King of Prussia, men were shot without questions. At Vilna women and priests were being arrested and thrown into dungeons.

The Russian Court was just going into mourning for the celebrated Countess Branitska, a niece of Potemkin, who had died on her estates of Biala-Cerkiew at the age of eighty. Catherine the Great had showered favours upon her and the Emperor Alexander had called her 'little mother' and would stand in her presence until she bade him be seated.

The woman had shown herself as shrewd as the toughest market operator. One million pounds sterling in specie was found in her château and a current account of 60,000,000 roubles stood to her credit in the Bank of Russia. She had discounted bills, sold gold, disposed personally of the immense products of her lands and lent money on mortgages to almost every big landed proprietor in the Empire. Her business acumen was keen and ruthless. Discovering in Paris that human hair was a valued commodity, she broke short her stay to return to Russia, and as the first frosts of autumn covered the land, eighty thousand female slaves knelt down for their heads to be shaved.

Travel across the Atlantic was relatively fast. A good liner would dock at Bristol thirteen days after leaving New York. The arrival of a liner meant news. The hawsers and the gangway gave the same sort of promise that the envelope of the cablegram does to-day. It was a moment of anxiety, the few seconds of trepidation that precede tidings from the other side. While the clocks of Bristol struck midnight and the "Great Western" started to unload her passengers by the light of spluttering oil flares, the mail and newspapers would be hurried to waiting coaches. There would be papers from New York, Quebec and Toronto. The news from Canada would be reflected in the Stock Exchange next day.

America was pulling out of the panic of 1837. Confidence was slowly coming back and the prospects of the Fall trade were good. The wheat crops had been realised abundantly. America would have grain to export and because of the ravages of the wheat-fly in the Canadian crops, prices would not be likely to fall.

New peoples were beginning to pour into America in a slow, steady stream that during the next fifteen years was to reach mighty proportions. The first carts and covered wagons were rumbling towards the West, new cities were springing up, a new era was beginning, everything was in movement. Machinery and railroads had not grown out of the infant stage, but their influence was already far-reaching. An almost wholly agricultural population looked upon these new devices with a tinge of curiosity. Only a few hands were as yet leaving the land for factories and mills, and nobody on that vast continent was in a position to foresee the immense natural resources that lay undreamt-of below the farmer's plough.

The first bunch of American millionaires was headed by the German-born John Jacob Astor, whose fortune was assessed at £5,000,000. Like most rich men in America, he had traded with the Indians. His traffic was the shipment of furs to China by a fleet of his own ships. No financier had yet risen to dim the fame of the Rothschild family, whose members persisted in keeping out of American business.

There were bigger fortunes just around the corner. It was seventeen months ago that an unknown adventurer called Bill Rockefeller had driven up to the house of that stern Baptist, John Davison, to fetch away his daughter, Eliza, and marry her in the home of a friend. It would be another year before a chubby baby to be called John D. Rockefeller would see the light of day in the village of Richford, in New York.

But in a modest brick cottage on Asylum Street, Hartford, Connecticut, there would have been found a kicking, crying youngster not yet old enough to answer coherently had you addressed him as John Pierpont Morgan.

CHAPTER FOUR

THAT summer Mrs. N. M. Rothschild spent some time at an estate in Gunnersbury purchased by her husband not long before his death.

Nathan had been moved by the same urge as his brother James had felt in Paris. He wanted a place in the country within convenient driving distance from his office at New Court. Gunnersbury suited him admirably. Though it was only eight miles from Hyde Park Corner, the drive from London was through the depths of the country.

Nathan took immense trouble with Gunnersbury Park, but he never lived there. He died too soon. His widow turned her husband's dream into reality. The place became a favourite resort for the family, and was to be the scene of brilliant gatherings such as Disraeli was later to describe: "A delightful fête at Gunnersbury—Madame de Rothschild mère. A beautiful park and a villa worthy of an Italian prince. Military bands, beautiful grounds, temples and illuminated walks. All the world present."

Gunnersbury was famous long before Nathan bought it. It had been the home of Princess Amelia, daughter of George II. This princess held many receptions there for kings, statesmen and poets of the eighteenth century. Horace Walpole had been invited to stay there as Princess Amelia's guest. The invitation reached him at short notice and he sent to town for a dress coat and sword. They played cards until late, but Walpole was tired. The next day, while visiting the dairy, the Princess insisted that he should make some verses on her home. He pleaded in vain to be let off, but he was finally obliged to compose several stanzas that he delivered at the hour of her breakfast. One stanza ran:

GUNNERSBURY PARK.

The home of Madame de Rothschild mère.
Disraeli called it a beautiful park and a villa
worthy of an Italian prince. Here started the
FitzRoy–Rothschild romance.

"O! Why is Flaccus not alive
    Your favourite scene to sing?
To Gunnersbury's charm could give
    His lyre immortal spring."

"If these verses are poor," he said later: "Consider I am sixty-nine, was half asleep and made them by command."

By the time the Rothschilds went there, little was left to recall Princess Amelia's days with the exception of a large wall surrounding the kitchen garden that she had built with her winnings at cards and some ivy-covered ruins in which was her bath. These ruins, some distance from the main house, were now full of cobwebs and queer echoes. Moss clung to the damp walls and trees spread their branches thickly overhead.

It was at Gunnersbury that Hannah spoke to her mother about FitzRoy. His political future was assured. He had been nominated Deputy Lieutenant for the County of Northampton.

When the question was broached Mrs. N. M. Rothschild, who managed all the members of her family even when they were fully grown, violently opposed the idea. There is no doubt that Hannah showed a dogged determination. She was ready to defy the traditions of her family and to take the consequence.

In his dealings with the Rothschilds, FitzRoy acted with loyalty and frankness. Though he was determined to win his bride he realised the dangers of a hurried or impetuous marriage. The wedding would doubtless be solemnised according to the rites of the established Church and Hannah would thus be obliged to renounce her faith and adopt her husband's religion. These considerations must have weighed heavily with him, for there was the danger that Hannah might have cause for regret.

Lionel was now thirty years old and father of a baby daughter. He knew that his sister was capable of acting without his consent, but it was the first time that a member of the family had threatened rebellion and it was clear that this might estrange her from her nearest relations.

Some time in August, the Rothschilds, hoping that Hannah

might be made to forget, invited FitzRoy to Piccadilly and asked that he should leave England for six months. If at the end of that time Hannah was still determined to go through with the marriage, the matter might be reviewed.

FitzRoy accepted this banishment with a broken heart. There was obviously no other solution. He was then living in chambers at South Street, and as soon as Parliament had adjourned he mapped out his journey. It so happened that Lord and Lady Southampton were also planning to leave England, for the Dowager Lady Southampton had died that summer and there was nothing to keep them in London. FitzRoy fixed September 1 as the day of his departure. He booked a passage on a three-hundred-tons steamer called the *John Bull* that plied regularly between the Port of London and Hamburg. He would travel slowly to Berlin, waiting for his brother and Lady Southampton to join him, so that they could all travel South together. Somewhere on the Adriatic coast the party would break up, Lady Southampton going to Naples, where she was to stay with friends, and the two brothers continuing their journey by sea to Athens and Constantinople.

As August drew to a close the position appeared less desperate than FitzRoy had feared. One evening twenty-six-years-old Nathaniel Rothschild knocked at his door and brought him a letter from Hannah in which she stated that she would patiently wait for his return. Nathaniel had a great affection for his young sister and was sympathetic in the matter of her marriage. This letter gave FitzRoy great encouragement. He told Nathaniel of his plans and gave him a list of the places he would visit, so that Hannah might send him news.

During the whole of his journey FitzRoy kept a diary in a plain copy-book. The writing is occasionally difficult to read, but that is because of storms at sea.

CHAPTER FIVE

SEPTEMBER 1, 1838. Sailed from the Custom House at ½ past six a.m. on board the *John Bull* bound to Hamburgh. Wind light from W.S.W. reached the Nore about ½ past eleven. There were about twenty-five passengers chiefly Germans; by dint of a bribe of two pounds to the Steward, I secured a state cabin for my exclusive occupation; this together with the beauty of the weather that was extremely favourable during the whole of our passage, enabled me to support its very unnecessary length with more patience than I had imagined myself to possess.

Sep. 2. (Sunday) The morning was thick and hazy with rain, the wind from the north, but about mid-day the mist cleared off and a beautiful fresh breeze sprang up. We came up with a Swedish brig standing N.E. under Jury Masts; from her appearance she had been long at sea.

Sep. 3. Entered the Elbe at 4 a.m. the weather wild and boisterous, with heavy rain. At first the river was hideous but as we neared Hamburgh, the left bank appeared prettily disposed with pleasure grounds and villas. Poor as the sandy soil looks, not one inch is allowed to remain unemployed. We anchored about 2 p.m. having been 56 hours performing a journey that with all the favourable circumstances attending us should have been completed in 48 at the utmost. Engaged a room at the Alte Stadt London, that is apparently the best hotel here being (as indeed they all are) beautifully situated on the Alster.

At 6 p.m. after eating the eternal German dinner at the *table d'hôte* I went to the Tivoli Gardens where I saw part of an amusing play: *Der Reisende Student*. Went down the Montagnes Russes and then strolled back through the pretty gardens that now take the place of the old Ramparts to the Promenade, where the most glorious moonlight was lighting hundreds of loungers. The cheerfully-lighted crowded Cafés, the extreme loveliness of the night, and the placid clearness of the water as it reflected the moonbeams from its bright surface, made it quite a fairy scene— and yet, what a sadness forces itself on one who under such a sky, and in such a scene, treads alone where all beside have their friends, and perhaps partners with them. To walk on such a night with her whom my soul loves, would be worth whole years of other enjoyment without her, but I feel that all that is most lovely will now only make me sad. What is there that peculiarly leads us to reflect on all we love with the greatest tenderness under the most beautiful summer night? Why should the stillest aspect of nature stir up the remembrance of a passion that has nothing of stillness in its nature? How inconceivable are the workings of our inner man and yet, undefinable as they are, I love most especially to try to trace the connexion and the spring of thoughts and feelings, that are in themselves also undefinable.

Sep. 4. (Tuesday) Walked over the Town to see what little is worth notice, such as the Exchange, the large Churches (all miserably bad) and in the Evening went to the Opera where the *Nozze di Figaro* was respectably given. A certain Herr Reichel has a good bass voice and the orchestra was very good; the House a fair size but dark and heavy. Walked afterwards on the Promenade the night fine but not so clear as the preceding one.

Sep. 5. (Wednesday) After losing myself some hours in the streets in search of the plays to be performed in the evening, took a drive outside the Ramparts by the water where I saw a number of the prettiest and gayest villas that one could wish to summer in. With dear Hannah how happy I should be there! Or anywhere with her; I should never perceive the absence of the sun when she was near to cheer and gladden me. Shall I ever be so blest?

Hearing of the reviews at Magdebourg which I was first told were now going on, I went to engage a place by the Steamboat from hence, but finding that the great day would not be till the 12th, formed the sudden resolution to start to Berlin by the Schnell Post after dinner, hoping to find the Baron von Leuden

September 1. 1838

Sailed from the Custom House at ¼ past one a.m. on board the John Bull bound to Hamburgh. Wind light from W.S.W. reached the Nore about ¼ past eleven. Passengers about 25 in number chiefly German, many of them en route by Leipsic for the Fair; by dint of the bribe of two pounds to the Steward I secured a State cabin for my exclusive occupation. this together with the beauty of the weather which was extremely favourable during the whole of our passage, enabled me to support its very unnecessary length with more patience than I had imagined myself to possess. Sunday 2nd the morning thick and hazy with rain — the wind from the north. It was cleared off about twelve, and a beautiful fresh breeze springing up, came up with a Swedish brig standing N.E. under jury masts, from her appearance had been very long at sea. 3rd Entered the Elbe at 6 h. the weather mild and boisterous, with very heavy rain, the Rain at first hideous, but as we neared Hamburgh the left bank very prettily disposed as pleasure grounds, villas in, indeed, for as the sandy soil looks, not one inch is allowed to remain unemployed. Anchored about two P.M. having been fifty six hours performing a journey that with all the favourable circumstances attending us should have been completed in 28 at the utmost. Engaged a room at the Alter Stadt London, apparently the best Hotel here being far indeed they all are, beautifully situated on the Alster at one, after eating the eternal German dinner at the Table d'hote went to the Swiss Gardens where I saw part of a very amusing play "der wiesende Student" went down the Montagnes Russes, then strolled back through the pretty gardens that now take the place of the ramparts of old to the Promenade, where the most glorious moonlight was lighting hundreds of loungers on the prettiest Boulevard I ever saw. the cheaply lighted and crowded cafés, the extreme loveliness of the light, and the placid clearness of the water in it reflected the moon beams from its bright surface made it quite a fairy scene — and yet what a sadness forces itself on one who under such a sky, and in such a scene treads alone, where all

---

ACROSS EUROPE IN 1838.

There was trouble when dark-haired Henry FitzRoy proposed marriage to Hannah de Rothschild. He was banished from England for six months and travelled from London to Constantinople. Both he and his diary were nearly drowned in the Mediterranean.

there, and go with him to Magdebourg. Had it not been for the kindness of Mr. Ree here who procured for me change for one of Hammersley's notes, I should have been much embarrassed as to my departure, the Banks being closed before I knew that I should start so soon. *N.B.* Always keep a certain supply of money in my dressing case.

Although I was No. 15 and consequently expected a miserable journey outside a calèche, on arriving at the Poste, the officer informed me that he had secured for me Number Five, the best place in the coach! Why or wherefore he showed me this kindness I have no idea but it entailed upon me numerous white lies as all my fellow travellers were very angry at this preference shown me, and asked me when I had written, how I had written, to all of which I gave evasive answers for fear of committing the officer.

We started at 9 o'clock a most beautifully clear, moonlight night, and as we drove all round the water, and out at the Gate by the Tivoli Gardens, I thought to one entering from Berlin at that hour, Hamburgh would appear the most beautiful fairyland in the world.

Sep. 6. (Thursday) Breakfasted at Ludwigslust, the village by the Palace of the Grand Duke of Mecklenburg-Schwerin. It is a pretty little village, small and resembling one in England, built near the Château of some grand Seigneur who made it his hobby to have everything neat and pretty round him. I thought of Whittlebury, Southampton's place, although I fully believe the extreme ugliness of the preceding and surrounding country made me view this little exception with too favourable an eye.

We dined at Perleberg and supped at Friesack, these numerous stoppages are very annoying, although I must own I made good use of my time in the eating line on every occasion.

At 5 a.m. on Friday *Sept.* 7, after a night of very heavy rain the morning light woke me to a view of the very fine entrance into Berlin. We were just then a mile from the town and the whole of that distance the road, that is magnificently wide and level, passed through an Avenue of fine trees that form the border of the Park, public property as they now tell me, but I shall know more of this in a few days.

The Gate and entrance to the Town are just what such an approach would lead one to expect—very fine, the Arms of Prussia over the Gate in good taste. Everything is beautifully clean, the streets so wide and airy, the houses so large, the buildings (all of which that are the best worth seeing, being passed in review as you drive down to the Poste) so noble that I was quite in raptures with the whole thing.

It appears to me so much finer than Munich, at least, I feel sure, quite as fine without any of the effort that Munich always seems to me making to be so.

I went to the Picture and State Gallery but I am no judge of either. I only stayed two hours in the Gallery as I shall look over it again once or twice more at my leisure. In the afternoon drove out to the Tivoli Gardens to see the Iron Pillar or Monument in memory of the different battles and victories achieved by the Prussians.

In the evening took a stall at the Opera to hear *Norma* and I never listened to it with greater pleasure. The orchestra perfect and Demoiselle Lorne, the best singer I have heard in Germany, and a first-rate actress, her figure peculiarly adapted for the rôle of Norma. The theatre is good, the King's box almost too large in proportion. He was there but I could not see him. There was a species of *divertissement* introduced in the second act. I cannot say much in its praise but I never saw anything so perfect as the acting of the Prima Donna. To-morrow they give *Oberon* and I trust she is to play in it, though however beautiful it may be, I like no musick so well throughout as *Norma*. How much every scene in this reminds me of Hannah. I have so often turned from a passage that peculiarly pleased me, to try and read the expression on her pretty face as she sat at my side. What would I not now give for one glimpse of that countenance!

Sep. 8. (Saturday) Had a German Master for one hour, the stupidest ass I ever saw; what a good Reformer he would make for when I had written a sentence he invariably found fault and said it was not intelligible, yet frequently after ruminating over it for some time he could make no better of it, and was forced to leave it. I then went to the Manége to hire a horse for Monday, and then over to the Grosse Schloss, where I went through the usual routine of rooms filled with all the venerable relics of the King's ancestors; afterwards through a most splendidly adorned hall, hung on one side with massive gilt plate, superb lustres of rock crystal, mirrors framed in silver and doors carved in wood, I never saw a place so light, so striking. There was a silver vase with coins set in it from which one of the old Kings surrounded by his troops, would drink beer. There is a model of a monument at Potsdam of the Fête given in 1829 to the Empress of Prussia, containing the crests and devices of the noblesse who attended it. There are, in fact, a great many pretty things particularly a Secretaire made nearby Cologne that contains more secret deposits for papers etc. than I should have imagined any human ingenuity could invent, and now that it is done it must tax the memory severely to find all the springs. There is also a complicated clock which shows the day of the year, the age of the moon and the stars. We then progressed to the Long Gallery in which I saw some fine pictures. A Madonna riveted me. What a divine countenance and quite different from the every day Madonnas that throng every gallery in Europe. I could have watched it for ever, could have talked to it, prayed to it and those lovely eyes must have answered.

In the afternoon I went to the Riding School, hired a horse and a man to teach me to ride as I wished to feel the Prussian seat which to a beginner is certainly as awkward as it looks. In the evening went to the theatre to see Mlle. Enghaus from Hamburgh, play in *Preciosa*, the plot being as far as I could discover a gypsy girl who after all the bitters and sweets of loving and being loved by a Noble Knight, whose friends oppose the union, is discovered to be the daughter of some Don of Spain and is married accordingly without further trouble.

Sep. 9. (Sunday) German Master came late which disturbed my equanimity as I was bent on going to Mass, the loss of which to me is really a great privation, however, thanks to my servant mistaking the hour I arrived in good time and sooth to say I should have almost been better pleased to miss it for I who (dare I own it?) love the Catholic religion and all its prestige and grandeur, cannot bear to see it here where it ought to be in the ascendant, so meanly decked and so meagrely attended. The plainest, though not badly proportioned church I ever saw, a poor organ, a congregation almost exclusively of the *bas peuple* and soldiery, all made me long again to arrive in Orthodox Saxony or Bavaria or Austria, where the Christian service is performed as it should be.

Went from thence to hear the band at the Great Guard Mounting I was disappointed. I find myself inclined to say this so often to-day, very much against my usual habit, that I must really stay to think. Was I out of temper and determined to be disappointed? No; I really think not and yet it has been (with a few moments of exception which I shall presently notice) a day of Blank—no real enjoyment, no pleasure, for how badly defined and yet how wide the line between that and content. I only find real pleasure in those objects that by association carry me back to Her. Such moments I found, strange to say, in the Mausoleum at Charlottenburg, where I went more prepared to criticise than to admire the figure of the late Queen executed by Herr Rauch. The countenance is so lovely, the 'rapture of repose' spoken of by Byron, so charmingly delineated in the pose of the limbs and in the expression of the face, that the quarter of an hour I passed in examining it, was the only time upon which I shall look back with gratification.

I then walked round the gardens, very ill kept with nothing striking either in the lay out of the grounds or in the botanical specimens. Dined badly at the Café near at hand and then went to another garden close by the Palace where they told me I should see a multitude of people and that it would be gay.

True, there were plenty of people but only eating and drinking, and I am convinced that the inhabitants of Northern Germany are of a quite different race from the Southern ditto, and have not the germ of life and pleasure in them. Bavaria for ever!

Came back by another part of the Park or Thier Garten from that through which I had gone out. Some of the villas in it are quite beautiful and the people dining before the doors looked happy and enviable. Why have we English no outdoor habits? I suppose I must ask, why have we no outdoor climate?

Went to the Opera to hear *Oberon*. The Overture beautifully played and encored. Demoiselle Lorne does not lose by acquaintance and plays superiorly. The dancing was wretched but vehemently applauded. By the way, I gave myself to-day the very unnecessary trouble to go to the top of the Palace to see the view. The view round Berlin! It was what it is, self-evidently must be, no view at all—not a single feature in the country if you except the two little hills in the direction of Frankfort-on-the-Oder, both nearly two hundred feet high! *N.B.* Never take anything on the report of a Laquais de Place, and never do what he recommends you.

Sep. 10. (Monday) Started at 7 a.m. to see the troops exercise. Rode out to the ground with the Artillery. Saw them go through part of their exercise (not, I think, quite as quickly as our Artillery), then galloped across the plain to where the Lancers were drilling most beautifully. Their advances breaking into divisions and skirmishing and charging were all beautiful. A regiment of light dragoons were also good and their Band composed only of trumpets, trombones and an opialeid. The Cuirassiers marched off the Field first just as I rode up to the Lancers and I did not go near the Infantry which of course looked splendid from that distance while the band sounded both very strong and very soft. Rode home with a regiment of Lancers whom also I had no time to see manœuvre and was astonished to find how effective the music was though the Squadron by which I had placed myself had only five trumpets by way of a band.

Went again to the picture gallery which, to an ignoramus in the art, is certainly not a pleasing one. I saw there the strangest picture that man ever conceived, divided into the three subjects of 'Eve's Temptation,' the 'Day of Judgment' and 'Hell' by Bosch. He certainly intends those who enter the place of punishment to have no sinecure. The tortures inflicted are both various and recherchés. I left the gallery as my eye soon tired of an abundance of picture and went over to the Arsenal which appeared superb. It is arranged with the best possible taste and come what may, Prussia will certainly never be conquered for want of arms wherewith to supply her soldiers.

I have been told there are eighty thousand hand of arms in the arsenal! After dinner I took a carriage and walked through the wood at Treptow but I grieved to see so many fine young oaks spoiling for want of care and thinning. This is certainly not the fault at the farther end of the wood near the river where they have indiscriminately cut down everything for what object I cannot conceive.

I am nearly tired of Berlin. I find all the buildings bad bricks and the apparent cleanliness accompanied by the most intolerable stench. It is a fine garrison but the interminable length of the streets fatigues the eye, and I am anxious now to get to Dresden as soon as I can. I begin to feel that the six months are already so long that I shall scarcely get through them. What chance is there that she will write? It is indeed a trial and Bosch might have put it in his picture of Hell. Perhaps hereafter we may look back on it with satisfaction as certain proof of the reality of our mutual affection, but should it end in separation, and unhappiness, how bitterly will both repent having made the concession. I dare hope for no good result.

Sep. 11. (Tuesday) The Lehrer came at ½ past nine. I think he will make me progress a little but I much fear I shall never learn to speak correctly and before I return to England I shall have forgotten all. It is a desperately difficult language but as I never use a word of anything else from morning to night, perhaps I may soon speak it in a sort of way with facility. I shall do no sightseeing to-day as I start this evening to Magdebourg and must write some letters before I go, and cannot force myself to hurry about. I like to live quietly here and go for two or three hours in the day to whatever is extraordinary.

Started at 7 p.m. in the Schnell Post to Magdebourg and on Wednesday *Sep.* 12 arrived there at noon. Every bed and sofa in the town taken, and I was very glad to put up with one in the Hôtel Pétersbourg, a vile hole, for which I was compelled to pay the price of one Louis per diem. *Il n'y avait pas à choisir,* so dined at one and afterwards went over the Cathedral, a fine plain building most substantially put together of solid stone. I think the exterior imposing but like other Protestant Churches, it is somewhat like a large barn inside having no ornaments unless one might reckon the splendid pillars which support the roof. Went afterwards to call on Fancourt whom I found unwell. Learnt from him how great was my mistake in bringing no uniform. Cannot in consequence dine with the King of Hanover or of Prussia—which is disagreeable as they are very hospitable and kind. Sent to get a horse, no easy task, but succeeded, on paying four Louis and a half for the three days.

Walked round the town to see the preparations for the illuminations that were imposing, most of the houses being festooned with garlands. The pillar erected in the place opposite the Emperor of Russia's house beautifully illuminated. Saw him arrive about 6 p.m. He is certainly a most imposing-looking man, and seems to bear the weight of all the Russians with easy dignity. I must own that after scanning his features closely, his is not what I conceive to be a pleasing countenance.

Sept. 13. (Thursday) The Parade to which this day alone was to be given up was ordered for nine. I started in consequence at half-past eight in company with a Mr. Walker of the Artillery, and a brother of Lord Ward. When we arrived on the grounds on which it was supposed there were 80,000 spectators, I was fortunate enough to get inside the lines though without uniform. The King of Hanover came first, next the King of Prussia and thirdly the Emperor of Russia. I rode round the troops with the three Kings, their Courts and Staff. Certainly to a man who had never before seen more than 7,000 men together, it is a most imposing, I might almost say a wonderful sight to see 25,000 and such troops. I must own, however, that the effect was still more striking and gave me a much greater idea of their number, on both the succeeding days on which they were differently disposed. The divers bands taking up the National Air and other fine pieces of musick as the Kings rode by had a beautiful effect combined here with a harmonious accompaniment by the men and certainly every time I heard those bands, they seemed to be more perfect. We then returned to our Station when I was lucky enough to be placed on the Sovereigns' right hand; and the troops marched past in slow and quick time. Their dress is generally beautiful. I do not like the blue shako worn by the Green Hussars and I think the Lancers almost too plain but generally it is the most soldier-like thing I ever saw.

There are several distinctions between our mode of marching past and that used by them; for instance the march of the Infantry is quite different, being all done with a bent knee. Then again they never open the Ranks and the Adjutant who covers his Commanding Officer does not salute, but the line that both Infantry and Cavalry keep is mathematically precise and the bands as they relieved each other, seemed one more beautiful than the other.

I was much struck by the extreme youth of the soldiers, and still more at their splendid style of manœuvring though they only serve two years. No wonder the Prussian officers arrive at perfection! Their whole life is one continuous repetition of drill. This is not left, as with us, entirely to the non-commissioned officers. The Landwirth are only embodied for one month before the manœuvres take place and the cavalry ride perfectly unbroken peasant horses, but their appearance and work are equally good. Of Artillery there was little nor can I say much in its praise.

In the afternoon had a long interview with the King of Hanover who received me in the kindest possible manner and enquired with the greatest interest after all his political friends. I am sorry to see how implicitly he trusts the policy of the Emperor and how little he seems to believe the possibility of any danger from that quarter. This seems to me singular in a man of his superior talent.

After we had talked together for an hour, he bade me farewell with the kindest manner and words. The combined bands played after the theatre before the Emperor's windows. I cannot describe the effect of such a magnificent crash there being, I believe, the bands of at least ten battalions. The light from the wood fires by which the men played giving strongly on the windows and outline of the Cathedral the form of which was rendered even more beautiful than usual in the red glare, the thousands of people over whose heads the illuminations from the town threw a fitful and picturesque light, the numerous staff in brilliant uniforms on the steps of the Palace and the Sovereigns with the Princesses on the Balcony, combined to produce a scene that I shall never be able to forget.

Sep. 14. (Friday) An attack on a supposed enemy was the order of the day, and on arriving on the ground, the disposition of the troops preparatory to the attack made it appear as if there were more soldiers than the day before. Their advances were splendidly made and if the dust would have permitted the whole manœuvre to be seen, it must have been prettily executed. The Artillery was terribly slow. I am persuaded that ours would have turned their guns round, fired and reloaded and fired again before these could get one shot fired. I found a most intelligent Hanoverian officer who had a plan of the attack and who explained to me any part of it that I was unable to follow.

On my return from the Field I found an invitation to dine with the King and go afterwards to the Ball. I was compelled to decline the dinner having no uniform but at six p.m. went to the Ball at which there were about 1,400 persons and from the beauty of the women, the style of dress (if you except the total absence of jewels on any but the Royal Family) and the abundance of the uniforms though all of one colour, I should almost have fancied myself at St. James's Palace. The King was there when I arrived but the Royal Family did not appear for half an hour. They then went into the interior room which became more or less the sanctum headquarters during the evening. I remained in the first room some time so cannot say which of the Royal Party opened the ball. I soon went in however and was shown the different Princesses by name and after a short time the Baron von Senden came and introduced me to the Princess Charles. She is a fine woman and seemed friendly with everybody there. She said two or three words to me and passed on. The Baron then introduced me to the Grand Duchess of Mecklenburg who has a pleasing countenance and manner, soft, graceful in every way. She asked me several questions and struck me as clever and agreeable. The Baron then introduced me to the Chamberlain of Princess Albert who presented me to his Royal Mistress. She was full of life and talent and I was sorry when the few minutes with which she honoured me were over.

Saw the King of Hanover again who was equally kind as before. I felt his kindness the more sensibly as I was an isolated Bourgeois in a crowd of splendid uniforms. A little kindness from one in the highest rank, shown on such an occasion is remembered with gratitude for the rest of one's life.

The supper was well arranged and Fancourt and myself who sat together got so plentiful a supply of Champagne from a good-natured old colonel opposite who filled our glasses as incessantly as he told innocent lies in bad French, that I scarcely remember what passed after supper. I got home about 1 a.m.

Sep. 15. (Saturday) This was the cream of the affair. There were two armies, the one of the Elbe and that of the West. The army of the Elbe occupied the little heights, lined the rivulets at the bottom and a village opposite. The first attack was made on the village with the intention of weakening the enemy's right flank by forcing it to send assistance to the village and then attacking the right wing and carrying the heights. This was accomplished with great difficulty. It was beautifully done. I like the cheer in charging. When the attackers had driven the enemy over the next heights, the Campaign was finished and the Emperor left immediately to inspect, so I was told, the Prussian regiment he commands at Brandebourg but I do not see how he could have arrived there by daylight.

After dinner I went to the top of the Cathedral to look at the Citadel, fortifications and surrounding country. From the facility with which the latter can be flooded I suppose Magdebourg is a strong place. They say it would require 60,000 men to invest it. I believe it but from the extent of the works it would require but little less to defend it.

By the by, why do they not repair one of the pinnacles carried away from the top of the Cathedral during Tilly's Siege?

Started at 7 by the Personen Wagen which is half as cheap as the Schnell Post, quite as fast and twice as comfortable. Reached Potsdam at 10 a.m. As in Magdebourg not a room to be had for love or money. At last found a pig-sty in a public house where I managed to dress, making the man believe I wanted it for the night. Hired a carriage from him which I found so disgracefully bad that, hot as I was, I was positively compelled to get out and walk as being less fatiguing. Ordered a carriage from the Hôtel Pétersbourg intending to see Potsdam and return by the 8 p.m. Schnell Post in which I had taken my place, but to my great disgust found that I could see nothing that day so went off to take a place by the earliest conveyance to Berlin and had just time to walk to the Great Park, look at Sans Souci and swallow my dinner when the Post arrived. I had sent my servant to get my things from the pig-sty and expressly warned him not to pay for the carriage which I had not used. On my arrival at the Post he told me he had been compelled to pay or the men would not give up my things. How I have been cheated this week! However if it had cost me even double I would not have given up going for I may never again have an opportunity of seeing such a splendid sight. Do I wish it? NO. Give me a small cosy home with Hannah and I never wish again to move. However, here or there would all be equally blessed and happy where she was. We shall certainly be compelled to live on the Continent for cheapness but the worst is I dare scarcely hope that we shall live anywhere together and without her I cannot be happy. Could I but have the offer how happy I should be!

It has been the finest day I think I ever saw in any country but almost too hot! I do not think I ever felt it quite so hot as during our drive from Potsdam back to Berlin. Even now at half past 8 p.m. on looking out of my window, I see the men walking without their hats. I met the Empress of Russia on her way to Potsdam with a long retinue of carriages—six and four. The drinking gardens (for here there is nothing else) looking very gay on each side of the road. They were crammed with women in pretty dresses many of whom had pretty faces. It all looks gay but here they do not dance or amuse themselves at all. As soon as I got home I had so much to write that I gave up the idea of going to the Opera. I received a letter from Harriet. Shall I wait here and see the fun, or shall I go on to Dresden and await them there? I must decide to-morrow.

Sep. 17. (Monday) Called on Sir George Hamilton who lives comfortable here and is in fact Minister as Lord W. Russell is seldom or never here. Went to dine with him at a quarter before 5; the first comfortable good dinner I have eaten since I left England.

Sep. 18. (Tuesday) Went first to the Bankers and drew £50. Ordered uniform for the Reviews, sent my things to a new apartment and then went to Herr Rauch's Atelier where I must confess I was not much charmed, there being little but the Busts of the King and the Emperor finished. Went to dine with Fancourt at the Restaurant where French cuisine was abominably mixed with the German—an unhappy combination. Went to see the new ballet of the Corsair at which all the Court was to be present. Found only the Grand Duke of Mecklenburg and Prince August with the Ladies and Chamberlains of the different Princes. The ballet was well got up, the music new and the grouping perfect. The house inordinately full and the heat insufferable. Came home to my new apartment where I still had the ill fortune to find my bed too short for me, a circumstance that I fear will not vary during my stay in this country. They talk of travelling as a sovereign cure for worry and for unfortunate affection. I wish I could find it so but change of scene has lost its charm for me. I cannot forget. I endeavour to be both occupied and amused with what I see but how gladly would I change all that is supposed to be amusement here for one single glimpse of her my soul loveth. What will be the desolation of my future life if I am debarred from that which makes the joy of my existence? All besides is secondary if not totally indifferent. I wrote to her to-day but I scarcely hope she will answer my letter. She never will resist the long and indefatigable siege that will be laid against her affection for me. Can I trust that my love will suffice to compensate her for all she must undergo, all she must sacrifice for me? Yes, I will subdue every inclination, every feeling to her wishes. My only object shall be to live for her.

Sep. 19 *and* 20. Went about the Town with Fancourt, left my name with all the Princes and after calling on Wellesley went to the theatre to see the Postillon de Long. The weather quite delicious but to-night rain with lightning tho' very warm. Find that unfortunately the Diplomatic Bag went off last night so must send my letter to Hannah under cover to my servant by Post. To-day Southampton and Harriet leave London. What a splendid passage they will have!

Sep. 21. (Friday) Went out with Count Rossi and Fancourt to the Manœuvres on the ground by Tivoli. The King, the Emperor and a large staff were there, Prince William commanding the infantry and Prince Albert the Cavalry. There was a supposed enemy in the wood who drove in the advanced Guard of the attacking army, who, however, brought up all their forces and drove the enemy thro' the wood. Then came the Parade. The marching past of the men was better, if possible, than at Magde-bourg. It is impossible to imagine anything more splendid and more perfect—more like machinery than a body of men. What would they be if they were to serve as long as ours? Some of the horses in the Cavalry are extremely good and in general the men and their officers ride well. The other day, however, the King sent to tell some of them that they rode like old women on rocking horses!

Received an order to dine with Prince Albert at 3 and went there with Rossi and Fancourt. About eighty sat down in as pretty a room as I have seen. The Salon de Bal on one side and the dining-room on the other are both consistent and pleasing. The dinner purely German, the wines excellent. After dinner talked a while in the drawing-room and then the whole thing was over. I cannot help hoping that Southampton will come here in time to see one good manœuvre. If not I shall start for Dresden as soon as I hear from him.

Sept. 22. Went to buy some artificial flowers I had been asked to get and went to dine with Prince August at 3. A comfortable and noble palace, a good French dinner with abundant and excellent wines. Prince William and Prince Albert interested themselves about my being asked to Potsdam to-morrow, which I had no right to expect. In the midst of this gaiety one object only is constantly before my eyes and were that for ever hopeless, I should have neither spirits nor power to go into such scenes. At times I think I am wrong in going out at all since she is all this time shut up in sorrow at home, and perhaps, did she not know now how impossible it is for me to avoid my present surroundings, she might think me unfeeling and forgetful. If she realised how much more earnestly it makes me look forward to the happiness of living with her alone in undisturbed privacy, she would not fear that I should be led astray even for a moment. It is three weeks this morning since I left the land where she lives and breathes. How slowly the time goes by and yet how awful it is to wish oneself six months nearer the grave; and still I must do so. The suspense of these dreadful six months is too much to bear. May Heaven bless thee, dearest! May no pang ever wring thy heart! Above all, God grant that pang, if it must come, may never come from me. I had rather suffer anything myself than expose thee even to an acquaintance with what sorrow is. Good night, my own, my best beloved. May the God of Israel watch over thee!

Sep. 23. (Sunday) Went to Potsdam at 2 p.m., where I was invited by the King to the Theatre and afterwards supper in the new Palace. Dressed in a wretched hole in a bad inn and then drove to the Palace. Found the King and the Court assembled in a splendid room called the 'large Grotto.' Was presented to the King and the Prince Royal. We then adjourned to the Theatre where the scene opened with a short *divertissement* in which the two Paglionis danced. This was followed by the Black Domino, musick by Auber. Demoiselle Lorne played gracefully. The theatre is prettily shaped with a cornice of cupids holding a wreath. The heat was tremendous. Between the acts the King and the Royal family left their places and ice and tea were handed round.

As soon as the theatre was over we went into a splendid room built of marble round which they say (and I believe with truth) a coach and four horses may be driven. If they mean that the horses should be harnessed *à la Prusse*, this requires no insignificant space. We supped at small tables and when the King rose he and the Princesses went round to speak to their different acquaintances for a short time. Then they and we severally retired. My friend, the Princess Albert, kindly came and said a few words to me.

The Emperor's daughters are pretty but too fair to endanger my tranquillity of mind. The Empress appears reduced to a skeleton. Princess William, who is far advanced in pregnancy, is amiable and I regret not being presented to her. This new Palace is certainly a splendid building! It was built at the close of the Seven Years war by Frederick the Great to silence and contravene the supposition, both among his own subjects and the enemy, that he had no money and truly he must have had enough and to spare, if he paid for this structure out of his superfluous cash! We got home at half past 2 a.m.—a lovely night but a little cold. I cannot determine whether it would be better for me to go to Leipzig to try to find my brother or to wait for him here. It is a great pity he should not see the manœuvres on Thursday and Friday, but if he has determined to join me here, he will scarcely come by Leipzig but by Halle or by Magdebourg. It is most unpleasant to be in uncertainty.

Sep. 24 *and* 25. (Monday and Tuesday) Did little or nothing but take my German lesson and look once more at some of the pictures. Rode with Hamilton by Charlottenbourg and dined with him.

Sep. 26. (Wednesday) Took my place for Dresden hoping to start that evening; found that the Schnell Post left on the following morning. After performing the laborious task of packing, dined with Hamilton, where I met Charles Villiers who went home with me afterwards and we sat for a couple of hours discussing sundry political matters.

Sep. 27. (Thursday) Left Berlin at 9 a.m., travelled through hideous country, but at sunrise the following morning approached Dresden where the improvement became immediately visible. Found an agreeable and gentlemanlike Frenchman in the Schnell Post, Le Comte Gabriel de la Rochelambert, with whom I came to the Hôtel de Rome where I am now staying. The approach to Dresden is gay and pretty and really a relief after the uninteresting plains that surround Berlin.

Sep. 28. After dressing went off immediately to the Gallery in which I found more pictures to interest me than I have seen in any other gallery. I shall make out a list of those which most pleased me, with some remarks on those that struck me in divers manners, as it will recall to me in after days what I have seen, and I must here express my regret at not having always preserved catalogues of the pictures I have seen as well as a register of what I have done in my travels.

In the afternoon went with the Count to the Palace where I found a remarkable collection of stag horns from twenty even to fifty points each. There are a lot of 32 and upwards! In the Hall below are strange specimens of heads of stags that have become entangled in fighting and died interlocked. In some cases the brow antlers have penetrated the eyes and heads mutually and in others the animals must have died of starvation. Drove afterwards to the new Pavillon à la Chinoise where a quantity of Pheasants are said to be kept, of which I saw none though I examined their house carefully, and in returning saw two fine stags close to the road.

Sep. 29. (Saturday) Went immediately to the Gallery after breakfast, then went to call on Mr. Forbes who had invited me to dinner but I could not leave the Count. Went to the famous Rococo warehouse and then to Mayer's where I saw some Dresden china that almost equalled the old Sèvres. Procured some engravings and descriptions of Saxon Switzerland where I shall go to-morrow and where I expect to find much satisfaction. Walked later on the Terrace whence there is a beautiful view down the river. I am grieved to say the Gallery is closed for the Season.

Sep. 30. (Sunday) Went to the Catholick Church where the musick much disappointed me, the trumpets being out of tune. After dinner drove to Attewalde and thence to a guide and walked through the Attewalde Grund to Bastei. I regretted at the time that the sun was so far down when we entered the Valley of Rocks but was afterwards convinced of my error for the effect was finer by twilight than in full sunshine. Took a survey of Saxon Switzerland from the platform of Bastei from whence in the bright moonlight the heights round Schandau loomed splendidly in the distance.

October 3. (Wednesday) Started at half past 5 a.m. to see the silver mines at Freiberg and arrived at 10 a.m. Sent for permission to see the works and then started off to descend. I am sorry we wasted the time. The descent by a dirty wet ladder is laborious and the heat in parts quite insufferable. One fine line of ore I certainly saw but they seem chary of giving information. Walked across the field to the offices which were shown to us by an intelligent young man. Finding that the band of the Officers of the Mines was about to play, we stopped an hour and heard a concert of superior style. Left at half past 5 p.m. and reached Dresden at 10 p.m.

Oct. 5. (Friday) Went again to the Gallery where I am every day improving my knowledge of pictures and really think that I shall in a short time become a connoisseur; but there are so many beauties that the eye becomes puzzled and wearied before it has time to get through a tithe of them. After dinner went shopping, then to the bank and later in a Hackney coach to the Baths where they told me there was to be musick but owing I presume to the badness of the weather, I found there was none. Returned on foot and being too late for the theatre sat down to write a letter and read a French book. Shall I soon have an answer to the letter I wrote from Berlin? She surely cannot allow me to pass the whole dreary months of separation without one line of encouragement or of remembrance; and yet I almost dread to receive her letter upon the tone of which hinges my fate. If she is still unchanged then I am secure and happy, but I cannot get rid of a certain fear. It is almost too much to expect. From anyone else it would be hopeless to dream of attachment so durable but she is so different from all beside, that I dare hope. I am much disappointed at not seeing Southampton and Harriet yet. I had made sure of their arriving to-night at the latest. I trust they have not changed their route.

Oct. 6. (Saturday) Went to see the Huguenots which exceeded my most sanguine expectations. In the evening found that Southampton and Harriet had arrived.

Oct. 11. (Thursday) Walked about and bought some books etc. I am so disappointed at not hearing from Hannah. She has at last yielded to annoying remonstrances and determined to give me up to her family prejudices. I could scarcely doubt it and yet, God knows, how hard will be the blow if this is indeed the case! Never again will I seek the love of woman and that which was my pride and happiness will be my deadliest bane. From her I have not deserved this. Heaven knows how ready I am to sacrifice all for her; but this silence bespeaks if not total forgetfulness, at least indifference.

Oct. 12. (Friday) Went for the last time to the Gallery (shall I ever see it again with her I love?) and in the evening went to the opera but as Schroeder did not sing I found little interest in it.

Oct. 13. (Saturday) Left Dresden and went across the river with Southampton to Bastei, re-crossed and arrived at Teplice at 10 p.m. Passed in the dark the scene of the surprise of the French by the combined Austrians and Prussians, or rather by the Prussians as they alone remained with 8,000 men to check the French.

Oct. 14. (Sunday) Left Teplice at 8 p.m. and reached Prague after passing through a generally plain and uninteresting country although with partial spots of beauty. Certainly the town strikes me as one of the finest I have ever seen. In the evening went to the Platz and saw a scene from *Faust*.

Oct. 17. (Wednesday) Left Prague at 7 a.m. and after endless difficulties from want of horses reached Pilsen at 7 p.m. A wretched inn but not so dirty as to beds as I expected. Left at a quarter past 6 a.m. on Thursday *Oct.* 18 and after a provoking day of stoppages from want of horses etc., reached Ratisbon at 2 o'clock the following morning.

Oct. 19. (Friday) Walked about the town to see the buildings but being (wonderful to say) rather unwell, went home and turned in early.

Oct. 21. (Sunday) Left Ratisbon at 7 a.m. and descended the river through some fine scenery particularly as we approached

Passau when the sun broke out and showed us smiling valleys with snug chalets lying under the shelter of the wooded rocks. For a description of the scenery in detail I shall buy Murray's book. Reached Passau at a quarter past 5 p.m. It was too dark to see much so I went to the theatre but finding no room and little interest came home at 8 p.m.

Oct. 22. (Monday) Went on board before tea but the fog so thick we could not start till nine. Fortunately the thickness did not last long for the beauty of the scenery was delightful.

Oct. 23. (Tuesday) Went on board at 6 but there was again thick fog and we did not start till 10. In consequence of this delay we were compelled to stop at Stein that night, a miserable village. Southampton and I slept in the carriage. Harriet and her maid found a bed in the cabaret.

Oct. 24. (Wednesday) Arrived at Vienna where I had the happiness of finding a letter from my beloved Hannah. I read and reread her dear kind letter with a joy I cannot express. Thank God she is not yet changed.

Oct. 25. (Thursday) Walked about the town and dined with Esterhazy and then went to the Opera.

Oct. 26. Went off at 9 a.m. to shoot with Nicolas Esterhazy at Potendorf; came home late and dined with him.

Oct. 27 *to Oct.* 29. Passed our time in seeing the Arsenal, the Esterhazy Gallery and the Prater Riding School.

Nov. 1. (Thursday) Went to try to see the Gallery of Prince Lichtenstein but it being a Feast Day was not allowed to do so. Walked afterwards on the Ramparts where I saw the Emperor and Empress walking quite unaccompanied and most cordially saluted by the crowd. On Thursday last wrote to my dearest love. I shall hope to find the answer at Constantinople. How wretched it is to hear from her only once a month! How I long for the end of these long months of trial. Three months and eighteen days still! and when these are expired what will be the result? The suspense of the last few weeks will be almost insupportable. I dread the issue but thank Heaven, we are not free agents and in the hands of

Providence, I can leave it with confidence, certain that we should not have been permitted to go so far, were it to lead to nothing.

Nov. 2. (Friday) Went to Eisenstadt to shoot where we remained Saturday and returned home on Sunday evening. Shot deer the first day and pheasants on the second; the bag being 400 head.

Nov. 6. (Tuesday) Spent this day in writing letters and in packing and on Wednesday *Nov.* 7 left Vienna for Trieste as we were informed that the boats from there to Constantinople were so superior.

CHAPTER SIX

NOVEMBER 16, 1838. Trieste. Embarked on board the *Baron Eichoff* having engaged all the ladies' berths. There were about forty passengers most of them forward cabin gentry. Amongst those with us were Mr. and Mrs. Branbridge who have some property in Athens and have travelled a great deal. Our misfortunes began immediately we stepped on board. The most soaking rain I ever beheld and on our endeavouring to get under way, we found no steam and what was worse the coppers, being heated empty, had set fire to the boards and we were delayed more than four hours in ascertaining the extent of the damage. Sailed at half-past eight p.m. with the hope of Ancona at eleven on the following morning, but alas a strong head wind had arisen in the night and we did not reach Ancona till 9 p.m. after a disagreeable cold day. The coals or machinery or probably both so much damaged that the ship was unable to make more than four miles an hour in smooth water. We could not get Pratique so by force remained on board.

Nov. 18. (Sunday) Breakfasted on shore, then visited the Fortress, Trojan's Arch, dined at 3 and went on board (having left Harriet bound for Naples). A most lovely still evening very warm.

Nov. 19. (Monday) The damage having been repaired, and it being a most lovely day, we made rather better way, although she was in such bad time owing to the Cabin being filled with merchandise, that her progress was miserably slow. Past Lissa and the little islands round it at 10 a.m. and spent a pleasant day, anticipating arriving at Corfu the next evening.

Nov. 20. (Tuesday) On going on deck found the wind dead against us and a heavy sea which promised to impede our way so much that the Captain decided on running into the Bocca di

Cattaro for provisions and coals, as it was evident we had not enough of either. We made this Bay in a manner to me perfectly incomprehensible, as we kept no reckoning and it was too thick to steer by the land. Arrived just at sunset, the scenery and the weather being equally lovely and soft. A small bay quite wind-locked girt round with high hills all covered thickly with the most luxuriant myrtles and arbutus; the only cultivation being small olive gardens; saw the remains of the oft-disputed castles at the north side of the Bay, but did not get up to Cattaro, the scene of Sir J. Hoste's valour.

Nov. 21. (Wednesday) The weather quite perfect and we walked a little on the south side of the hill, but did not sail till 2 p.m. thus wasting the most lovely and to us (as it turned out) invaluable hours, through their laziness in bringing us provisions. The sun set with a wild fearful appearance which I pointed out to our Captain but he ridiculed the idea of its foretelling wind. However, in the course of the night we were turned out of our berths by a most tremendous burst of thunder and lightning, accompanied by wind that nearly drove us back. It was the first storm I had ever seen at sea and the effect of it was far beyond my expectations as to the sublimity of the scene and I must add also its fearfulness. The rain poured down at last in such torrents that even the force of the wind was insufficient to raise the sea.

Nov. 22. (Thursday) On waking found the wind so strong and at the same time so contrary that our only hope was to make for the shelter of Cape Linquetta, behind a small island called Sasseno where we hoped to cut wood enough to supply the dearth of coals without dread of quarantine, to carry us into Corfu. Found good anchorage but too much sea to approach the shore.

Nov. 23. (Friday) Found the wind equally strong and adverse. Began to think of shortening our expenditure of provisions and consequently took off one dish from our dinner. In the course of the night when all were just turned in came a repetition of the thunder of the preceding night, with redoubled fury, but luckily for us the thunder broke in one fearful clap on the rock under which we were anchored and consequently its force subsided. The wind, however, raged so fearfully that we gave up all idea of sleeping and cowered together in the cabin, every moment expecting to part from our anchor. Sleep seemed banished from every eye; we all felt that our existence depended on one cable.

Nov. 24. (Saturday) Went on deck early and found the wind still blowing fresh but in a short time it veered round a point in our favour and at ten a.m. we got under way and sailed with a prosperous wind to Corfu where we arrived at 8 p.m. Thus being nine days from Trieste. On reviewing the events of those nine days what cause of thankfulness have I for almost miraculous escapes! How little can anyone imagine till he himself feels it, the horror of being roused from sleep by crashing thunder accompanied by a wind that howls through the rigging with an ominous wailing that finds a ready echo in the breast. I own I feared and cannot envy the man who remained unmoved during those nights of sublime horror.

We got Pratique very shortly and landed in search of a good inn at which to sup. After trying many we found the Bella Venezia the most capable and ordered supper, during which Claud Hamilton and Colonel Dawkins found us and kindly proposed to us to sleep at the Palace. It was however too late for this and we returned to our berths.

Nov. 25. (Sunday) Found the Governor's boat waiting alongside to convey us to the Palace where we breakfasted and then started off in pouring rain with four-in-hand to Pianta Leone. The weather soon cleared and the view though limited by mist, was very fine and I had a good idea of the circumference of the island which was, however, much improved by ascending the Citadel which I did after an excellent luncheon while the band of the Rifles was playing. We dined at the Palace and I went to the Opera where they were torturing the Italiana in Algieri.

Nov. 26. (Monday) Sailed at 7 a.m. with a fair wind and had a very prosperous voyage although after the first four or five hours, we lost sight of land and the view of one's fellow creatures in the act of vomiting was not agreeable. However, owing to our complaints, the time of the vessel had been altered and she sailed in good style. At half-past 11 p.m. we reached Patras having done this distance in sixteen and a half hours.

Nov. 27. (Tuesday) Foolishly determined not to go round with the steamer but hired a small boat and after laying in necessary provisions, we started at one p.m. hoping to reach Loutraki the next morning. In the afternoon our old ill luck attended us and we found the wind dead against us with a soaking rain so much so that they informed us after a time that further progress was impossible and wet and wretched we were compelled when they dropped the anchor, to creep into the filthy hole called, I imagine, by courtesy, a cabin. Here I sat on a box, Claud Hamilton on the floor, far too short for him, and I crept most valiantly into a niche used by the crew as their refuge.

Nov. 28. (Wednesday) Got under way with the wind still against us, endeavoured to make the point beyond Galaxidi but after fruitless attempts, made up our minds to run into Vostitza which we had passed in the morning, giving up all idea of reaching Athens unless by almost miraculous speed in time for the steamer. Here I should have liked to bring the man who calls himself a traveller on the strength of a trip up the Rhine, or at the most to the beaten track of Naples and Rome. Four bare walls, not certainly of the cleanest, no sign of furniture, not even a stool; the substitute for windows being composed of deal boards with sundry large holes in the same; the floor (a space of about ten feet square on which our only hopes of rest were centred) being covered with a filth of the most abominable nature. Although we were wet through we saw the ludicrous side of the picture and looking at each other's faces fairly burst out laughing. In time, however, stools arrived and we arranged our quilts, capotes etc. on the floor in such a manner as to make a very tolerable bed in the midst of the filth, and after a good *Poulet au Roi* by Giorgio, we lay down meaning to start at dawn for the Convent, the first station on the way to Corinth.

On Thursday, finding that the Greeks wanted to profit by our apparent helplessness and charge us double the price for our horses, and seeing moreover a brig laying her course well up the Gulf, we determined again to try the boat, there being then a slant of wind which promised to take us to Loutraki in five or six hours. In about an hour it changed and finally died away. We now determined to make Itéa if possible and so ride across to Athens, as it was clearly impossible to adhere to our Corinth project. The night was lovely but dead calm, and after numerous tacks that scarcely advanced us we were compelled to use the oars which, owing to the clumsiness of our craft, were of little use.

On Friday morning therefore, we found ourselves in the bay with the sun shining brightly on Galaxidi and only a few miles from our point of debarkation; but no wind to help us. We bought some fine fish from a boat we passed and at noon arrived at Itéa. Here, for the first time, I saw camels at work, and their docility as they knelt to receive their burdens, joined with their savageness when strangers approached quite surprised me.

We soon procured mules and horses and started off through olive groves and vineyards to Kastri beyond which the road winds round a rocky ridge until one comes into view of Delphi and the famous plane-trees that grow around the Castilian fountain. Whether a draught from the Castilian fountain inspired me or whether the peculiar beauty of the evening, I never enjoyed a view so much.

Dec. 1. (Saturday) Started at 7 a.m., a lovely morning with the snow-clad hills over the Gulf just tipped by the sun. After passing Arakhova the mist cleared from Mount Parnassus. Our ride was beautiful all the way through bold defiles and lovely passes to Livadia where we slept. The Inn was too dreadful even for us now drilled to filth. We therefore procured a store-room in a private house where, as usual, we slept on the floor.

Dec. 2. (Sunday) Started at dawn, the first part of the route being rocky, the last five hours through the plain of Thebes. We lost our time in following eagles a great number of which we saw, and one of which I ought to have killed. We reached Thebes at dark and put up in a room the walls of which were actually white-washed.

Dec. 3. (Monday) Got up at daybreak to see the ruins of Thebes taking with us a Cicerone who professed to be acquainted with them. He may be so with their modern, certainly not with their ancient history. Saw the remains of a temple but in reply to a question as to what temple it was, received the usual answer: '*Chi lo sa?*' What a flourishing town this must have been with the rich, fertile, plain round it, aqueducts supplying the inhabitants, the soil arable almost with a bit of stick and such a climate! Changed our mules here for excellent horses. Started at half-past eight, rode first over the Plain of Platæa and then through some splendidly wild and well wooded passes, to Athens. The last four hours were tedious with fatigue but the effect of the fires lighted on the hills by the people employed on picking olives made so striking a picture that it revived us. We reached Athens at 10 p.m. and had supper at the Albergo Reale. Went to bed at half-past twelve, tired with the journey but charmed at the good fortune which had prevented us from going through without seeing all this part of the country.

Most lamentable indeed, from all I can gather, is the state of this unhappy country. Ruled by Othon I, son of the King of Bavaria, the people have no voice in their own affairs. This monarch, placed on the throne by foreign interests, is destitute of energy and talent. The wretched inhabitants see every office filled with hulking Bavarians of the lowest class. The Minister of Finance was a cobbler in Bavaria, a sous-lieutenant enjoys the King's entire confidence. English influence is more than con-demned. Every opportunity is laid hold of to insult our Minister either in the person of his own servants or of those confided to his care and no step can be taken in any affair of the slightest moment until the advice of Russia has been obtained.

Then there is a council of State of 25 or 26 persons of weight and character in the nation, but instead of being chosen by the people they are elected solely by the King who can remove them at his wish. That the form of government here should be despotic might be beneficial were the Despot a man of understanding but to attempt to thrust foreign institutions wielded by foreign ministers down the throats of a people who have always striven for liberty is playing a game that not even the continued presence of 3,000 Bavarian bayonets can make safe. It maddens me to see such a glorious career as was open to this young king, neglected for want of common sense.

Dec. 6. (Thursday) Was presented in due form to Their Majesties. Among other questions the King asked me whether I thought it would be better to leave or to remove the Venetian Tower that now encumbers the Propylæa. I answered: "In my opinion nobody could hesitate a moment in voting it to destruction."

"That is the feeling of all painters," said the King. "But it is a fine object from the sea."

The Queen, who also mentioned this subject expressed herself very strongly in favour of its preservation. She is a charming person, graceful and unaffected and worthy of a far more efficient husband than she is at present blessed with. I can find none of the 'fine figure and countenance beaming with benevolence not unmarked by intellect' which Quin in the second volume of his *Steam Voyage down the Danube* attributes to King Othon. I cannot but think that Quin was mostly enraptured at the uncommon occurrence (for him) of presentation to a king.

In the evening was tempted to try the Hôtel de France for dinner but found it still worse than my own.

Dec. 9. (Sunday) Went on board the *Koldwrat* at 3 p.m. and having left our things went in a boat to the tomb of Themistocles which is round the point but under water at high tide, and this,

of course, it happened to be just then. Saw two Russian Ships
of War in the harbour, one Austrian. The little *Magpie Cutter*,
the *Beacon* just beating out to Malta and in Salamis, the old
Jalavera. Started at four with the wind as usual against us and in
the course of the night a good deal of it, but we arrived at Syra
at half-past 3 a.m.

Dec. 10. (Monday) Syra looked beautiful from without forming an amphitheatre rising in the centre to a point and crowned by
the convent. We landed after breakfast and after lounging a little
in the bazaar, walked up the hill above the town from whence we
had a view of more than fifteen of the Greek isles under their own
peculiarly joyous sunshine. I never saw, I never can conceive a
more lovely view; far as the eye could reach, not a ripple on the
water and each island standing out with its tiers of white villages
glistening in the warm rays.

Dec. 11. (Tuesday) Went on board the *Mahmoud* and sailed at
noon, a most lovely day. Just what one would have desired for
the Archipelego. What a climate! The day almost too hot, the sea
like glass, the sky cloudless. Passed between Tinos and Mykonos,
leaving Icaria, the scene of Icarus's unhappy attempt at flight on
our right hand. Man will certainly never fly! We passed Samos
next, an island that although subject to the Sultan has its own
Governor called the Prince of Samos and makes its own laws,
produces good oil, *vin de muscat*, honey and wax. Ahead of us we
saw Chios between which and the mainland our passage lay. The
evening was perfect. I stayed long on deck watching the lights
from the fishermen's boats and drinking in the softness of the
night, and truly I found as the Captain told me, in this climate the
stars are as brilliant as the moon elsewhere.

Dec. 12. (Wednesday) Arrived at Smyrna at half-past 5 a.m. after
a most lovely passage of seventeen hours. The plague was pretty
strongly developed so that we dared not have any communication
with the shore for fear of quarantine at Constantinople. From the
spot where we anchored close in, could not form a very favourable
opinion of the Town. Saw four French Men of War, three

Austrians and a good deal of merchandise. Sailed at 3 p.m. the weather still delicious, passed a French corvette and a lumbering Turkish Frigate just below the Port in which I saw some of the cannon for throwing the marble shot. Here a Pelican, the first I had ever seen on the wing, came right across our Bow, almost within a shot. Hoped to be in the Dardanelles by next morning at 10 a.m. but alas, on *Dec.* 13 (Thursday) on going on deck, found a strong head wind and no chance of getting through in the course of the day. Stopped at Tenedos to take in a cargo of slaves from Tripoli with the brutes who had bought them. It was bitterly cold and these poor wretches had literally nothing on but a piece of coarse woollen cloth wrapped round them. They all huddled together on the deck and in the evening a tent of sailcloth was rigged up for them. The sea rose so much, as well as the wind, that it was quite disagreeable on deck. I could not, however, resist looking at the ancient plains of Iraq, the tombs of Patroclus, Achilles and Ajax; it was too dark to see Mount Athos; turned into the Hellespont, misnamed by Homer 'the Broad Hellespont,' and, a few miles from the fortress, just at the mouth and on the very spot over which Byron must have swum, anchored for the night as they were afraid to go further. The Cape of Abydos sheltered us from the wind. In the morning of Dec. 14th again started, the wind dead against us and blowing a hurricane. The current here running five miles an hour and the wind blowing strong from the E.N.E. our progress was of course wretchedly slow and we did not reach Gallipoli (a town just at the mouth of the Sea of Marmora, formerly of some importance) till four o'clock. After proceeding about four miles, the Captain informed us that it would be necessary to return to Gallipoli to anchor for the night, for that we were then making only two miles an hour, and if the wind came any stronger we should not be able to hold our way. He said in that case we would not make Marmora, still distant 40 miles; that between Gallipoli and this island it was too narrow to tack about all night, and that if we tried to run into Gallipoli after dark it would be very dangerous.

We could, of course, say nothing more than our fellow passengers, the Turks: "Allah is Allah!" The ship put about and again we anchored for the night. May I ask, why should not sailing vessels answer every purpose for the Austrian trade, as the more expensive process of steaming? The moment the wind is contrary, they are in some snug anchorage. They might as well do this in a sailing vessel! The French ship which had not lit her fires when we left Smyrna, is now in Constantinople. Here we are a hundred and ten miles from it and but little prospect of ever reaching it. Thirty days from Trieste! It is the most unattainable land of promise I ever tried to reach. The moment I arrive I must leave it again or I shall be too late for the opening of the Session.

Dec. 15. (Saturday) The wind changed to N.N.E. so we weighed anchor at half past 9 a.m. and started in hopes of reaching Constantinople to-morrow morning. It is blowing very hard and is still so cold that I can scarcely hold my pen. The mountains to leeward are very dark and heavy but the sky looks a little better in the wind. They say we shall not have snow, but that it has fallen farther north. The poor wretched negroes are all huddled together under a scrap of flannel, trying to impart the warmth they want to each other. They give them nothing but bread and seem to treat them just like beasts or any species of merchandise.

Dec. 16. (Sunday) The wind freshened very much during the night and the morning was extremely squally and wild and the cold more severe than any I had ever felt in England. Unfortunately it was almost dark with clouds as we approached Constantinople, but as we turned the Seraglio Point, the clouds lifted and showed us the far-famed gilded minarets and mosques— Santa Sofia on our left, with the beautiful Seraglio gardens and the Palace. We anchored at 11 a.m. having been so many days in consequence merely of the timidity of the Captain, the French steamer having arrived on Saturday morning. Went to try for rooms at an Englishman's house but found none so came to Madame Giuseppini's where in hot weather all must be comfortable, but in this piercing cold, the absence of stoves is sensibly felt. Mr. Cartwright, the Consul, brought us some letters that had come by way of Vienna but none were from London. The courier is due to-morrow but this weather will probably delay him. We went after dinner to a theatre—or rather to a room where a third-rate conjuror was performing the hackneyed sleight-of-hand tricks. Only two women were present, all the rest of the spectators dirty Turks.

Dec. 17. (Monday) The weather more horrible with the wind blowing strongly from the North-east. Sleet, hail and rain nearly cut my nose off and prevented me from seeing any distance. However we started on horse-back to take a superficial view of the town and after crossing the wooden bridge, went up some bad, narrow streets until we came opposite the Palace of the Generalissimo, the porch of which is magnificent. From thence we went to the Mosque of Sultan Achmet and rode across the yard admiring the domes and minarets which had apparently been recently gilded. Thence to the Sultan's Porte where we were first introduced into the Grand Vizier's room which is well furnished and in the wall of which nearly over the door, is a hole where formerly the Sultan hung his sleeve into which Ambassadors held conversations supposing it to be the Sultan himself. After a short *pourparler*, our fat Turkish Cicerone told us that if we would give him a *cadeau* he would show us the Sultan's own room in which he holds Council. This is an extremely pretty and really comfortable room, well cushioned and carpeted, in the centre of which is a table with a gilt stand for the Koran. Here sits the Council while the Sultan decides on the measures to be adopted. Next to this is a place where the Sultan makes his ablutions. The Palace is large but the wind howls miserably through the long corridors and bare rooms and there seems no more means of warming this than any other house in this wooden town.

Rode into the far-famed and justly celebrated Bazaar or rather Bazaars, for although all under one roof, or within one enceinte, they are separated into depots for particular articles, one for shoes, one for pipes, one for embroidered clothes, one for saddlery, one for bonbons, etc. The Turks seemed much put out at our riding through, and I think justly, for there is so much business and such a crowd that it must have been really inconvenient to them. I shall in my future visits prefer walking. Many of the shops were shut in consequence of the Bairam which was to take place next morning, but certainly the magnitude and oddity of the whole place exceeded my most sanguine expectations. Passed the burnt Pillar of Constantine and other mosques and then returned home, the cold being intense.

Dec. 18. (Tuesday) Got up at five to go to the shop we had secured the previous day to see the Procession of the Bairam. The streets were in such a dreadful state from the snow and ice that it was almost impossible to get along. On arrival at our shop (after a great quarrel with a brutal Turk) we found that owing to the state of the weather the Sultan would only go to the Mosque of Santa Sofia, it being so much nearer his Palace. We left our horses and went to the corner by the fountain at the Gate of the Seraglio, and seeing a window unoccupied we arranged with the master of the house to allow us to take possession of it. The street opposite the Gate of the Seraglio was lined with troops (of which more anon) half way between the two mosques, as it was not positively known to which he would go. On the side of the fountain were several carriages filled with women, and in the clear space intended for the horses of dismounted men, a number of Turks were selling the puddings of rice, butter and peas, of which the soldiers as well as others constantly partook. In about a quarter of an hour signs of the commencement of the Parade made themselves visible. Several men whom we were told were Colonels and Generals rode to the door of the Mosque and then, after being assisted to dismount, their horses were taken to the rear; some of the horses were pretty, but most of them though showy in their splendid saddlery were not apparently well-shaped. Presently appeared the Bishop in a rich sort of robe, or to speak in plain English, a dressing-gown and turban, followed by three others, two of whom instantly threw themselves off their horses and rushed to assist him in dismounting. These were also in dressing-gowns but less splendid than that of the Bishop. After a few minutes we heard the band inside the Seraglio strike up. The word was given to all the soldiers to take off their cloaks which were then hung on their shoulders and to the marines to unsheath their cutlasses and place the blades in their muskets instead of bayonets. They did not obey these orders in unison but one after the other, or rather as each could, one putting the butt of his musket on the ground and lugging at his cutlass with both hands, some giving the whole thing up in despair and quietly leaving theirs in.

When the order Present Arms was finally given the Marines did obey after a fashion but the men in brown who were opposite did not appear to have the slightest idea of doing so. The band now struck up and the procession appeared headed by a host of general officers who threw themselves helter-skelter off their horses, the mounts being taken away in equal disorder through the ranks of soldiers to the rear. Next came the main part of the procession. The bodyguard of the Sultan wore feathers far beyond me to describe, these being the size and shape of an eagle's wing, a bouquet forming the lower edge and then long feathers of green, blue and white, the effect of which in the mass was very striking, although singly they appeared ridiculous.

The Sultan himself followed and his horse was beautifully caparisoned with a yellow plume on its head. He looked neither right nor left but rode at once into the Mosque. After he arrived there, the Regiment of men in brown was relieved by a regiment of cavalry, and such cavalry! I wish even Lord R's Yeomanry could have seen them. About two among the whole corps had black belts. Their brass might once have shone but now the fiercest ray could not call forth a twinkle. Breeches that I imagine were intended to convey and warehouse the provisions of a campaign. Some of the men were talking, others were laughing. One would have a blue glove on his right hand and a green one on his left while many only had one glove for both hands. If possible the officers were more ridiculously dressed. When the ceremony was over the Sultan rode forth from the Mosque with the same retinue as before. Then began a race of warriors, officers and soldiers, cavalry and infantry, each endeavouring to outdo the other in the laudable effort to cast away even the pretence of order that had previously existed. Some men ran off with two muskets, many with none. The soldiers pushed their officers and the officers ran and joked with their men so that the confusion and disorder would have satisfied the most insatiable pickpocket. We left disappointed at the result of the whole business for what might have been an imposing spectacle was destroyed by the carelessness of the troops. On our way home we were compelled to halt while a regiment of marines passed the gate into Pera and we had additional time to comment on their appearance. The trousers tucked in the boots, the total irregularity of step, the running of the men into the Arsenal boats, the soldiers pushing their officers out of the way to avoid stepping into the snow. We had the greatest difficulty in preserving our gravity. This was the first day the troops had worn their shakos. Tilted at the back of shaved crowns, they gave a burlesque character to some of the faces that clowns at pantomime time would have willingly copied.

This is what comes of putting Asiatic barbarians into European uniforms. The Sultan is forcing civilisation down the throats of his subjects. He believes that the man who had courage enough to massacre the Janissaries and sense enough to seize the consumers of opium can, like the Creator of all, call light in the chaos of barbarity. Returned through the snow and dined with some merchants and two officers from the Tyne Frigate.

Dec. 21. (Friday) Mustapha came at 10 a.m. and took us to the madhouse, the cells of which are built round an inner court. In the cells are confined one, sometimes three men chained round the neck. Such a chain, made of iron, was broken by one more violent than the rest who, to-day, was hidden from view. The constant exposure to ridicule must tend to prevent the chance of recovery and the wretched manner in which these men are caged, invests their sorrowful condition with more than its accustomed horror. I was peculiarly touched with the countenance of one poor wretch who lost his all in a vessel. He seemed perfectly quiet and was eating bread, some of which he offered us. There was no one to tend him, no one apparently to care for him. The place was full of spectators and there were many there whose amusement it was to jeer at the poor wretches who were in a violent state and try to excite them like wild beasts.

Went into the Bazaar again for a short time and then returned to Pera to see the ceremony of the dancing Dervishes. We were shown into a plain little Mosque with an outer circle railed off from a polished wood centre. The spectators took their places sitting on their hands. There was a space latticed off for the women and a gallery above for superior people. The dress of the Dervishes is strange enough—a conical beaver hat, a short jacket and a capacious petticoat. Most of them are barefooted. On their entrance they made a profound obeisance to the cushion spread at the end on which, after a short interval, the chief accompanied by two others, took his seat. A prayer was said by the chief after he and the other two had prostrated themselves till their foreheads touched the ground. Then commenced a most extraordinary sort of music accompanied by what was meant for singing. After this had continued for some time they all made a circle round the enclosure bowing opposite the cushion on which they had sat while the others twisted around it as they passed. Eighteen danced at the same time in this small enclosure and although it seemed impossible to walk round without confusion, they made three separate circles into which they broke off at once never swerving the least either to the right or to the left. One who seemed high in authority walked round inside the outer circle bowing profoundly every now and then but though his arms were extended and the others were whisking round at a rapid pace, none ever ran against him but each kept exactly to his own orbit.

Dec. 22. (Saturday) Mustapha came at 10 a.m. and we started off to the Mosque of Solyman the Great into which we entered without difficulty. The simple grandeur of the building, the light softened down most perfectly by the extreme richness of the painting in the windows, the enormous height of the dome, the size of the pillars, the perfect stillness in consequence of the foot falling on the thickest Turkey carpet, produced a feeling of veneration such as I have seldom experienced even in the finest cathedral. The effect at night when the innumerable lamps are lighted must be striking and I left the mosque with great regret. We paid another long visit to the Bazaar of Arms and of Pipes and then returned to dinner.

Dec. 23rd. (Sunday) Went on board the steamer we had hired to go up the Bosphorus. Got under way immediately and had a beautiful though somewhat clouded view of the European bank, the new palaces, the small port of Therapia, the batteries and the lighthouse at the *embouchure*. We went about ten miles down the Asiatic coast.

Dec. 24th. (Monday) Rode all round the walls of the town and ascended the tower at the gate of which Constantine entered. We saw the hills on the other side of the Sea of Marmora covered with snow and glittering in the sun. We then returned and rode home through the Jews' quarter and the Greeks' quarter in both of which were seen at almost every window most lovely forms and faces. This was a real spring day.

Dec. 25th. (Xmas Day) Got on our horses intending to ride to the Seraglio but on reaching the bridge found that it was being repaired and we were therefore obliged to cross in a caïque and order our horses to join us afterwards. We walked to the Gate of the Seraglio and were then conducted, by order of the banker, over part of the Mint. The money seems principally composed of copper washed over with silver. The people employed are almost entirely Armenians. From thence we went into the court which contains the chamber in which the Sultan, after being crowned, was viewed by his subjects. We later went into the Cavalry barracks to see the troop horses. I bought a horse from one of the officers which had been given him by the Sultan. We then went into the Saddlery Bazaar and bought a saddle and bridle for the little horse and returned and had a most excellent and jolly dinner and Christmas party at Mr. Cartwright's.

Dec. 26. (Wednesday) Packed up, got money, paid bills and went on board the *Stamboul* (Captain Vord) and sailed at half-past 4 p.m. with a light, favourable wind down the Sea of Marmora.

Dec. 27. (Thursday) Wind still favourable and a beautiful passage. We stopped at Cape Baba at the entrance of the Gulf of Mitylene and then at Mitylene itself which lay basking in the sun and well screened from any blast of wind. The whole island looked beautiful, studded with villages embedded in olive groves, the revenue from which is considerable. The weather continued lovely and we anchored at Smyrna at twenty minutes past 6 p.m. having made the passage in 26 hours. The landlord of the Pension Suisse was in attendance and in a few minutes we were in a very comfortable inn.

Dec. 28. (Friday) Sent to enquire about shooting and found that it was impossible, without devoting to it a longer time than we could spare, to do more than chance a stray shot. We determined on going to Saint Nicol to sleep where it appeared we might be certain of sport. Prior to starting we went through the town and then returned to dinner after which we got on our horses and rode for three hours over a beautiful plain under a most brilliant moon, passing five or six large caravans of camels bivouacking picturesquely, and arrived at 8 p.m. at the village where we found better accommodation than seemed likely at first sight. Made arrangements for starting at daybreak.

Dec. 29. (Saturday) Got up at 6 a.m. and started after a cup of tea to the top of the hill, in ascending which we saw numerous marks of boars or sows. We posted a short distance above a ravine down which piggy was said to intend coming, and after waiting some time, heard him roused a short distance on my right. Unfortunately he went up the hill. We followed over mountain and over plain but returned empty-handed to our bower having seen but one quail that we brought back in triumph. On our return we found waiting for our inspection an Arab slave, whom I should conceive to be the best living representative of human obesity since the days of Daniel Lambert. I must own that the disgusting, considerably preponderated over the extraordinary. Breasts larger than those of any woman except Lady Stafford, stomach more protuberant than that buttoned on the drab breeches of Baron Patterson, legs to which Lady Caroline Stanhope's are a joke, hands broader than Mrs. Cotterell's, feet larger even than Mrs. Anson's completed a figure embodying the worst conception of a Hoffman. I was nearly buying him for five pounds. He was only eighteen and his countenance bespoke a strange compound of sheepishness and good-natured quickness.

After an early dinner we rode home, diverging a little from our route to see the Aqueduct and the rampart of the Citadel. On our way passed several caravans of camels as picturesquely planted as those of the preceding night. Arrived by a new road through the ford of the river at our Host's house, when we found that the steamer had not yet appeared.

Dec. 30. (Sunday) Walked about and saw the people of Smyrna parading the streets or sitting before their doors. In the evening went to a Jewish wedding. The bridegroom was 17 and the bride 13. They had been married the day before and according to the custom in their church, kept open house for seven days. At the moment we entered, a conjuror was amusing the company with specimens of his art and, I must own, very effectually as far as I could judge both from the applause he elicited and the proficiency of his attempts. After he had concluded his somewhat too protracted operations, coffee, liqueurs and some sweetmeats were handed round. This was preparatory to the music which consisted of a tambourine, an ancient species of lute and a fiddle. We were introduced into an inner room where the bride held her court as, through a window, she looked at the gaiety without. She was seated on a divan and was dressed in gorgeous brocade. She looked as much at home and as thoroughly bored as if she had sat there for years. The bridegroom, though a mere boy, was good-looking but we soon wearied of this wedding and returned home.

Dec. 31. (Monday) Went on board the French steamer *Dante* at 8 a.m. and sailed at half-past nine. Went round inside some of the small islands as our Captain had despatches to deliver to Admiral Lalande who was here with *l'Hercule* and other vessels belonging to the French squadron. A beautiful day with scarcely any wind but we soon found to our cost that the march of the *Dante* was very different from that of the *Stamboul*, her maximum in a perfectly smooth sea, being eight miles an hour. In the evening passed Chios. The sailors grouped themselves about and sang: "Le Beau Pays de France."

Jan. 1. (1839). Anchored at Syra at 6 a.m. where we remained till 2 p.m. but of course in quarantine. The captain prophesied bad weather and in fact it began to rain and became thick immediately after we left the island. On going on deck at 7 a.m. on Wednesday 2 I found that we had experienced a great deal of wind in the night and were only then off Cerigo whereas we had hoped by this time to have been off the redoubted Cape Matapan. Being unwell after breakfast, I went to my berth and slept till nearly dinner time after which I returned to my cabin. It rolled dreadfully all night and it was almost impossible to lie in a berth.

Jan. 3. (Thursday) Blowing a heavy gale of wind right in our teeth. The vessel not making more than one mile, or one and a half, the greatest part of the day. Very cold and disagreeable and although I did not feel actually sick, I dined on deck instead of going below.

Jan. 4. (Friday) Blowing much as yesterday except that we were able to carry sail for two hours. The casing of the pistons was worn so that the engine could not work with full power and the hold had to be pumped all day.

Jan. 5. (Sat.) Wind still the same though less of it, provisions getting rather scarce and the dinner principally composed of haricots under different forms.

Jan. 6. (Sunday) The wind half a point more on our beam; about noon saw the land of Malta and bore down for it, as we certainly had been steering rather wide of it before. How happy we all were at the idea of a quiet night's rest after all the tossing and rolling. Off the lighthouse at 6 p.m. and anchored at the end of the Quarantine Harbour at ½ past 6.

Jan. 7. (Monday) Went on deck early hoping to see something of Malta which however was impossible from our situation. Had an excellent dinner, no small pleasure after the bad living we had on the *Dante.*

Jan. 8. (Tuesday) Harriet arrived in time for dinner.

CHAPTER SEVEN

THE six months were over and once more the old, familiar drone of London echoed in FitzRoy's ears. Visions of gilded minarets and Grecian shepherds faded before the noise of clattering cabs. The February sun was pale and half-hearted but a bright fire and an English breakfast must have helped to make life seem solid and real. Piccadilly lay just round the corner and it was only eight miles to Gunnersbury.

FitzRoy was now obliged to take up the threads of his political life. The country was greatly excited by the opening of Parliament. The speech of the twenty-years-old Queen of England was eagerly discussed.

The ceremony had lacked none of its habitual grandeur. A vast crowd of people lined the route leading from the Horse Guards to Abingdon Street and the balconies were filled with eager sightseers. The Royal Gallery and the passages leading to the House of Lords were packed.

At ten minutes past two a discharge of cannon announced the arrival of the young Queen, who appeared in excellent health though somewhat paler than usual. Having passed through the lobbies and robed, the Queen entered the House, being preceded by the heralds and great officers of state.

The Sovereign made a lovely picture as she bowed graciously to the peers and peeresses. She wore a white-and-gold satin dress over which were her robes and round her throat was a necklace of diamonds. The Deputy Usher of the Black Rod summoned the members of the House of Commons and in a few minutes these appeared in large numbers, the noise occasioned by their entrance contrasting strangely with the almost breathless silence which previously pervaded the House.

These people listened with polite attention to the young girl in her white satin dress and sparkling diamonds. But as soon as the speech was over the opposition fiercely attacked it. The Queen had begun by announcing that matters of great importance demanded the serious attention and advice of the Legislature. Nothing very vital followed this statement.

As FitzRoy poured out his morning cup of tea he doubtless tried to construe his party's policy in the light of some of the newspaper criticism. There were many foreign entanglements to keep clear of. The Queen herself made mention of the continued war in Spain. The Spanish unrest had been going on for so long now that it figured annually in the Sovereign's speech. Russia was considered to have hostile designs against Great Britain, and there had been military and naval demonstrations. The affairs of France were approaching a crisis. Louis Philippe had resolved not to submit to the expressed opinion of his Parliament and had appealed to the constituency by dissolving the chambers. People were forecasting another French revolution, and Englishmen were wondering just what repercussions such a tragedy would have upon their home affairs. There was an Irish problem together with the broad principle of religious liberty throughout the Empire. Of more personal interest to FitzRoy was the news that Her Majesty's Government had concluded treaties of commerce with two nations he had just visited. They were signed by the Emperor of Austria and the Sultan of Turkey.

The old Duke of Wellington, who so often had called on Nathan Rothschild to drink wine with him, got up in the House of Lords to say a few words about the Royal speech. In the Commons Sir Robert Peel exhorted members to get down to business.

FitzRoy put his papers aside and ordered his servant to bring him a steak. He was a big man and had returned to London with tremendous vigour and a huge appetite. He was also in high spirits at the thought that the end of his probation was drawing to a close. He was about to start breakfast when young Nathaniel walked in. The two men greeted each other with obvious pleasure. What was the position with the Rothschilds?

To begin with, Hannah was still desperately in love. The long banishment increased her determination to have her own way and the strain even told on her health. Nathaniel said: "She has been pining and has not slept all night or eaten a crumb of bread."

Presumably the Rothschilds were of opinion that nothing could any longer stop the marriage from taking place. It was now a question of discussing financial details and giving a tacit permission. This did not signify that the Rothschild family was in any way reconciled to the marriage. They could no longer prevent it.

Nathaniel had undoubtedly exerted his influence. He did more. He had a charm of manner that was irresistible and a big, frank smile that could smooth things over during moments of difficulty. He returned to his sister during the morning and told her jokingly that he had found FitzRoy at his lodgings looking extremely jolly, and breakfasting on a large beef-steak, which certainly did not look as though he were dying for love!

As the days wore on FitzRoy saw many difficulties fade away, and it appeared that the marriage was now assured. He had several meetings with Lionel, during which he gave an account of his financial position, and on the whole this seemed to meet with approval.

Suddenly an unexpected difficulty arose.

Lady Southampton took swift action. She told her husband that as his brother was about to marry the daughter of Europe's wealthiest banker, there was no longer any reason to continue his allowance. This was sufficient to shatter all hopes of the marriage. Lord Southampton being childless, FitzRoy was considered heir to the title, but as their father had died when FitzRoy was only three years old, no provision was made for him in the will. He was therefore dependent on his brother's generosity. The position was aggravated by the fact that FitzRoy had already told Lionel about this allowance and the Rothschilds would now be justified in thinking that he had over-stated his condition in order to force their hands.

HANNAH MAYER ROTHSCHILD

The two brothers who had been close friends since childhood faced each other across the table. FitzRoy was roused and did not mince his words. He was fighting for the only thing in life he really cared about. When the Rothschilds originally opposed his marriage he faced them with a courteous doggedness. The attitude of his brother was so unexpected that he threw discretion to the winds. This was a threat that must be met without flinching or all his dreams might fall about his head like a crumbling house of cards. That Hannah should be deprived of her dowry by her parents was only to be expected, but that he should lose what was clearly his birthright was indefensible. His father had certainly never intended to leave him penniless.

The quarrel was fierce and went so far that no words could mend it. FitzRoy turned on his heels and left the room. He was not to speak to his brother again for fourteen years.

This event did not break the lovers' troth. It cemented the bond between them. But FitzRoy was cut off from all that remained of his family except his sister, Anne Caroline. She had married a minister called the Rev. Humphrey Allen. This man had a tall, conical, bald head, a sanctimonious drawl, and was often to be found leaning back in his chair with his hands placed together in the attitude of a praying saint. Like her mother, Anne Caroline wore a black poke bonnet and distributed bibles. She had a merry disposition, wore her dark, shiny hair in three long curls on each side of her face, and twisted the rest over a comb at the back. Her husband was incumbent of a chapel at Clifton and she seldom came up to town.

For FitzRoy and Hannah there followed two months of ecstasy. During this period they drove out in Hyde Park, went to the theatre and had ample opportunities to make plans for the future. Perhaps the most surprising sidelight to this was that Nathan's widow, who more than any member of the Rothschild family had been violently opposed to the marriage, now showed signs of being won over by the charm and goodness of her prospective son-in-law.

It was arranged that the wedding should take place at the Church of St. George, Hanover Square, on April 29, and though Mrs. N. M. Rothschild was careful in no way to relent from her officially hostile attitude, she showed considerable understanding of her rebellious daughter. Moreover, Nathaniel, who had never wavered in affection and loyalty towards his young sister, declared his intention alone among the Rothschild family of attending the wedding.

This momentous day opened sadly for Hannah. Instead of the wedding dress of white satin and lace that is the dream of every woman, she put on a simple morning gown and bonnet. Instead of the rich carriages filled with gifts from all her cousins scattered over the capitals of Europe she received letters of withering condemnation. These touched her deeply, because they came not only from near relations, but also from utter strangers of her own faith who were shocked by her defiance. The great house in Piccadilly was silent that morning. There was none of the bustle and excitement, the laughter and warmth of a big family. Her eldest brother, Lionel, left the house; her mother, though understanding, was of a sudden strangely distant, for fear, no doubt, of revealing the conflicting emotions within her breast. However masterful, however authoritative was Mrs. N. M. Rothschild, she was that day to hand her daughter into the care of a man who by race and religion was a stranger.

FitzRoy left his flat in South Street with his friend, Lord Castlereagh—two men with grave faces who might have been driving to their offices rather than to a wedding. Lord and Lady Southampton remained at Whittlebury. There would be no bridesmaids to bring a smile to Hannah's lips with their laughter and gay voices. There would be none of those spring flowers that just now made Gunnersbury a fairyland. The primroses would stay unpicked on the mound beside the lake, the hothouses near Amelia's ivy-covered bath would not give up their carefully tended plants. Mrs. N. M. Rothschild decided to leave the house and then turned back. This lovely woman, so striking in appearance, with her wonderful blue eyes and fine brow, must have suffered severely under the strain. Calling her daughter to her side, she declared her intention of accompanying her in a four-wheeler to the church door.

The two women were doubtless lost in thought as they drove to Hanover Square. In a short time Hannah would have adopted the name and religion of her husband. She would go out into the world with no longer the support of a powerful family. FitzRoy would be taking her for better or for worse, and not even her own mother would be present to witness the scene. For over a year she had been fighting for freedom, during which time her determination had never wavered nor her love for FitzRoy grown less. Possibly she was afraid. Here was Nathan's widow sitting rigid but red-eyed in the corner of a common four-wheeler in order to facilitate her daughter's runaway match.

The carriage clattered across the road and drew up beside the church. When Hannah looked up to see the tall figure of FitzRoy hurrying forward she doubtless felt reassured. How young and healthy he must have looked! Mrs. Rothschild rose slightly from her seat in the corner of the carriage, made a friendly gesture to her future son-in-law and then kissed her daughter before turning away her head. In a few minutes Hannah was standing between her brother Nathaniel and FitzRoy, while the sound of the four-wheeler died away carrying Mrs. N. M. Rothschild within it.

As the curate in his surplice came forward to ask if the party was ready, there were not more than a dozen people in all. It is probable that the words of the prayer-book's impressive service struck Hannah with all their solemnity: "I Hannah take thee Henry to my wedded husband, to have and to hold from this day forward, for better for worse, for richer for poorer, in sickness and in health, to love, cherish and to obey, till death us do part, according to God's holy ordinance; and thereto I give thee my troth."

As Hannah Mayer FitzRoy looked up into her husband's face

she doubtless knew she had been right. This was the moment she had waited for. How small was the price she had paid!

The Rev. W. H. Dickinson closed his prayer-book and led the way into the vestry. Eliza FitzRoy, an elderly aunt, took in her wizened fingers the quill pen handed to her by the curate and appended her name to the register under that of Lord Castlereagh. Nathaniel broke an awkward silence by going resolutely to his sister and kissing her warmly on the forehead. He then shook hands with his brother-in-law and congratulated him. Hannah often spoke later of this brotherly gesture. Her gratitude was immense. As the verger threw open the wide doors allowing the daylight to pour into the church, all these people must have got back their nerves. Nathaniel, for one, had a joyous temperament that was never quenchable for long.

The married couple drove over to a small villa at Petersham, near Richmond, where FitzRoy had prepared a surprise for his young wife. A cart stood outside the door laden with spring flowers. They would bring joy and fragrance to every corner of her new home.

CHAPTER EIGHT

O N the evening of December 15, 1842, the watchman making his round of Berkeley Square might have heard the clatter of a cab coming with speed from the direction of Piccadilly. The night was raw and foggy, and the trees in the gardens in the centre of the square looked like skeletons of fantastic shape.

The cab drew up at the house numbered 43. It was a fine house of five storeys with long rectangular windows, a balcony on the first floor and some wrought ironwork for the links and their extinguishers on either side of the porch. Hardly had the cab come to a standstill than a tall, dark, broad-shouldered man jumped out, took the small steps leading into the house at one leap and opened the door. A servant in livery hurried to his master from the end of the corridor.

"What is the news?" asked the man breathlessly.

"It's a boy, Mr. FitzRoy."

"A boy!" repeated FitzRoy: "May God be praised."

Inside the house the family doctor was bending over the bed where Hannah lay, her baby next to her. The doctor was so much a relic of bygone days that he actually wore a coffee-coloured coat with brass buttons and a frilled shirt-front. The boy he had helped bring into the world was to be called Arthur Frederick FitzRoy.

More than three years had passed since the wedding in Hanover Square. At times it must have appeared difficult for FitzRoy to remember what obstacles he had been obliged to overcome. Fortune seemed to smile on him. His political career showed even greater promise. Now he was blessed with a son.

The boy was to have two godfathers. The first was Lord Castlereagh, who brought back some water from the river

Jordan for the baptism. The other was Viscount Dungannon, who lived across the Square in Grafton Street with his wife and her two maiden sisters. The three women made a strange trio, invariably dressed in long trailing robes of black silk garnished with black lace. Their cheeks were delicately rouged and they remained always together in a long, deep drawing-room, perfumed and semi-darkened, and filled with a multitude of silver ornaments that they would spend the best part of their lives cleaning and rubbing up. Lady Dungannon wore round her neck, even in the morning, a string of pearls of which she was extremely proud.

Some days after the baptism, FitzRoy was obliged to travel to his constituency at Lewes. Thoughts of his infant son must have preoccupied him, for he spent some time of the journey carefully writing out a poem on a sheet of paper. They were bad verses, but this was a period when men broke into rhyme at the slightest excuse.

"A blessing on thy head, thou child of many hopes and fears
A rainbow welcome thine hath been, of mingled smiles and tears
Thy father greets thee unto life with a full and chastened heart,
For a solemn gift from God thou com'st, all precious as thou art.

I see thee not asleep, fair boy, upon thy mother's breast,
Yet I am sure how guarded there shall be thy rosy rest;
And how her soul with love and prayer and gladness will o'erflow,
While bending o'er thy soft sealed eyes, thou dear one, well I
    know.

A blessing on thy gentle head, and blessed thou art in truth;
For a home where God is felt awaits thy childhood and thy youth.
Around thee faith and holy thoughts dwell as light and air
And steal into thine heart and wake the germs now folded there.

Smile on thy mother, while she feels that unto her is given
In that day-spring glance the pledge of a soul to rear for heaven.
Smile! and sweet peace be o'er thy sleep, joy o'er thy wakening
    shed.
Blessings and blessings evermore, fair boy, upon thy head!"

CHAPTER NINE

BY the late summer of 1843 Arthur had blossomed out into a fine baby of seven months. Hannah was supremely happy, while her husband planned ahead for his son and heir. He would be taught riding like all the FitzRoys, so that in later years he would have the seat of a born horseman. For the moment the child squealed with the full strength of his lungs.

Anne Caroline Allen travelled up to London from Clifton and bent her dark, shining curls over the infant. He was wrapped up in a blanket and driven to Piccadilly to see his maternal grandmother, who paid him compliments.

During the first week of August, with Parliament in recess, FitzRoy decided that his son should travel abroad. Hannah was anxious to visit her sister Charlotte, who lived with her husband Anselm in a villa on the outskirts of Frankfort. Right in the heart of that city, in the narrow and tortuous Judengasse, a frail, lace-capped old lady had just been celebrating her ninetieth birthday. This was Gudule, Nathan's mother, who ever refused to leave the humble house where her children had been born.

The journey was a long one, and required a good deal of preparation, but the infant had a solid constitution and his parents were filled with joy. FitzRoy was also consummating a wish he had expressed five years before—to travel on the Continent with Hannah. How often during his wanderings in the winter of 1838, when he had been placed on probation by the Rothschilds, had he longed to have Hannah by his side! This was now to come true and indeed there would be a third person with them—a son.

Instead of travelling by way of Hamburg, they decided to cross the Channel by the Antwerp steamer. Hannah kept a rather scrappy diary of this journey, in which, on August 7, she makes this entry:

75

"We left London at 12 o'clock precisely by the Antwerpen steamer. Henry had engaged a private cabin for our use, but the weather being fine I only saw our bags safely deposited and then went on deck. The vessel was very full of passengers, but the only persons of our acquaintance were Sir John and Lady Burgoyne with their two children, who were on the road to Spa. Baby spent the greater part of the day on deck greatly amused with the bustle around him. We landed at Antwerp at 9 a.m. after a good passage of twenty-one hours, which ought to have been accomplished in less time had we not been detained in the river on account of the tide being against us. The custom house officers would not let us pass our desks without being examined, and greatly to our annoyance we were obliged to leave them with the courier; however, he managed so well that the carriage and parcels were not tumbled and disarranged as they frequently are. We walked to the Hôtel du Parc."

The railroad was already a much more common form of transport than it had been when FitzRoy was last on the Continent. But as yet the comfort of these trains was elementary. One way of travelling in comparative privacy was to bring one's own carriage and place it on a truck at the end of the train. Hannah had already planned this for the infant and his nurse. She had chosen a Briska, a light, well-balanced carriage adapted from the Russian chariot of light cane. It would allow Arthur to sleep during the most tiring part of the journey.

"We got up at 7 o'clock the next morning," Hannah continues, "and, after breakfast, proceeded to the station and took our places in the public carriage; baby, his nurse and Muffatt being in the Briska, the carriage being fastened on to a truck. We got out at Malines and went on another train. We passed by Louvain, Tirlemont and got to Liége at about half-past 2. At Liége we went in a carriage to the Hôtel du Pavillon Anglais where we dined; they made us pay for the honour of our country, but they did not feed us in honour of theirs. We got back to the station at half-past 5 and at 6 we started again."

76

From Aix-la-Chapelle they continued their journey by road.

"We travelled in our own carriage and arrived at Cologne at about 3. We dined at the table d'hôte, strolling about the town and then came home, amused ourselves by looking out of the window, nearly the whole population of Cologne promenading up and down gazing at the bright lights and fireworks which are enlivening the charming scene before us. There is a fête in commemoration of some event that took place 1,000 years ago. There is a dreadful noise what with the firing of guns, the blowing of horns and bells being rung every moment either at the door or to summon people to the steamer."

The FitzRoys journeyed down the Rhine to Mayence. Here FitzRoy appears to have had a moment of hesitation. Mayence is no distance from Frankfort. It is possible that he did not wish to break in, unheralded, on a branch of the Rothschild family that had shown some animosity against his marriage. Hannah took the railroad to Frankfort, while FitzRoy remained at Mayence. Charlotte received her young sister with great affection and, escorted by her two sons, drove Hannah back to Mayence, where she was sufficiently persuasive to make Henry come to dine with them. FitzRoy capitulated joyfully at this barrage of kindness. Thus little Arthur, at the age of seven months, made his triumphant entry into Frankfort—cradle of the Rothschild family.

CHAPTER TEN

BY the summer of 1848, the FitzRoys had moved from Berkeley Square into Upper Grosvenor Street. Arthur was now nearly six years old and when FitzRoy sat in his study he would hear from the nursery the shrill voice of a later arrival in the family—a little girl approaching her fourth birthday. Her name was Caroline Blanche Elizabeth.

As FitzRoy listened to his daughter's happy laughter, he would doubtless think of the moments he had been able to snatch with his children. Once he had taken a place called Garboldisham Cottage in Norfolk. Hannah had put the children one on either seat of a little green go-cart and they all went off to a country fair. There was a slippery mast with a leg of mutton on the top which aspiring yokels were trying to reach. In all this festivity, Hannah and he had taken turns to drag the go-cart home, laughing and quarrelling, each eager to do it. Hannah had teased him by singing:

> "Oh, dear, what can the matter be?
> Johnny's not come from the Fair;
> He promised to bring me a bunch of blue ribbons
> To tie up my bonny brown hair."

The point was that this song was invariably played at the departure of an unsuccessful candidate at election time.

The two children brought back a toy horse from the fair, but the next morning Arthur invited his sister to help with the funeral of the horse, which was decently interred within a few yards of FitzRoy's study window. Blanche in a loud voice had begged to exhume it, but Arthur was adamant. "Why bury it if I dig it up again?" he asked with logic.

Blanche was a cheerful child even when reprimanded. There

78

were times when Hannah would say to her at lunch: "Don't scrape your plate, Blanchy: always leave something for manners." FitzRoy at that time had a good friend called Mr. Manners Sutton. Blanche concluded that all the scraps of food left over at meal-times were for this gentleman.

"Does Mr. Manners always collect the scraps when he calls at our house?" she asked her father.

Most mornings the two children came down while FitzRoy and his wife breakfasted. Blanche was devoted to her brother and invariably tried to extract a promise from him that they should spend their future lives together. It was a real sorrow to her when Arthur expressed a wish first to become a sailor, secondly to marry a lady with black ringlets. She was even jealous of their cousin Annie, whom Arthur admired. Hannah had found her daughter sobbing in bed one night because Arthur had painted a valentine for Annie, who, in return, presented him with a large chalk drawing representing the head of a knight which filled his little sister's soul with envy.

Generally the two children played quietly together during their parents' breakfast. Once when Blanche was so little that she sat curled up in a waste-paper basket, Arthur insisted on her learning all the names of the kings of England, with their dates. After breakfast FitzRoy would open a drawer and give each of his children a chocolate drop. These chocolates were flat and about the size of a half-crown, with pictures of animals stamped upon them. Blanche decided that she liked chocolate better than chronology.

Occasionally FitzRoy would take his daughter out with him. Wishing to call at his club in St. James's Street and not knowing where to leave her, he had taken her in, the porter making no objection. Holding her by the hand, FitzRoy walked into one of the principal rooms. Everybody looked up in astonishment, but he, without saying a word, lifted his daughter and deposited her on a long leather sofa. He warned her to be absolutely silent and Blanche, looking grave as a judge, sat staring at her toes, which, because of the wide seat and the shortness of her legs, stood straight out in front of her. Presently, one by one, the other occupants of the room began to thaw and to approach the little girl. At the end of ten minutes she was the centre of a delighted and voluble crowd until FitzRoy thought it high time to carry her off. They went out, hand in hand, followed by many invitations for Blanche to return.

Nevertheless at dinner that evening Blanche had fallen into disgrace. Arthur was allowed the use of a knife at table, but she was limited to a spoon and fork. Stewed pears with deep red juice and cream were served and Blanche demanded a knife. When this was sternly refused, she set up a howl and became so obstreperous that Hannah carried her upstairs to the nursery, drove her in and locked the door. How great was Blanche's triumph a moment later when she discovered that her old nurse Lavallée, who had been quietly sewing by the window, had been locked in with her!

Nurse Lavallée was French and taught her small charge to speak French in the nursery. She was a good-natured old thing and extremely superstitious, interpreting each morning her dreams of the night before with the aid of a book. She told Blanche dreadful stories of chimney sweeps; how small children were constantly stolen to be sent up chimneys and how one little boy was forgotten in a narrow chimney, so that when the fire was lighted he was roasted. Whenever Blanche looked at the fire in the nursery grate, she expected to see a little black sweep come tumbling down. The worst story of all was about the fine lady who envied the beautiful teeth of a little sweep and who, having paid a large sum to his master, had her own black stumps extracted and the lovely white ones inserted instead.

Possibly as FitzRoy thought of his children his mind would also turn to the woman who was such a faithful companion. There were two carefully folded notes that he had received from his wife shortly after their marriage. These he specially treasured, and indeed he read them so often that the paper was already worn.

The first was a letter she had sent to him at the House of Commons asking forgiveness for some trifling slip of memory.

My very dearest Hubby,

I have been very thoughtless and I hardly know how to ask you to forgive me, and I do so with tears in my eyes, for I am so very sorry—I implore you, do not scold me; be kind and indulgent. You cannot be half so sorry as I am. But I must summon up courage to tell you my unfortunate misdemeanour!

I called on Mitchell when I went out, but as I did not let him know in the morning, he let our stalls, and the theatre is so full to-night that he could not exchange them for others.

Dear Hubby, I write to you because I am afraid to tell you. Do not be cross with me. I am so sorry. I know I ought to have sent the first thing this morning and so I always will in future. Do not be angry or too much annoyed about it. I can send if you please for a box at the Haymarket or elsewhere instead, but do smile on me and do not call me, although I fully merit it, a neglectful little thing. I may be in this instance, but I love you most tenderly and believe me, I study to prove it to you.

The second letter was about a miniature that the painter, William Ross, had started making of FitzRoy. Originally it was to have been a surprise for Hannah during her absence whilst drinking the waters at Ems.

My dearest, sweetest, darling Hubby,

I have so great a favour to ask you and I am so frightened you may be inclined to refuse me, that I must write my request which is most urgent and which I shall regard as a proof of your love if you agree to. You will frown when you hear it, but after all it only requires a trifling portion of self-denial and you would indeed be conferring on me a real favour.

Mr. Ross was here this morning and the portrait looks so dark and unlike my dear own hubby that it would be considerably improved by one half-hour's sitting. I sent it back; the frame and case were both so inferior and the picture itself in so unfinished a state. Consider, dearest little man, this picture will be with me through life and will belong to our children afterwards, and I much wish it to delineate faithfully my dear Hubby's handsome countenance. I was ready to cry when I saw it, for I have been expecting it so long: I am to go to Mr. Ross to-morrow afternoon; may I say that you will come for half an hour on Monday about two o'clock? Do not, dear little man, refuse me, I earnestly beg because I really do wish the picture to be like you. Now I am sure you will say 'yes' at once, without hesitating. Am I not right, Hubby?

Ever your fond little wife,

H. M.

This summer the columns of the newspapers were filled with details of the French revolution. Louis Philippe and his Queen had fled to England and the Paris Rothschilds were wondering whether their House would be able to weather the storm. Nathaniel was travelling often between London and Paris. He could not make up his mind whether the revolution would be sanguinary.

From Ireland came the news of shootings and murders, trains held up by political gunmen and houses fired. The papers were making much show of their despatches sent by electric telegraph, and this method of news-gathering was featured in much the same way as later the first wireless telephone. FitzRoy saw in much larger headlines than he was accustomed to such lay-outs as:

LATE NEWS
IRELAND
(*By Electric Telegraph*)

"The police, who have been armed with cutlasses, took a number of pikes and guns throughout the city of Dublin yesterday."

When the FitzRoys dined at Piccadilly conversation was mostly of the French and Irish news. Discussing the Chartists' meeting and Ireland, FitzRoy claimed that the loss of Ireland would be England's gain.

One morning there was a sudden commotion outside the house in Upper Grosvenor Street. It is probable that FitzRoy was working as he usually did before lunch in his study while Blanche

HENRY FITZROY.

While William Ross was making this miniature, Nathan de Rothschild's daughter wrote: "Consider dearest little man, this picture will be with me throughout life and will belong to our children afterwards, and I wish it to delineate faithfully my dear hubby's handsome countenance."

and Hannah were upstairs. Arthur had gone riding with a groom. Just as they were about to cross Park Street, the little boy's pony shied and threw him on a heap of flints prepared for mending the road. The groom, who ran terrified to his young master's side, found his face white and apparently lifeless. Arthur was brought back to his parents' home and a doctor quickly summoned. It was clear that the boy had been badly shaken, but the doctor certainly did not diagnose anything of major importance. The child was put to bed and was not long in regaining consciousness.

CHAPTER ELEVEN

IN the minds of the doctors little Arthur made a remarkable recovery from his accident. Although not one of them was able to discover exactly the extent of his injuries, it was the general opinion that violent exercise would best bring him back to his former health and vigour. They therefore prescribed gymnastics, running and bathing, but at the same time they were of the opinion that towards the beginning of winter a change of air would be suitable.

For a short time FitzRoy breathed a sigh of relief. He sought a mild and agreeable climate, so that one morning in early autumn the whole family set out for Pau in the South of France.

Blanche was still young enough to be surprised and a little frightened by the rush of the journey. At Calais she was carried ashore in the midst of darkness and noise with her arms round the neck of the Butler, Parry, who later was drowned in a beer vat! The journey from Paris to Bordeaux was made by train. This was the time of year when the vineyards are hives of activity, when the peaches fall off the trees because they are too ripe, and the September sun is still warm enough to bask in.

The iron road had not yet made its appearance between Bordeaux and Pau. The family set off in what was then known as a diligence. One can picture that journey through Nérac and Auch—the horses clattering in a cloud of dust past the vineyards and chicken farms and distilleries of Armagnac. Hannah and her husband occupied the coupé in front; Arthur, his sister—redcheeked, good-humoured, dressed in a voluminous travelling costume with cloth gloves, a close 'cottage' straw bonnet and a gauze veil—and their nurse Lavallée, occupied the interior. The servants were perched up on the *rotonde* at the back with enough luggage to last three months.

84

Blanche and Arthur slept on extemporised beds of wooden boards and shawls at night, whiling away some of the long hours of the day in cutting out pink and blue paper flowers with blunt scissors.

So the autumn passed and the two children played on the big terrace that gives a fine view of violet mountains in the distance. They ate a tartine of bread and a bunch of grapes at midday and ran in the park with velvet hoops covered with bells and gold tinsel. They sipped of the wine of Henry the Fourth and climbed past Argelès to Gavarnie on the back of a donkey; but the exercise did not seem so good for little Arthur. He lost his strength and red cheeks.

FitzRoy returned to work in the first days of 1849. He was going to be plunged into a drama of the House of Commons in which his brother-in-law took the leading rôle.

Lionel and Charlotte now had five children. The eldest was a little girl of twelve called Leonora, the youngest a boy of four called Leopold. Charlotte and Hannah saw quite a lot of each other and corresponded frequently.

There was at this time a great deal of work to be done at New Court, but Lionel had not only financial interests. Even before his sister's marriage he had certainly explored the possibility of standing for Parliament. He definitely decided on this early in 1847 and was returned without any difficulty for the City of London. This only got him half-way. There was an oath that every new Member of Parliament was obliged to take before being admitted that read: " . . . on the true faith of a Christian." Lionel was determined to pave the way for Jews to enter Parliament freely. He had already discussed the question quite frankly with his electors by saying that he wanted freedom of commerce but that he was still more anxious to secure perfect liberty in religion. "My opponents say I cannot take my seat. That is rather my affair than theirs. I have taken the best advice. I feel assured that, as your representative, as the representative of the most wealthy, the most important, the most intelligent constituency in the world, I shall not be refused admission to Parliament on account of any form of words whatever."

Armed with a large majority Lionel was a member without a right to cross the threshold of the House. He waited until the following December for the first reading of what was known as the Jews' Bill. If this passed both houses it would sweep away the offending words.

He was disappointed. The Bill received majorities for all three readings in the Commons, but was thrown out by the Lords, chiefly because the clergy had risen up in arms. It was nearly Christmas time. Londoners were thinking of roast turkey and pies. "We may guess how the clergy will spend Christmas," wrote a commentator. "The sacred time will be spent by many of them petitioning against the Jews. Two courses will be served before the mince pies: the roasted heretic and the disfranchised Jew. We shall be told of the angels singing peace on earth and goodwill to men by those who are showing the ill will that would keep a Jew a slave and prolong the reign of discord and persecution. Whose birth is it that the Church commemorates? Is it not a birth in Jewry—the birth of a Jew?"

It was just as FitzRoy returned from Pau that efforts were made to introduce a new Bill to solve the difficulty. It had been drafted by Lord John Russell, and passed all three readings in the Commons, only like its predecessor, to be thrown out by the Lords. The Bishop of Oxford turned the vote by exclaiming: "If you destroy the groundwork of Christianity upon which this legislation is based in order to gratify for a time a handful of ambitious men, you will destroy Christian England."

The game of battledore and shuttlecock went on. One summer day in 1850 rumour spread through the House of Commons that Lionel had decided to walk to the floor of the House and see what would happen. He would go to the table and demand that he should be allowed to take his seat as one of the members of the City of London.

The Serjeant-at-arms took his place and announced that a new member was waiting to take the oath. There was tense excitement. Lionel appeared at the bar and, after a pause, walked slowly to the table. The Clerk rose to tender him the usual oath.

Baron de Rothschild: "I desire to be sworn on the Old Testament."

Sir R. Inglis (much excited): "I distinctly object."

Lionel then slowly withdrew and the House started to discuss his admission.

Sir R. Inglis: "I believe that I heard distinctly the words pronounced: 'I desire to be sworn on the Old Testament.' (Loud cheers.) I am not mistaken as to the purport of the words? Sir, from the time that this has been a Christian nation and that this House has been a Christian legislature, no man—if I may use the word without offence—has ever presumed to take his seat here unless prepared to take it under the solemn sanction of an oath in the name of our Common Redeemer. I for one will never give my sanction to his admission."

A few days later the Baron was called to the table again and asked:

"Why do you demand to be sworn upon the Old Testament?"

He answered: "Because that form is the most binding upon my conscience."

* * * * *

At a quarter-past twelve the next day, the Speaker rose and said: "Baron Lionel Nathan de Rothschild, I have to inform you that the House has come to the following resolution: 'That Baron Lionel Nathan de Rothschild having presented himself at the table of the House and having previously to taking the oaths requested to be sworn on the Old Testament, the Clerk be directed to swear him on the Old Testament accordingly.'"

The Clerk brought a copy of the Old Testament to the new member and when he had placed it in his hands, he administered to him the first oath of allegiance. Baron Lionel, who was uncovered, repeated the words very audibly after the Clerk, and at the close he put on his hat according to the Jewish form and solemnly said: "So help me God."

Exactly the same thing happened for the oath of supremacy.

When the Clerk proceeded to administer the oath of adjuration, Baron Lionel repeated all the words without hesitation. But instead of saying: "Upon the true faith of a Christian," he said: "I omit these words as not binding upon my conscience," and kissing the book with his head covered, he concluded: "So help me God."

The Speaker then said:

"Baron Lionel Nathan de Rothschild, you may withdraw."

Many members, however, began to cry out: "No, no: take your seat," intermingled with cries of: "Withdraw," during which the Baron withdrew.

Sir F. Thesiger: "I beg leave to move that Baron de Rothschild, one of the members returned for the City of London, having refused to take the oath prescribed by the law before a member can sit and vote in this House, Mr. Speaker be instructed to issue his warrant to the Clerk of the Crown to make out a writ for a new election for the City of London in the place of the said Baron Lionel Nathan de Rothschild."

CHAPTER TWELVE

THE little boy with the injured spine for whom the doctors had at first prescribed violent exercise was now condemned to lie on his back. Many surgeons had been called in. They trussed up his body and placed him on a plain wooden board with a hole for his head. He fell off this board once and injured his knee. The knee broke out in boils. Then he was given a mattress to lie on.

Little Arthur bore the pain bravely. There is a miniature painted of him at the time. It shows him with rather long flaxen hair and bright blue eyes. He is lying on his side on a couch, his slender right hand reposing on the velvet mattress. His sad little face is almost feminine and his cheek is resting on a thin white cushion bordered with lace. He wears a soft, cream-coloured shirt fastened at the neck by a button, a grey waistcoat in which may be seen his gold watch-chain and a short jacket of indigo. There is no smile on his tightly closed lips, but his eyes look at one with a sort of resigned sadness. A low table stands at the side of the couch so that he may reach it by merely stretching out his arm. On the table is an open book, a long gold pencil and a couple of blue flowers in a bowl.

Hannah now lived only for her son. When, less and less frequently, FitzRoy gave political dinner-parties at the house in Upper Grosvenor Street, she did her best to play the rôle of hostess, but she bore with difficulty the society of others. FitzRoy worked extremely hard and because of late hours in the Commons and more especially in committees, he tried to keep fit by working off steam, as he called it, rowing, riding, shooting, fencing and single-stick. Nevertheless, the tragedy of his son brought him closer than ever to his children. He began taking his daughter out with him whenever he had a spare moment and there grew

89   G

up a sort of understanding between them that was quite remarkable. FitzRoy was Blanche's best playfellow.

Often in summer he took his daughter out driving in what was called a cab, a kind of phaeton with a hood, at the back of which a groom hung on standing. Mostly they would take long drives towards the country beyond the Harrow Road or Hampstead. Once the horse kicked and plunged and endeavoured to climb a bank. As the groom jumped out to grasp the bridle, FitzRoy muttered to his daughter: "Sit quiet," and Blanche sat like a frightened mouse. FitzRoy did all he could to quiet the horse, but the animal kicked without ceasing. Then FitzRoy hurriedly lifted his daughter out and told her to go and sit on the bank. This she did, crying silently, until Sambo, her faithful retriever, came to sit by her side, looking pathetically up at her face trying to comfort her. Meanwhile FitzRoy and the groom struggled with the horse, but it kicked the cab in splinters and the end of it was that FitzRoy and his daughter were obliged to walk home.

As they crossed the Regent's Canal, FitzRoy said to his daughter: "Two-shoes [that was his pet name for her], I have eight shares in that canal."

"Dear me," thought Blanche, "what a lot of water." But aloud she only said: "Oh, really!"

"Yes," added FitzRoy, with a twinkle in his eye. "I will give them to you some day if you like."

"Oh, thank you very much," said Blanche, thinking that she ought to feel desperately grateful and scarcely knowing why.

When she reached home she forgot all about the accident, flew upstairs and cried to her mother: "Oh, Mama, Mama; Papa has promised to give me eight shares in the Regent's Park Canal! Whatever shall I do with all that water?"

"My dear child!" exclaimed Hannah, and could say no more from sheer amazement.

On Sundays they would walk together. Hannah disliked walking intensely, much preferring to remain with her son. FitzRoy might have taken the carriage, but now he was becoming

LITTLE ARTHUR.

The boy who had been thrown from his horse
on a heap of flints in a London street was now
condemned to lie on his back.

more religious and refused to bring out even the phaeton on the Sabbath. On the same principle he objected to use cabs, for, as he would explain to Two-shoes, if their horse ought to have a day of rest, cab horses should have one too. Occasionally they would have to pay a return visit, and in this way they would call on Lady Molesworth. While the good lady entertained a large circle of friends, Blanche would sit on the floor playing with her pet parrakeet.

Nevertheless, there was something about Lady Molesworth that made Blanche uneasy. This was the redness of her parting that was doubtless due to the electric hair-brushes then in fashion. One day FitzRoy assured his daughter that it was caused by the application of hot sealing-wax to keep her wig on. Lady Molesworth would certainly have been horrified if she could have guessed why Blanche, on her next visit, looked at her with such profound interest.

One day in early spring there arrived, on a week-end visit to the FitzRoys, Caroline, wife of the Rev. Humphrey Allen. Blanche received her aunt, took her by the hand to her room and stayed curiously in the background as Mrs. Allen stood before the looking-glass combing and twisting round her fingers her dark shiny curls, of which she wore three on each side of her face (her back hair was in a twist over a comb), and meanwhile looking round from time to time and talking merrily to Blanche. In the evening when the family were gathered together, Mrs. Allen presented her niece with a Bible, whereupon, to the embarrassment of everyone, the giver included, Blanche sat down immediately to read it in the middle of the drawing-room.

Her visit lasted only two days. Shortly afterwards the FitzRoy family was plunged in sorrow. Mrs. N. M. Rothschild, Hannah's mother, died from a fit of apoplexy brought on by running down a green slope with two of her grandchildren. She had ended by being reconciled to the marriage and had shown a lot of kindness to Blanche and Arthur. On many mornings Blanche had been taken by her nurse to visit her grandmother at her house in

Piccadilly and had scarcely ever been allowed to go away without presents and toys of some kind. On occasion also she played two or three little tunes on the piano, such as 'Buy a Broom.'

Though Blanche was scarcely six at the time she felt the loss of her grandmother deeply and would lie awake at night thinking of her and sobbing.

This devotion did not prevent Two-shoes from getting into serious trouble at times. Every now and then the old family doctor (still with his coffee-coloured coat and frilled shirt-front) would come to see her. His visit would be followed by that of a chemist, who would bring a multitude of grey powders, rhubarb and magnesia draughts. At breakfast, Hannah asked her daughter if she was taking all these medicines. "Oh yes, Mama," she answered. Then one morning Hannah went into Blanche's bedroom. There, on the top of the chest of drawers, was a mighty collection of bottles and pill-boxes of every size, still neatly papered and sealed up as the chemist had sent them.

Some time in the summer of 1852, Arthur suddenly got better. It seemed miraculous, but the surgeons looked him over and decided that he must be made to walk. They still thought that the injured spine needed exercise, more and more exercise. Arthur got up and felt a bit stiff, but after the first few days he was able to move with ease and, what is more, his appetite increased.

Hannah could hardly believe it, but the doctors assured her that little Arthur was now cured, and that he must lead a normal life. Sunshine came into the house in Upper Grosvenor Street. Arthur was going to be a sailor after all and Blanche was going to have a playfellow of her own age. FitzRoy decided that his son should do some of the things that he had never been able to do before. For instance, the whole family would go to the theatre. Arthur and his sister were taken to see the real blood-and-thunder dramas of the time: *Richard the Second*, played by Charles Kean, who rode on a real horse through Old London and had a long soliloquy in the castle of Pontefract; *Henry the Fifth*, in which the audience had their patriotic feelings aroused to the utmost and their clothes scented with gunpowder for days; and *Sardanapalus,* whose palace fell to pieces in the flames. They also went to the Coliseum in Regent's Park and witnessed the earthquake of Lisbon, holding each other's hands tightly in a dark room where there was a great noise of hail and thunder and a tremendous rustling of the paper waves that made the sea.

After this riotous holiday it might be a good thing for the convalescent to get pure country air. Limbs that had been inactive for three long years must not be allowed to relapse.

The children were sent down with a nurse and governess to Tunbridge Wells, while FitzRoy and his wife, overjoyed, decided to spend a brief holiday at Wildbad in Germany taking the waters.

The FitzRoys now had a second honeymoon. Of a sudden life seemed truly wonderful. After a few days they were delighted to receive a letter from Arthur with the Tunbridge Wells postmark. They read in a pencilled handwriting:

Tunbridge Wells,
July 27th, 1852.

My dear Papa,

I hope you had a comfortable passage across the Channel, and that both you and dear Mama have been enjoying yourselves in Germany. I should indeed like to be with you.

For ourselves we are very happy. The sun is too hot to go out in the morning except under the trees, but in the evening we have nice walks or rather rides for me, and sometimes Blanchy goes on a donkey. We have not had any drives since you left because our governess thought they were dear, but she says we shall have one this week.

There will be a grand cricket match on Thursday and we may go. To-day I had such an enormous appetite for dinner. I do not remember ever having been so hungry before. I must now bid you good-bye.

Believe me, dear Papa,
Your devoted
Arthur.

At the Hôtel Belle Vue at Wildbad, Arthur's parents read the news and drank to his health in German wine. Then FitzRoy went to his room and took a large double sheet of thin notepaper on the top of which was engraved a handsome etching of a portly gentleman in white trousers and a top hat looking at the Hôtel Belle Vue and the tree-covered mountains behind. Upon this FitzRoy wrote to his daughter:

My darling little Pet,

I hope you are going on very well and are happy; I long to see you again and hope to find you much fatter and better than when I left you. Mama hopes to hear that you are the very best girl in Tunbridge Wells. Write me word if the two little teeth are coming down fast. We are at Wildbad in Würtemberg, a picture of which you will see at the top of this page. We drove all the time through the Black Forest—nothing but uphill and downhill all the way. We never saw anything of the Black Huntsman of whom Arthur has read and thought so much; we only saw children picking raspberries, strawberries and black-berries with which the whole ground is carpeted. It is very fine and may well be called the Black Forest, for most of the trees are fir and the sides of the mountains being very steep, looking down into the valley is like trying to look into the night.

Wildbad is a little valley with a clear rapid mountain stream running through it. I hoped to catch some trout there, but it came on to rain so that I could not. There are beautiful baths here where the water comes up fresh from the springs into the bath. The water is quite hot. It is raining in torrents; I wonder if it is still sunny with you. You must write to me and tell me if you hold yourself very nicely and are the best girl in the world. This letter is for both of you. Give my kindest love to dear Arthur. Tell him I hope he is getting stronger every day and that I send him a thousand good wishes. God bless you, my darling children.

Ever your affectionate
Pa.

FitzRoy folded this sheet in three, but he did not put it in an envelope. Most of his letters from abroad reached the children

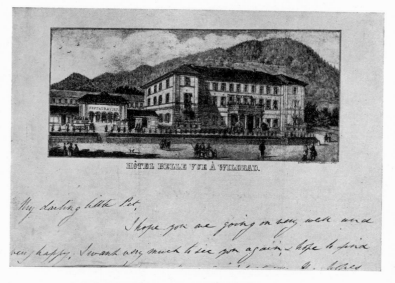

HÔTEL BELLE VUE À WILDBAD.

IN THE DEPTHS OF THE BLACK FOREST.
"FitzRoy took a sheet of notepaper on which was engraved an etching of the Hotel Belle Vue at Wildbad and wrote to his daughter: 'My darling little Pet.'"

with a big red seal at the fold on which was embedded the mark of his signet ring. The letter bears the postmark of Baden with the date of August 7, 1852.

Hardly had the FitzRoys returned to England than the riding and walking that the doctors had prescribed for Arthur began to exact their toll. The enfeebled spine suddenly gave way under the strain. Once more the hard couch was brought out and feverish pain rent the little boy. Doctors stood at the bedside and declared that the relapse was due to the weather.

Thus on the eve of his tenth birthday Arthur again saw his hopes of being a sailor fade away. When he was three years old his father had taken him on his knees and said: "Arthur, your papa is a Lord of the Admiralty. He hopes that one day you will go to sea." The boy persisted in his optimism. But now his mother knew otherwise. Hannah looked down on her son's upturned face with a tremendous surge of love.

Towards mid-December his condition became worse. On the night before his birthday a great storm broke over England and the wind howled round the house in Upper Grosvenor Street. Hannah stayed up all night with her boy, who suffered tortures from his thigh, so that the doctor, called to the bedside, covered the dwindling body with leeches. The next morning Hannah bent over her son, implanted a light kiss on the white forehead covered with perspiration and murmured: "A happy tenth birthday, my darling."

A happy birthday; what irony in these words! FitzRoy had not slept much either that night. Not only had he been worried to distraction about his son, but also things in the political world were coming to a head. The Earl of Derby's ministry was in difficulties. Four days later Lord Derby resigned. Christmas passed, while rumours thickened that FitzRoy was going to be Secretary to the Admiralty. That was a Cabinet post he had wanted for a long time. Little Arthur, slowly recovering from his fever, heard the news and was overjoyed. He longed for his father to hold a post that had something to do with the sea. Lord Aberdeen, the new Prime Minister, went to the House of Lords and explained the circumstances under which he was undertaking to form a new administration. Then the Cabinet was announced. FitzRoy's place had been given to somebody else. Instead he was made Under Secretary of State for the Home Department.

CHAPTER THIRTEEN

ALTOGETHER it had been rather a stormy Christmas, but FitzRoy did not forget his children. Now that it looked as if Arthur must remain for long on his back, FitzRoy decided to make a little man of him. He engaged a tutor whom he instructed to teach his son the classics. If the body must remain still, the mind must be active. He chose his Christmas present with care. It was a wooden box covered with leather, very similar to the despatch boxes used by Cabinet ministers. Arthur found it well fitted with writing material, but there was sufficient space to accommodate all his personal treasures. There was a tray divided into a number of compartments. The pencils, the pens and the ruler were in a subdivision. There was an inkpot on one side and on the other a space in which Arthur placed his purse of silk brocade. The purse had two rings that slid over the material in such a way that the gold coins might be kept on one side and the silver coins on the other. Arthur kept it well filled. On the silver side were coins ranging from the silver penny to the sixpenny piece. On the gold side were a few English sovereigns and a couple of louis d'or. This desk was placed on the table by his couch.

Meanwhile FitzRoy took good care that Blanche should lead an active, healthy life. He could not always be taking her for rides and walks, but Lionel's children were much the same age and he wanted her to go to parties and mix with others. There was a queer old spinster called Miss Mitchell, who lived in Berkeley Square and who, possibly because she had none of her own, gave the most imposing parties for children. When Blanche received an invitation that Christmas, FitzRoy urged Hannah to let her accept it. Blanche was naturally delighted and on the great day drove with her nurse Lavallée in Hannah's carriage.

Nearly a hundred small guests were shaking hands with the hostess in the brilliantly lighted hall when they arrived. Tea was spread out in the dining-room, where several tables were covered with cakes, creams, jellies, jams, fruit and sugar plums. There were games, prizes and dancing to a band in uniform, while in a corner was a Punch and Judy show.

When tea was over the folding doors were thrown open and a giant Christmas tree was revealed, lighted with hundreds of candles and covered with toys. The younger children clapped their hands while the older ones, conscious of dignity, smiled affably and, encouraged by their hostess, walked round the tree peering up at the treasures hanging from the branches.

"It is superb, *magnifique!*" exclaimed nurse Lavallée.

When the candles had burnt down, Miss Mitchell enlisted several helpers to cut down the presents. Blanche, in her wanderings, had noticed, somewhat high up, a blotting-book that took her fancy. She thought she had never seen anything so lovely. Her eyes turned to the dolls, work baskets, harlequins and bags all about the tree, but these things did not interest her. That morning she had sat beside little Arthur on his hard couch and heard his voice thicken when she told him about this party. All the usual amusements of his age were now being denied him. Finished were the days of theatres and horse-riding. He could never go out except on his couch.

Blanche had decided that, come what might, she would bring him something home. This blotting-book appeared just the thing. It had a black, shiny surface upon which were embossed a pink moss rose and three prickly green leaves. Suddenly she heard her name called.

"Miss FitzRoy," came the voice. "This is for you. You are lucky to have such a fine work basket."

Blanche stepped forward and saw that the basket was indeed pretty, made of straw trimmed with sky-blue ribbons with a small doll inside.

"Won't you take it?" asked the woman who had been cutting down the presents.

Blanche stood glued to the ground and unable to lift a finger. Of course she would like the work basket, but then she would never have a chance of obtaining the blotter. Her cheeks grew hot, and as she hung her head some of the children whispered among themselves. Miss Mitchell came forward, having perceived the drama from afar.

"Don't you like it?" she asked. "What else would you like better?"

That was just the question that Blanche had been waiting for. But Nurse Lavallée had also seen that something was happening. She hurried over from a group of nurses with whom she had been talking in voluble French and hissed: "*Mais répondez! Répondez!*"

Blanche held out her hand and, in a choking voice, said: "Thank you."

"No, no," answered Miss Mitchell. "Tell me what you would like. You need not be afraid."

Blanche looked up and saw the blotting-book dangling from its high branch. "I would like that," she answered.

Miss Mitchell gave her the blotting-book, but Blanche noticed that many of her small friends drew away from her. Even Nurse Lavallée looked at her with a sullen expression. The little girl, her heart throbbing, tightened her grip on the gift and slunk over to a dark corner where her hostess, puzzled by her strange behaviour, went to question her.

"What is it, my dear?"

"I wanted it for my brother," Blanche explained.

"Oh, I understand," answered Miss Mitchell; "why on earth did you not tell me that it was for Arthur?"

Suddenly Nurse Lavallée's shrill voice could be heard.

"Blanche, *mon enfant*, we shall be late; come fetch your cloak."

The little girl bade her hostess farewell and on her way home nestled up against her nurse's friendly arm. She was glad to escape her shame in the welcome darkness of the carriage. On

her return she ran to her brother's room and presented him with
the blotter. She did not tell him how she had obtained it, but the
next day she noticed that Arthur had placed it at the bottom
of his square wooden box where it was to remain always.

The period that followed this party brought the children
nearer to each other than at any time before. Blanche saw her
brother bending over his Greek dictionary and decided that she
would be a poet and took to composing her poems by night. This
was discovered and night-lights and pencils were taken away so
that she was left after bed-time in total darkness. Deeming her
poetical thoughts too valuable to be wasted, she invented the
laborious plan of pricking the words with a pin on a large sheet
of paper which she took from the bottom of the chest of drawers.
Her first poetical effort was discovered and much laughed over.
It ran:

> "I wish I were a little bird
> To fly above the sky,
> For then, I'm sure I would be glad
> To find myself so high.
>
> But then, perhaps, I might be shot,
> That would not pleasant be,
> So I'll be content and no more wish
> The sky so near to see."

The discovery vexed Blanche. She took to writing a history
of England for the benefit of her nursery maid.

One day Hannah came into the nursery and asked Blanche if
she could keep a secret. FitzRoy was eager to take his daughter
to a court ball. These balls that began at nine o'clock in the
evening were given for the little princes and princesses, and the
Queen was anxious that everything should be done as though the
functions were for grown-up people. The same ballroom was used,
the same band, lights and supper arrangements. Hannah had
agreed to let her daughter go, but she insisted that Arthur
should not be told for fear that he should be disappointed at

not going also. That is why she had come in to obtain this promise from her daughter.

When the evening came the family started off in great glory, Blanche feeling rather nervous and scared, dressed in white tulle, crowned with white jasmine and standing up (so as not to spoil her frock) between her father and mother, who were dressed in full court attire. In this way they were whirled along in a yellow chariot with the old coachman in his wig on the box and two footmen standing up behind. Presently they found themselves in a long gallery at Buckingham Palace, where all the fathers and mothers stood about holding their children by the hand and showing them off to each other. After a short time, during which Blanche began to feel as if she were at the dentist's, all the children were arrayed in two long files. On every side one heard the anxious mamas murmuring: "Mind you curtsy low enough! Mind you bow to everyone." Some doors were thrown open, the band struck up "God Save the Queen," and the Royal Party entered. The Queen and Prince Albert advanced, surrounded by the young princes in Scotch tartans, and the little princesses, dressed in blue tarlatan with wreaths of blush roses. After the Queen and Prince Albert had shaken hands with everyone they passed on into the ballroom, whither all the children followed. The Royal Party then ascended thrones under a sort of dais in the middle of the room and the dancing began, the Lord Chamberlain and other officials being actively engaged in finding partners for the children. In the course of the evening FitzRoy beckoned Blanche towards him; he was standing talking to a man to whom he wished to introduce her, but before he had time to explain who it was, Blanche had tumbled up against Prince Albert, for it was he, and trodden on his toes, much to her shame and contrition. The Queen came down from her throne and danced a reel. One of Blanche's satin shoes was tight round the instep and hurt her. She wandered to a rather secluded end of the long gallery and bent down to take it off in an effort to loosen the edge. A kind old lady came up and asked her what was the matter. When Blanche told her she exclaimed: "Ah, my dear, that is exactly what happens to my shoes and I always cut them a little at the top; shall I send for a pair of scissors?" Blanche refused, fearing that the consequences might be awkward when she got home, so, smiling kindly, the old lady went away. Hannah came up at the same moment. "What have you been saying?" she asked. When Blanche told her she said: "That was the Duchess of Kent, the mother of Queen Victoria." They went back into the ballroom where Prince Arthur, who was to become the Duke of Connaught, was present. He was extremely young, dressed in a little scarlet frock. Being both frightened and sleepy he became naughty, and his Royal Mama then and there administered a slight corporal punishment which had the effect of making him scream, whereupon he was carried hastily from the ballroom.

It was the following autumn that FitzRoy took, for his children, a house at Roehampton. The gardens had fine lawns and big cedar trees, in one of which was a staircase leading to a seat high up among the branches where Blanche delighted to perch herself and play at being one of the 'Swiss Family Robinson.'

In this house she and Arthur would engage in tremendous battles with tin soldiers of which Hannah had given them several boxes full. They would arm themselves with a couple of paper bags of dried peas and the soldiers would then be ranged on either side of the schoolroom table, the Britishers at one end and the foreigners at the other. Whoever won the last game had the privilege of commanding the English troops, and as Arthur invariably won, Blanche was reluctantly compelled to lead what he called the 'dirty foreigners.'

Arthur was, of course, obliged to lie on his invalid couch, but the table and the room were soon filled with dried peas. During these battles they generally locked the doors and let all the birds out of their cages. They had two canaries, a Java sparrow, a blue bird whose name was Bluey and, most loved of all, a ragged and very tame English bullfinch which they had saved from a fall out of the nest. Arthur was already in the hands of his tutor, a man called Sims, a good classical scholar and learned in the art of stuffing birds. Nevertheless, he had a mocking spirit that enraged Blanche, who every day had to spend an hour in her brother's schoolroom to receive a solitary lesson in English grammar and literature. Blanche grew to dislike this hour. On her ninth birthday, which fell that September, Blanche received from Mr. Sims a book of stories inscribed to: "The modern Dido," in painful allusion to her habit of saying: "I did do it, but I did do it, really."

What Blanche hated most was reciting Gray's *Elegy* to Mr. Sims. She cried bitterly one day, so he said there was no use in her learning poetry whatever. Blanche retired in dudgeon, but she was so sorry for her sins that, remembering she had once heard him praise *John Barleycorn*, she learned the whole of this lengthy poem by heart before the following day, when she grew very red and proposed to recite it to him.

Arthur's tutor laughed, which hurt her feelings again. Nevertheless, she got satisfactorily to the end of the poem, which probably pleased him after all.

Both she and Arthur wrote long letters to their father. They would ask him to bring down his dog Cæsar, who invariably waited up at night until his master came home from the House of Commons.

Arthur wrote to his father from Roehampton:

Sept. 13.

My dear Papa,

I thank you very much for your letter which I received yesterday. I am better and can move my feet. Mama desires me to say that she will not write to you to-day but that she sends her love.

Our cousins, Natty and Leonora [Lionel's children] came to see us on Monday and brought us a great many presents; mine were an inkstand made in ivory like a cottage in Switzerland, a thermometer that is a very pretty one made of carved buck horn, and two green froggies which in raining weather go to the bottom of a bottle in which they are kept, and climb to the top when it is fine. These creatures are much addicted to small game in the shape of flies.

It has been fine lately but we had some rain during last night, the wind being in the south-west.

I have asked Mr. Sims to make me a list of the eggs I would like best for my collection.

I remain, dear Papa,
Your affectionate son,
Arthur.

*   *   *   *   *

As the months succeeded one another, FitzRoy sent his son from place to place in the forlorn hope of finding a climate that would suit him.

One grey morning in March, 1854, a man wheeled an invalid's chair along the Marine Parade at Brighton. Little Arthur, who was now twelve years old, had been sent here with his tutor in search of bracing air. Lying on his back the boy scanned the horizon with a pocket telescope.

"I see no signs of the French fleet," said Arthur to his tutor, who walked slowly by his side.

Mr. Sims laughed. "Wait until you are in the navy," he said: "there is plenty of time to give the French another beating."

Arthur put down his telescope and, closing his eyes, listened to the surge of the waves against the pebble beach. His tutor, looking down at the frail figure in the chair, wondered how it was that such a keen intelligence could still believe that a cripple could become a sailor.

As the invalid chair came level with the chain pier, little Arthur put his hand in his pocket and brought out a commemorative medal that he had been treasuring for some time past. It was like a very large coin made of some cheap, light metal, and bore embossed upon it the drawing of a Chinese junk. On the other side were words to say that this was the first ship constructed by the Chinese to reach Europe. An enterprising Englishman had purchased it at Canton. He had sailed it from Hong Kong round the Cape of Good Hope to England, where it arrived some fifteen months later.

Here was a story to fire Arthur's imagination. The opening up of China and Japan was already turning public attention to the Far East. Britain's new twelve-square-miles colony of Hong Kong already beckoned across two oceans and a continent to the mother-land. Great Britain had not yet declared war against the Manchu dynasty, but each year brought new treasures from the distant East. Merchants in Europe found a growing demand for China silks, teas and porcelains.

The boy, strapped to the wooded plank in his invalid's chair, thought of these things as he heard the waves of the sea breaking against the pier and his heart grew sad. He also longed to sail away across the horizon to discover the romance of Cathay.

As midday struck, the boy and his tutor returned to their lodgings on Marine Parade. There was a smell of roast beef in the sitting-room, where a bust of Queen Victoria dominated the fireplace and two bird-cages hung in front of the window. On the table little Arthur found a letter from his sister Blanche. It was written in a small, clear hand, and there were affectionate greetings from her canary Twee-wee to Arthur's Java sparrow Dick. Dick and Bully, the bullfinch, looked at one another from their respective cages in front of the window and chirruped as their young master read through his letter.

Then Arthur asked his tutor to bring his box and place it on the table beside him. While the beef was roasting he would answer his young sister's letter.

He searched in the long narrow compartment where he kept his writing material for a pen. There was a six-inch ruler in bone, half a dozen differently coloured pencils, each with his name inscribed on the outside: "A. F. FitzRoy, Upper Grosvenor Street." These pencils were light as a feather, and the lead did not reach from end to end but stopped within half an inch from the top, for the sake of economy. But the lead was as light as the wood and crumbled easily. With these there was a half-used piece of red sealing-wax, a miniature drum with the name Arthur at one end in order to form a signet, six marbles, a commemorative medal like that of the Chinese junk but smaller, made when the Queen had opened the London coal market in 1849, and a number of quill nibs.

The boy took one of these nibs and inserted it into a silver penholder by the strange method of lifting up a joint which he then snapped back and locked by means of a ring that slid over the end of it. Thus armed he licked the nib, placed it in the inkpot that lay in the box alongside the compartment for writing materials, and started his letter.

At the top right-hand corner he wrote slowly and methodically the address: 63, Marine Parade; and then:

My dear Blanchy,

Thank you very much for your nice letter. I am glad to hear you like Edgar Clifton; for my part I am reading *The Betrothed* and have just finished the *Talisman*. I like both very much. How many dolls have you got now that a new one has come from Paris? I hope you enjoyed yourself at the party; were there many little girls there? Mr. Sims says the primrose is to be watered every other day. I have not got any flowers of my own but there is a fine camelia of Mr. White's in the room. I have only been once on the chain pier.

It is not at all fine to-day and if you have a yellow fog we have a grey one. I write in my pocket-book every day but I keep a larger diary besides. It is very uncomfortable sleeping in my stays. I have got a horrid gumboil which goes all up on the inside of my cheek. Tell Mama that as soon as we got her letter Mr. White got a filter and all the water we now drink is passed through it.

Yesterday I began to drink beer at dinner and I like it very much.

We went to Folthorp's and (please tell it to Ma) they said that although it was their custom to consider the subscription continued so long as any book of theirs was in the house, yet they would make this an exception.

The boat I am making for you does not get on very well but I hope still to succeed. I suppose that Mama has told you that I went in a boat on Saturday, but that the *Nelson* did not behave herself at all well. Do Mama and Papa intend ever to bring you to stay over Sunday at Brighton? If they do, then write to tell me when and if you can come at 2 o'clock we will order such a grand dinner for you—not such a one as poor Mama got, but we did not really know she was coming. Dick and Bully have asked me to enclose a note to Twee-wee, to whose mistress I send my best love, and remain,

Her affectionate brother,
Arthur FitzRoy.

A smile spread over little Arthur's wan face.

He took a small tortoise-shell paper-cutter and ran it up the side of a double piece of notepaper. Then he folded this single sheet and again cut it in half. He made what remained into a piece of notepaper that might be in proportion with a dolls' house and, making his writing very small, first appended the date at the top: "March 9th, 1854."

Then he wrote:

Dear Cousin,

I thank you very much for your letter. This is the first time I ever got a letter, and also that I have ever written one. I entertain as high an opinion of you, dear Twee-wee, as you seem to do of me. I believe I was once in the same house as you are now lodged in but my master found it spoilt my tail and I was removed to the room I now inhabit.

I and my brother Bully have been hung up in chains in front of the window and although I think it very pleasant, Bully does not seem to be of the same opinion and they have taken him down. My master has given us some plants which are very good for us and which we like. They are called water cresses. Sometimes I can come out but my brother Bully does not. I believe that you are of a bright yellow colour and sing very nicely. But have you ever heard brother Bully? Ah, he's the fellow for singing!

But Good-bye, dear Twee-wee,

I remain your affectionate,
Dick, alias Richard.

Little Arthur read over this missive with delight. He then folded the paper in three and, taking the stump of red sealing-wax from his box, sealed the letter with the end of his toy drum.

* * * * *

Arthur made a note of this correspondence in his diary. He wrote thus: "I sent a letter to Blanche, am well and intend to work further at her boat."

He then looked back through the pages and felt a certain pride at having kept his entries up to date. He wondered how long this good resolution would last. For a few minutes he perused what he had written. The new diary had started on his arrival at Brighton, in this way:

Tuesday. Fine day. Came to Brighton at 63 Marine Parade with Mr. Sims by the 5 o'clock express. Not done my lessons as everything is packed up. Ma at Paris, and I am well.

Wednesday. Beautiful day. Went out in the morning in a chair with Mr. Sims to several shows in order to buy paint and wire for the boat I am making for Blanche. I was unable to find some lead which I wanted. In the afternoon I went out again for the lead and found it. I made the oars and seats for the small boats and painted them. Wrote to Mama.

Thursday. Went out in the morning in a chair on the pier with Mr. Sims. Not gone out again but had my hair cut and wrote to Blanche. I had a headache in the afternoon from the sun but did a little carpentry.

Friday. Fine day. Went out in the morning in a chair, with Mr. Sims. Wrote to Pa and in the afternoon went in a fly on the London road to have a key fitted to the desk that Pa gave me.

Saturday. Went out in a boat this morning with Lavallée and Mr. Sims and tried to sail the boat I am making, but she did not sail well. Felt rather sea-sick so in the afternoon I had a half holiday, read and carpentered. I am pretty well.

Sunday. Went out in the morning with Mr. Sims; in the afternoon with Lavallée. Mr. Sims went to church this evening. Pretty well, wrote to Ma but did not go to church.

Monday. Fine day and went out in the chair this afternoon. It was foggy this morning. Worked on Blanche's boat.

Tuesday. Ma came to see me at 2 o'clock. I went out with her in a shut fly in the afternoon. We tried to get some jewels for Blanche's doll but could not. Afterwards we went to get cakes for tea. Ma brought me a letter from Blanchy. I showed Ma a trick with a sixpence but Ma did not find it out. Ma went away at 7 in the evening.

Saturday. Pa came to see me at 12 in the morning. Went out with Pa in a chair on the road to Rottingdean. I did not see the fleet as it sailed to the Baltic. It was foggy. Painted my boat in the afternoon.

Wednesday. Had a holiday nearly all day because I was not very well.

*   *   *   *   *

Before long Blanche and her governess arrived to keep Arthur company. Then their great delight was to visit the little shops on the chain pier where tiny red shells and other marine treasures were sold.

Up on the cliff, too, there lived an old sea captain who had pet fawn, which he kept in a green enclosure in front of his house. Blanche and Arthur made great friends with the fawn, and every now and then Blanche would work a blue bead collar for it.

The old sea captain had a very red face and a choleric manner, though he probably had the softest of hearts. One day he invited the two children into his house, but they were frightened and shy, and continued their friendship with the fawn rather than with him.

Just then the end of the esplanade was blocked up with a wooden hoarding. One day Blanche asked her governess what was behind it.

"All the old moons are put there," she said. So Blanche would always clamber about each time she was taken to the esplanade till at last she got up to where there was a crack visible. She peeped through and saw a great heap of oyster shells, so for a long time she firmly believed that all the old moons became oyster shells.

CHAPTER FOURTEEN

ONE cold, dark afternoon in December, Blanche sat
rumpled up in the depths of a large armchair in her
mother's drawing-room at Upper Grosvenor Street.

The story-book that she had just finished reading for the third
time lay half-open on the floor where it had fallen from her
listless hands. Her head was thrown back, her hair was untidy and
her eyes looked upwards at the star-shaped plaster ornament in
the centre of the ceiling.

Hannah was busy writing letters at an open escritoire that,
laden with masses of paper and envelopes, neatly docketed bills
and red house-books, offered to Blanche's mind one of those
grown-up mysteries wherein she had no desire to peer. Hannah's
work-basket, the lid only partly raised, revealed a tempting
collection of gaily-coloured satins, bright skeins of silk and steel
beads. But Blanche was not allowed to touch her mother's work-
basket, and this was not surprising when the state of her own was
considered, for Blanche kept her silks in chaotic knots.

Thus she felt dull while Hannah wrote on with the aid of one
taper she had lighted, the rest of the room growing darker as
twilight fell and fog covered the trees in the square outside.

As Blanche sighed, Hannah's heart was touched, so that she
wheeled round on her chair and exclaimed, smiling:

"My poor child, you seem to be in a bad way!"

"Yes, Mama," answered the daughter disconsolately.

"What can I do for you?"

"I do not know, Mama."

"What would you say if I gave you permission to invite a few
friends to a tea party?"

"Oh, Mama!" cried Blanche, as her face suddenly changed,
"May I invite Annie and May?"

"Yes, certainly," answered her mother.

"That would be delightful," exclaimed Blanche, who had scrambled out of her chair and was now joyfully hopping up and down the room on one foot:

> "My dear Annee
> Pray come to tea!"

"That's a good idea," remarked Hannah thoughtfully, her pen poised in her fingers. "You are always making nonsense rhymes. Suppose you write a poetical invitation?"

"Oh no, Mama!"

"Take this paper and pencil. I will light you another candle and you shall sit down and invoke the Muses. It is good practice and but a small penance to pay for the pleasure of your coming tea party."

Blanche nibbled the top of her mother's pencil till the wood cracked and the lead came tumbling out. After a quarter of an hour she handed up the following:

> "My dear Annie,
> I write to say
> Pray come to tea,
> And also May.
> Please come at four.
> I'll say no more,
> But now I'll end
> Your loving friend."

"That's all, Mama," said Blanche with a deep sigh.

"It is very nice," said Hannah. "Only . . . you haven't named a day!"

"May I not add it in a postscript at the end, Mama?"

"I do not think that would sound well," answered her mother. "Great poets polish up their work a great deal, you know."

"But, Mama, I am not a great poet."

"That is true," answered Hannah, laughing. "But try again all the same, and if you can't manage otherwise, we will put it in a postscript."

After another quarter of an hour, Blanche produced her amended work:

> "My dear Annie,
> I write to say
> Pray come to tea,
> And also May.
> Will Thursday do?
> Please come at four
> If that suits you.
> I'll say no more,
> But now I'll end
> Your loving friend."

"That is better," said Hannah, kissing her daughter. "Now run to the schoolroom and make a clean copy."

Nurse Lavallée entered into the spirit of the party.

She presented her pupil with a bunch of chrysanthemums to deck the table, while Sarah, the schoolroom maid, washed and ironed the white frocks of Blanche's two favourite dolls. One had a blue sash and the other was decked with blue ribbons. Blanche was herself dressed in white, while Nurse Lavallée put on her Sunday gown and also her favourite brooch which contained a minute tombstone and a weeping willow wrought in human hair.

Shortly before the party was to take place, Hannah entered the schoolroom carrying a large parcel tied up with golden thread that she handed to Blanche, saying:

"Your Uncle James has sent you this from Paris."

When the parcel was opened, there appeared a box containing a number of small toys fashioned of gilt metal and wire. There was a miniature chair, a table, a basket, a hat and a Lilliputian wheelbarrow, the top of which opened and shut with flaps.

Each of these toys was glued to a cardboard box covered with velvet containing sugar-plums.

Blanche, looking at these, drifted into a land of dreams, peopled with dolls and miraculous furniture, whence her mother's voice suddenly recalled her.

"How lucky that these things should arrive to-day, Blanchy. You will be able to give a toy to each of your friends."

Her daughter looked up quickly.

"Of course, you do not need to give them unless you want to," said Hannah as she went out.

At four o'clock there was a ring at the door and Annie arrived. A moment later Cousin Johnny, who had been left by his stout Scotch nurse, whose sounding kiss as she parted from him echoed through the passage, roared into the room. Then came Marian, a self-possessed little person who arrived alone in her mother's carriage. Finally two frail-looking sisters, Madeleine and Fanny, one on each side of their tall, angular French governess.

"How d'ye do, Blanchy?" said Fanny, stretching out her dainty white hand as she gazed sentimentally at her young hostess with large, lustrous eyes, her flaxen curls entangled in the white Shetland shawl wrapped about her head and shoulders.

Nurse Lavallée welcomed her flock and sat herself joyfully at the head of the nursery table with a doll on each knee, while Blanche waited on her friends.

Hannah came in for a few minutes and kissed the children all round, asking after their mothers. After tea, Blanche went silently across the room and fetched the box from Paris, requesting her nurse Lavallée to distribute the golden toys. There was a lump in her throat and she felt unable to face this ordeal.

Nurse Lavallée made a little speech and gave to each guest a toy; then, with a look that meant a great deal, she gave the empty box back to Blanche.

"Tell us a story, Marian!" said one of the children.

Marian was generally willing to oblige. In the course of her short life she had been abroad several times and she had read many books of adventure.

"In Sicily," she began as everybody settled down, "there are high mountains and deep ravines . . ."

"What are ravines?" asked Johnny.

"Well," continued Marian, "there are a lot of ravines and at the bottom of one of them, on a fine summer afternoon, there were two ladies travelling in a carriage. They were remarking to each other on the magnificence of the weather and the scenery. The two ladies were extremely beautiful. They both had golden hair and large blue eyes and they were dressed in the most lovely clothes. But they did not know that close behind them, in the shade of the rocks, lay concealed a most terrible, fierce and savage brigand."

"Oh!" cried Madeleine.

"This was quite the worst brigand," Marian went on complacently, "that had ever been heard of in Sicily. He had committed so many murders that nobody could count them. He could shoot people from miles and miles away and he had never been known to show any mercy whatever. He lay quite still behind a large bush, polishing his gun. Well, the carriage went on and one of the ladies was telling the other all about a beautiful pink bonnet that she had got packed away in her trunk with a necklace of pearls and a few other things. When suddenly the postillion threw up his hands and let go the reins. The horses reared, the ladies screamed and the brigand jumped out upon them from behind the bush.

"'Caramba!' cried the brigand in a horrible, hoarse, gruff voice."

"What was that?" asked all the children.

"Brigands always cry: 'Caramba!'" answered Marian. "The brigand drew his sword with one hand and pointed at the ladies with his pistol in the other. He held a long, shining knife between his teeth and in his belt were many more."

"More what?" asked Johnny, stamping his feet on the ground.

"More knives," answered Marian. "The ladies screamed for

mercy: they offered him the pink bonnet and the pearls, but the brigand shook his head and exclaimed——"

"Miss Marian's carriage has come!" said Sarah, the schoolroom maid, putting her head inside the door. "The coachman says, please not to keep the 'orses waiting as the night's very cold."

"Oh, dear," cried all the children in despair: "we shall never know the end of the story."

Ten minutes later, the schoolroom presented the appearance of a deserted banquet hall. Nurse Lavallée had gone to her room and Blanche stood alone in the midst of the ruins. She suddenly caught sight of a small, shining object on the floor. She bent down to pick it up and as she held it in her hands, she recognised a portion of her tiny gold wheelbarrow, crushed and flattened out of shape.

She bent her head and walked sadly from the schoolroom down the passage leading to her father's library.

All seemed dark and still; the gas in the passage was dim. She heard a low whine and then flop, flop went Sambo's swinging bushy tail, as he lay stretched on the coconut matting. Blanche ran towards him. He seemed a friend in need. She knelt down beside the big retriever and, putting her arms round his neck, leaned her face against his soft shiny head.

The library door opened and FitzRoy looked enquiringly into the passage.

"What on earth are you and Sambo doing?" he asked.

"Why, what's the matter, Blanchy?" he added, seeing the traces of tears on her cheeks.

The door was now wide open, and the lamplight from within fell full on Blanche's hot, flushed face. She had no courage to answer.

"Are you going out to dinner, Papa?" she asked, for the father was in evening dress.

"No, it is late and I am waiting for a friend who is dining here. I think I have a few minutes to spare."

He held out his hand as he spoke and Blanche followed him

into the library. There he sat down and, still holding her hand, asked:

"May I not do as well as Sambo for a confidant, Blanchy? Is this the effect of giving a party? I admit that polite society is depressing at times to the best of us."

He was gently bantering to give the little girl time to recover her composure. She smiled through her tears and then told him all about the golden toys.

"Well, Blanchy, next time I will explain to Mama that you are to keep all your things for yourself. Had you kept the contents of the box, you might now have been playing in state all alone in your schoolroom, with six different toys."

"Oh, Papa!"

"We shall know what to do another time."

"No, no!" cried Blanche.

"You will then experience no regret, no anger and no vexation." FitzRoy continued: "Sambo need receive no painful confidences."

"I do not regret at all," said Blanche.

"You do not regret even the wheelbarrow?"

"No," answered Blanche frankly. She looked up at her father, who gazed smilingly and lovingly down with an expression that filled her with contentment.

The next moment a servant knocked at the door. She announced that Mr. Manners was waiting in the drawing-room.

"Good night, little girl!" said FitzRoy. "Now I must hurry."

CHAPTER FIFTEEN

ONE fine April morning in 1855, the Rt. Hon. Henry FitzRoy, now chairman of the Ways and Means Committee, sat in the writing-room of the Hôtel du Rhin in Paris and wrote thus to his daughter, Blanche:

> My dear little Pet,
>   Very bad weather.
> We cannot go out together,
> So Mama goes out alone
> While I stay in till one,
> And now I write to you
> For of books I have but few.
> The Empress I have not seen,
> The trees are not yet green,
> The mutton is very tough,
> Of Paris I've had enough.
> The wind is very high
> And dreary looks the sky,
> Sometimes with disgust I recoil
> From the looks of the cod liver oil,
> But I find that it makes me eat
> My potatoes, my bread and my meat,
> So I take it all at a gulp
> Which softens my food to a pulp.
> I'm going to a party to-night
> Which no doubt will be a fine sight.
> I walk all over the Town,
> The Boulevards, the Quais, up and down,
> But there's nothing I like to see
> Half as much as my little Blanchy.
> I hope to be home before Sunday
> For the Emperor comes on Monday.
> Now I ask for your very best wishes
> That Mama may not feed the fishes,
> I have nothing more to say,
> So Adieu for the rest of the day.

FitzRoy was enjoying a short respite from Parliamentary work at home. He took advantage of this visit to Paris to see his Rothschild relations at Ferrières, and to ask their advice about some place to which he could send his children that summer, for Arthur was showing no sign of improvement.

It was finally decided that Hannah should take Blanche and Arthur to Dieppe early in July, and that FitzRoy should join them as soon as the House adjourned.

They crossed to Boulogne for the sake of the shorter sea voyage, but as there was no railway between Boulogne and Dieppe, they went by train to Abbeville, travelling in their own barouche, which was fastened on a truck at the end of the train. Both children wrote letters to their father, describing this dreadful journey, at the end of which they were bruised all over. For nearly eight hours they sat in their barouche with their backs to the engine watching the ground slip from under their feet with what appeared to them appalling velocity.

Hannah found a comfortable apartment on the first floor of a house overlooking the front. There was a broad balcony with an awning, and a garden where Arthur would lie for long hours watching the ships through his telescope.

Blanche found that a number of children occupied the floor above them, but, most of all, she longed for her best play-fellow, her father. She and Arthur wrote letters a few days after their arrival. The one from Blanche says:

July 9th, 1855.

My dear Pa,

We have removed from the Royal Hotel and are now at Madame Hallouin's pleasant little house where we occupy the rooms on the first floor. In the same house above us is a little boy, a little Count de Montebello. He has a large india-rubber ball, a kind of balloon, and he and I and another little girl who lives here also play together. Sometimes I stand on our balcony whilst they are in the garden and then we throw the ball to each other in turns. By the by it would be just the thing for you and me, would it not? There is a little fountain in the garden here which is now playing. I like Dieppe very much and I think you would like to sit out on our wide balcony under the awning. Do all my geraniums thrive with all the care I am sure you bestow on them? Did you take my dog Cæsar out for a walk on Sunday morning or did you abandon him to the coachman? I suppose you take no notice of poor old Sambo. Do you draw anything now when you cry: "Order! Order!" in the chair, the uncomfortable chair of the House of Commons?

Good-bye, my dear, dear Pa,
From your affectionate and ever loving
daughter, Blanche.

From Arthur: July 9th, 1855.

My dear Pa,

I hope you do not feel as lonely as you expected and that you have not had many late nights. I like Dieppe pretty well—it seems a sort of cross between Boulogne and Brighton. It has a nice walk by the pier, and has a much better harbour than Boulogne. There are very few vessels that pass, not more than at Brighton, but a good many colliers and that sort of thing come into the harbour. It is a rather old fashioned town and there is a pretty old cathedral and a funny-looking castle. The people look much the same as those at Boulogne.

I liked the journey from Boulogne here very much, that is, all but the first part when we were put on a truck, carriage and all, and tied to the tail of a train. We were so shaken we did not know what to do. Our house here is quite a modern little place painted white with a garden looking towards the sea. I have a donkey to draw me when I go out, but I think it would be a much better plan to buy a donkey because we could sell him when we go and it would save a great deal of bother, for sometimes the woman cannot give us hers.

I shall be very glad when you come and bring Cæsar. It will be such fun to send him into the water. You must teach him to fetch and carry and a lot of other tricks because you will have scarcely anything to do.

I remain, dear Pa,
Your affectionate son,
Arthur.

Dieppe was a pleasant place for the children. The picturesque harbour, the barelegged costumed fish-wives, the shops with their manufactures of delicately worked ivory, the market-place full of fruit and flowers, the old cathedral, and the ruined castle on a green hill overlooking the sea were all things to strike their imagination.

But there was one sight that greatly interested Blanche at that time. This was a certain flagstaff which could be seen from Madame Hallouin's balcony and which denoted, from an early hour every morning, whether bathing was practicable or no. If the flag was up hanging limply round its mast or floating proudly in the breeze, well and good—Blanche might be sure of bathing. Then the sea was, as old Léon, the bather, expressed it: *"Convenable."* But if the flag was not visible there was no use trying to melt the hearts of the stern bathing men. The bathing huts were locked and Blanche might go home.

She loved bathing; arrayed in a blue-and-red costume with straw slippers and a hideous oilskin cap, she sallied forth into the ocean hand in hand with her dear Léon, who, like all the other bathing men, was a weather-beaten elderly fisherman, who went out fishing at all times of the year except in summer, when he dipped the ladies and children and taught them to swim.

Blanche was not dipped, neither did she receive pails of water on her back or over her head. She used to run knee-deep into the sea and lie down under the first curling wave. The bathing men were jealous of each other and proud of their pupils.

Old Léon was a good, stern master. He used to hold Blanche by a leather belt that she wore round her waist while she learnt the movements of swimming. Every now and then he would treacherously let her go and when she came up again to the surface, panting and spluttering, he would nod his head and ask ironically:

"Ç'a du sel, hein?"

But as time went on Blanche swam away from him into the deep water where another old fisherman called Pierre, and not unlike

Charon, used to navigate in a small open boat, on one side of which was a short ladder whereon tired swimmers used to perch and rest, and from the upper step of which they took delightful headers into the sea.

One day she was very exhausted, and upon reaching the boat found the ladder crammed with ladies who were talking and laughing but did not trouble themselves with so small a child. Old Pierre, however, seeing her wearied condition, threw her a rope, but it is a difficult thing to climb into a boat by means of a rope and she had never tried it before. As a result, Blanche pulled herself under the boat, where she lay on her back utterly unable to extricate herself, bobbing about with every movement of the waves.

She would assuredly have gone under had not the watchful Léon swum from the shore to her rescue. He did not waste much time in words but, clutching her by the shoulders, bore her off, striking out so energetically with his heavy fisherman's boots that her shins were black and blue for many days afterwards.

A delightful epilogue to these bathes was the hot fresh-water footbath in the hut. Blanche would then go to a booth close to the beach where an old woman in a large clean white apron sold hot cakes powdered with sugar. And so home to breakfast.

Once Blanche went for a donkey race to amuse her brother. She and her governess each rode a donkey. Another of these animals was harnessed to Arthur's Bath chair and his tutor, Mr. Sims, bestrode a fourth. But Mr. Sims was tall and his legs so long that he could almost walk while riding the donkey, so it ended by his getting off and dragging the animal after him.

Blanche had taken a fancy to a white donkey which she begged to be allowed to mount. It was a pretty beast, and when she had started on her way she patted its neck affectionately and enquired its name of the boy.

"Mademoiselle Blanche," was the answer.

The market-place was their favourite resort. They bought there fresh flowers and ripe peaches, but the day they looked forward to was that on which the *place* was given up to the sale of trousers. There was always a strong smell of cloth and wool about the neighbourhood. Coats, waistcoats and other articles of manly attire were hung out to view, while a strong-minded female standing in an open cart sold garments by auction (chiefly trousers as it seemed to the children) and harangued the multitude.

"*Tenez, Messieurs, Mesdames,*" she used to vociferate: "*voici votre affaire. Un petit pantalon tout ce qui a de plus fin . . . magnifique, mirobolant! Un vrai pantalon d'Empereur!*"

If her sales were not as successful as she desired, this energetic lady apostrophised some unfortunate shy youth in the crowd, remarking on the shabby and baggy state of his lower garments, causing much derisive laughter and many jokes which warmed and cheered the country folk.

Once every week there was the travelling dentist. A loud booming drum announced the fact of his arrival and an enormous pink umbrella overhung a species of scaffold, from which he addressed the people beneath.

The drum lapsed into silence during the persuasive speech of the dentist, at the close of which there was always some unfortunate brought forward by friends who comforted him and patted him on the back, but were none the less ready to be amused at his expense. The wretch was, in most cases, a big hulking, good-natured lout in a blue-checked blouse, whose very swelled face was tied in a pocket handkerchief.

Amidst the applause of the populace he mounted the steps of the scaffold and the spider, having once secured his prey, pinned him down in a large armchair, and half covered his face with an enormous crimson pocket handkerchief which was probably to conceal the blood of the victim. He then extracted the tooth whilst the drum, at its very loudest, covered up all cries and expostulations. With a low bow, the dentist showed the tooth to the multitude, daintily holding it in his forceps. There was a murmur of admiration, whilst another victim was huddled to the front and even sometimes sarcastically urged on by his predecessor.

It was at the corner of this market-place that they first heard of the taking of Sevastopol. Hannah and her children were standing outside the pastrycook's when an old veteran with glittering eyes told them the news.

The whole town was in a state of great delight. The French and English were by way of being great friends and even the market women spoke with tears in their eyes of the dear English soldiers. Blanche and Arthur invested in a couple of coloured candles, which they stuck outside their window to aid the general illumination that took place at nightfall.

Soon after this FitzRoy arrived at Dieppe. He immediately had a long talk with his wife, having heard of a famous doctor living at Tours whom he thought might be capable of curing Arthur.

It was decided that no time should be lost, and towards the end of August the family once more set out on its quest.

This autumn proved a period of rising hopes. FitzRoy, having a long holiday from ministerial work, was in fine form. Both Hannah and he were optimistic about the new doctor. They settled in a large apartment on the first floor of a private house served only by a kitchen girl of the name of Angèle.

The whole family decided to take lessons in French.

FitzRoy made friends with his master, who came to spend the evenings with his pupil.

This teacher rejoiced in the grandiose name of Count Guérin de Tencin, and called himself one of the *Grande Noblesse* though he was much reduced in circumstances and was an artist vendor as well as a lover of bric-à-brac.

Hannah took her lessons from an elderly lady who had white curls on each side of her face and who read literature in rapid French, while Hannah thought of something else. These lessons came to a speedy end.

Blanche's instructress was a delightful one. Her name was Noémi Larthe, and she was only seventeen years of age (though that seemed a tolerable age to Blanche). Noémi was the eldest of ten children, her father being one of the masters of Tours.

Each day Blanche would sally forth to the home of Professor Larthe. The lessons would be held in a little salon where many claret-coloured velvet armchairs were ranged against the wall. These chairs stood on a shiny parquet floor with a little square of carpet in front of each. Professor Larthe stood in the middle of the room dressed in his grey redingote with his hands clasped behind his back. On his head reposed a black velvet calotte worked with rosebuds. He wore gold-rimmed spectacles and green bead slippers, and thus attired he surveyed his numerous progeny, while his wife, elderly and comfortable, sat and nodded affably in her chair. The little girls were in conventional black frocks and aprons with different-coloured stripes to mark their separate classes. They grinned from ear to ear and looked longingly at the big tray of refreshments, pastry cakes and *sirop de groseille*, of which the pupils were later to partake.

Albert, called Bébert, the youngest of the Professor's children, was the pet of the whole family and an exceedingly spoilt child—the only spoilt one, in point of fact, for all the other Larthes were brought up in a rigorous manner. Sometimes Blanche would be invited to join the Professor's family at play, generally on Sunday afternoons. In the middle of the games Albert used to interfere terribly, but he was never reprimanded. On the contrary, it was supposed to be a great honour to be the one momentarily chosen to kiss and fondle that very spoilt child who, to do him justice, was good-humoured and was perpetually going into fits of laughter at anything that he himself did or said.

On the fête-day of the Convent where the younger Larthes were educated, Mlle. Noémi begged that Blanche might accompany her to see the prizes given away. The kindly, elderly, very stout Mother Superior stood up at the end of the classroom surrounded by a bevy of smiling nuns to receive the children, who came two by two and presented her with little bouquets, most of which had written compliments—wonderful specimens of calligraphy—on large scrolls of paper.

During this time FitzRoy spent many hours visiting the prisons and reformatories of the neighbourhood. There was a large reformatory called "Mettray" close to Tours, upon which he wrote a report for the Prime Minister.

Often Blanche would go out with Arthur, who, though lying recumbent in his Bath chair, delighted in going to the '*tir*' where he practised shooting at little white plaster figures. He had a small pistol given to him and he became an excellent shot. At other times Blanche would go with her father to the market where the tall Englishman, who stood six feet in his socks, became a favourite. Smiling and benevolent market women who sat wrapped up in many woollen garments, their feet comfortably tucked up on their braziers filled with charcoal, would knit whilst volubly talking and chaffing.

"Come, my little man!" they would exclaim to FitzRoy. "We will show you something you have not got in England." Then they would show him their pears or their dairy butter.

* * * * *

One morning, when Blanche had returned to London, she received a wooden case containing a small and exquisitely wrought clock, supposed to have belonged to Marie Antoinette.

FitzRoy had purchased this for his daughter from the Count Guérin de Tencin, his professor of French at Tours.

The Count also sent a sealed letter addressed to the Hon. Henry FitzRoy, for his daughter, Miss Blanche, at 42, Upper Grosvenor Street, London, in which that worthy but indigent aristocrat described, in his picturesque hand, the packing of the clock.

"I am not ashamed to tell you," he wrote, "that my family and I kissed our darling clock before allowing it to be placed in the wooden case that was taking it from its native France—maybe for always! We reflect that our clock will be in your home, the emblem of the most complete felicity, and that if ever you pass through sadness, you may support it with greater resignation and courage, by turning your eyes towards the figures of Simplicity, Candour and Innocence sculptured upon it."

CHAPTER SIXTEEN

Arthur FitzRoy to his mother, Hannah Mayer.

Folkestone.
February 7th, 1856.

My dear Mama,

I shall most certainly come to London on Saturday as I do not particularly like Folkestone, and indeed it was only your apparent urgent wish that I should stay here which made me do so as long as I have done. I am also very anxious to see Dr. Tamplin as my leg seems to get worse instead of better. I could not now stretch it without its hurting me very much, so I no longer try. Josephine says it is rheumatism. I wish I knew what it was and had a means of curing it as it hurts me and is besides very boring, as I cannot even lie in all positions. I have spoken to Mr. Giovannini about a railway carriage (as at the station they told Josephine that we had best address ourselves to him) and he will get us one which we need not change, all to ourselves, by the train which leaves here at twelve and gets to London at 3 p.m.

I have not been anywhere to-day and I ate a pretty good dinner. We will bring all the luggage with us.

I hope they will soon let me get up though I would sooner lie down for six months longer than wear stays though I should not mind crutches. If they do not let me get up before autumn, I shall—I do not know what! perish away for want of exercise and any amusement. And there would be an end of me—and of you too, I fancy!

I shall not answer Blanchy's letter except verbally. I send you, Pa, and her my very best love.

And remain, dear Ma,
Your affectionate son,
Arthur.

In her room in Upper Grosvenor Street, Hannah, reading the boy's words, stained the paper with her tears.

*   *   *   *   *

In London, Blanche remained with her governess in the school-room. One April morning, after Sarah, the round-cheeked school-room maid, had combed her hair into two long sleek plaits, she ran, skipping and jumping downstairs. Mademoiselle was suffering from earache, and though she much resented the banging of the schoolroom door as Blanche entered, she had stuffed her ears full of cotton-wool and could not be said that morning to be ready for the joys of conversation. She accused Blanche of mumbling until, suddenly lifting the wool out of one of her ears, she found that her pupil's ringing tones were worse to endure than the pain.

"You have no heart, my child," she said with a sigh of re-signation as, after breakfast, she sat down opposite the fire, her large feet encased in ragged bead slippers and comfortably tucked up on the fender. Blanche strolled to the window. There was a fire in the room for the gratification of her governess, but it was a lovely morning and the sunshine out of doors appeared far more tempting to the little girl than the artificial warmth within. It was pallid London sunshine, beaming mildly through a light veil of greyish mist, flickering in and out of the branches of the hawthorn tree in the tiny garden, and bringing forward in dark relief the masses of ivy growing against the red-brick wall that formed the enclosure. In the middle of the garden was an oval grass plot, surrounded by a narrow gravel walk and a border of yellow crocuses wherein noisy, twittering groups of sparrows were making havoc, enjoying themselves as they picked off the golden petals and scattered them around. The schoolroom was a long, low room on the ground floor, built out from the rest of the house, to which it was attached by a passage. From one side of the bay window Blanche could see into another bay window, that of the library, from which there were two or three steps leading into the garden, an iron balustrade overgrown with jasmine and, just beyond this, a bench whereon FitzRoy sat to read his newspaper and smoke whenever he had the chance of a quarter of an hour's leisure. Blanche could see his writing-table in the window of the library—a large square table covered with blue documents and writing paper of every size and shape. A few books lay on the table also. Blanche knew their names by heart—*May's Parliamentary Practice*, *Burke's Speeches*, a volume of the *Annual Register*, and *Byron's Poems*. As the child looked on all this she reflected that in spite of the books her father seemed scarcely older than herself. He was so full of fun, his laughter came so easily and his jokes were so like her own. But she noticed also at the corner of his desk one of those leather boxes upon which, in gilt letters, were stamped the words: "On Her Majesty's Service." How she hated those boxes that messengers were liable to bring at any moment of the day! Their arrival always put an end to whatever game was going on and meant her dismissal from the library. For close on ten minutes she stood staring out of the window, flattening her nose against the panes, in the hope of seeing her father's dark head appear behind the writing-table. She would have liked to go and join him. Just now she felt in a refractory mood. Her life was mostly spent in extremes, in momentary efforts to be good, in lamentable failures or fits of remorse. Her father was seldom told of her delinquencies. Hannah used to say that he was so little at home that she did not care to burden him with household troubles. FitzRoy probably had an indistinct idea that all children were more or less difficult to handle, but that Two-shoes was almost certainly an exception. He remembered his own childhood and the innumerable whippings he had received and when, on rare occasions, Hannah would speak in his presence of her daughter's behaviour, he would say with a smile: "It's a pity that she's not a boy to give her a good licking."

"Blanche! Blanche!" cried Mademoiselle, seeing that her pupil remained at the window. She had been toasting her slippers one by one at the end of the tongs and replacing them in turn upon her feet, but clearly this occupation was not conducive to her pupil's education. "Come, my child," she continued impatiently looking towards the window: "let us practise the piano."

After a few minutes in front of the instrument, Mademoiselle's voice rang out angrily: "You shall play this piece all over again."

"I won't," said Blanche, veering round upon her music stool.

"Play the piece at once," shouted her governess, rapping the keys of the piano sharply with a ruler.

"I will not," answered the pupil, who jumped up and, seizing the composition with both hands, tore it down the middle.

"I am going to fetch Madame your Mama," announced Mademoiselle: "she will have to deal with you herself."

She walked with dignity towards the door, but Blanche, suddenly frightened, ran in front with outstretched arms to bar the way. Mademoiselle was about to brush her pupil aside when the child, by a quick movement, locked the door and deliberately put the key in her pocket as she faced her opponent with a countenance that was now as white as a sheet.

"Ah," murmured Mademoiselle, with a long-drawn breath, and stood as though she were turned to stone. Then, with a sudden thought, she walked quickly to the window.

Blanche knew that her governess was not sufficiently agile to meditate escape by the window, but guessed her more sinister intention. She followed closely and, looking out immediately behind Mademoiselle, saw the glass doors of the library open. Her father was sitting at his writing-table talking to an old gentleman who sat in the armchair close by. Blanche could just distinguish the thin hair at the top of the old gentleman's head, and the outline of his grey whiskers, but she recognised him. He was the Prime Minister.

It was the work of an instant. Blanche flung the key of the schoolroom door out through the open window. It soared over the low brick wall and disappeared among the bushes in the adjoining garden.

"Monsieur! Monsieur!" cried Mademoiselle, leaning as far out of the window as possible. Blanche crouched in the only corner of the room where, protected by an angle of the wall, she could not be seen by anyone outside the window. Then she heard FitzRoy's quick step crunching the gravel and his voice, in anxious tones:

"What is it, Mademoiselle?"

"Blanche is so naughty that I cannot continue," stammered Mademoiselle as she hung uncomfortably out of the window.

"I will come round to the schoolroom," said FitzRoy very gravely, and he began to retrace his steps, but Mademoiselle called after him: "It's no use. She has locked me in."

"Locked you in?"

"And she has thrown the key over the wall into the next garden."

There was a moment's pause. The Prime Minister, who was standing on the steps leading into the garden, gave a little chuckle of amusement which he vainly tried to suppress into a cough as he bent down to examine a spray of jasmine. Blanche sat huddled on the floor in her dark corner. There was an unwonted sternness in her father's voice that she was quick to notice.

"I will send for the key at once," said FitzRoy. "Pray tell my daughter, Mademoiselle, that I wish her to come to my dressing-room at seven o'clock to-night before I dress for dinner." With a slight bow he turned away and re-entered his study.

The staircase clock was striking seven as Blanche, trembling from head to foot, knocked at the door of her father's dressing-room. She knew how punctual he was himself, and what punctuality he exacted from everyone in his service, and she had been sitting waiting on the stairs for the last five minutes.

"Come in," said the well-known voice, and Blanche entered.

Below a mahogany press was an old military chest on which reposed two rusty duelling swords, crossed one above the other; close to the window was a big iron box, containing a fire escape. At a small table in the centre of the room, FitzRoy sat reading by the light of a lamp and his thin, white hand lay stretched across the open page. He was reading the Bible. Blanche knew the large book with its worn leather cover and silver clasp, but as she entered the room, her father closed the leaves and shut down the clasp. Then he rose and took her hand and drew her gently towards him.

"I wanted to say a great many things to you," he said, "but I can only think of one thing. I know as well as you do, Two-shoes, how difficult it is to be good." Then as the child stood mute with astonishment, he took from the breast pocket of his coat a tiny velvet case and, opening it, placed it in her hand. Within lay a gold brooch whereon were engraved the words:

"*Dieu vous garde.*"

"God keep you, little Two-shoes, always," said FitzRoy in a low voice; and then he bent down and kissed her forehead. "Now go, or I shall be late for dinner."

CHAPTER SEVENTEEN

DURING the spring of 1857 the children saw little of their
father. He went out early and came back in the small
hours. Hannah noticed that her husband was preoccupied. There were moments when he seemed depressed. At
other times he was brimming over with optimism. A political
storm had blown up. Lord Palmerston, then Prime Minister, was
defeated on a question of the China war by a hostile combination. He dissolved Parliament, appealed to the nation and was
returned with a large working majority. The first act of the House
was to elect a new Speaker. For a long time FitzRoy had dreamt
of holding this post and it now looked as if nothing could any
longer deprive him of the honour. He was a personal friend of
Lord Palmerston, whose secretary he had once been, and who was
a frequent guest at his house. More important still, FitzRoy
had for some time discharged the duties of Chairman of Committees and this caused people to believe that he was exceptionally
well qualified for the office. When the names of the three Government candidates were first announced it was found that he
headed the list. *The Times* spoke of him in glowing words,
said he was a thorough man of business and a hard-working one
and added: "We have no hesitation in making our choice."
Something happened at the last moment. Several times FitzRoy
saw high rewards in politics slip through his fingers. The
big, towering man who was so gentle a playmate to his small
daughter, had a warm temper that was apt to make him enemies.
This probably explains why it was Mr. E. Denison and not
FitzRoy who was elected Speaker.

Clearly FitzRoy felt bitter. He thought of quitting politics
altogether. Brand, Secretary of the Treasury, wrote him at this
time: "I am sorry on public as well as on personal grounds, for I

am sure you would have filled the office well. Let me ask you to pause before you give up either the Chair or your seat. If we cannot have you in the highest place, do not let us be deprived of your services altogether."

Like most quick-tempered men, FitzRoy did not bear a grudge for long. He was soon back on Committees working longer hours than ever.

One July morning Hannah, sitting before her escritoire, received a letter from Charlotte, who, with Lionel, was spending a holiday by the seaside at Scarborough. Lionel, mindful of his father's policy, had just given his daughter Leonora in marriage to Baron James's eldest son Alphonse. This was not the only link between London and Paris, for some years earlier Hannah's favourite brother, Nathaniel, had married James's daughter. Just now the Rothschild intermarriages were at their zenith.

It is the wish to hear from you and of the improved health of dear Arthur, that induces me to inflict an uninteresting scrawl upon your kind indulgence [writes Charlotte to Hannah]. We came to the seaside on Monday last and as we heard very indifferent accounts of the horses in this neighbourhood Lionel had his pony sent down and is thus able to spend the whole morning on the sands riding up and down and enjoying the views of land and sea. The children swim and bathe and in the afternoons we take long drives. Lionel takes shower baths of cold sea water; the waves knock him down against the bathing machines and he has given up going into the sea, but the marine breeze and infinitely more exercise than he can take in London agree with him to my heart's content. Your niece [Leonora] adores her husband and if he could stay with her constantly I believe she would never wish to see anyone else, but he leaves at half-past eight in the morning and does not return before 6 or 7 in the evening. Mr. James and Madame Nathaniel are at Venice. Madame James is at Luchon.

You can form no idea of the extraordinary number of persons here. They are all unknown to us and mostly, I believe, to fame. The round hats are countless and worn by ladies who have long ceased to be young and handsome but among the bathers and riders there certainly are lovely faces to be admired, and the whole scene is gay. The sea is quite beautiful and crowded with number-less pleasure and fishing boats among which are steamers plying between Scarborough and Hull that look like giants and are very black and ugly with their huge columns of smoke.

By the time that Charlotte wrote next, she was back at Gunners-bury Park, where she planned to spend part of the autumn.

Your kind letter [she wrote to Hannah] welcomed me on my arrival and should have been acknowledged ere now with a thousand sincere thanks for all the good, affectionate wishes therein contained, but I was in hopes that time, which is said by German poets to bring roses, might increase my budget of news and enable me to send you some agreeable intelligence. Lionel availed himself of a lull in the state of the ministerial atmosphere to leave for Paris. He wished us good-bye this morning. Mrs. James talks of coming to England on a visit to the Duke of Devonshire who had pressed her to stay with him at Chatsworth. She is anxious to see a great many country houses before she finishes Ferrières which, according to my small ideas is too colossal to prove enjoyable. Thank God, the intelligence from India seems rather better. Freddy Helbert is most fortunate in having secured a charming partner for life. The young bride will not hear of letting him go out to India alone but insists upon accompanying him. She and her maid are learning the use of fire-arms. I hope they may not be called upon to shoot Sepoys but that, on their arrival at Calcutta, the horrors of war may have subsided.

The autumnal tints are only just beginning to make their appearance and the garden, though not so bright with roses, is almost as pretty as in July. Is there anything, my dear Hannah Mayer, that Lionel can do for you in Paris? It will give your brother great pleasure to make himself useful.

Always most affectionately and truly yours,

Charlotte.

P.S. Everything is so black that Lionel, on the point of leaving, remained at New Court.

As the Indian mutiny flared up, the FitzRoys rented a country house in Wiltshire called Everleigh. It was a lonely, rambling place nearly two hundred years old with a good-sized garden and excellent shooting. On the garden side of the house was a large magnolia tree which grew up against the windows flowering beautifully. It was necessary to cut off some of the white, velvety blooms beneath Blanche's bedroom because of the strong perfume. On the gravel walk below this were two little pomegranate trees in pots which tried each year to put forth a few scarlet waxen flowers.

Everleigh was not a place with a particularly warm climate, however, and close at hand lay Salisbury Plain, with long tracks of green undulating grass where never a soul was to be seen and where Blanche and Arthur made occasional expeditions in search of mushrooms. FitzRoy would often take his daughter for long walks there, but at other times, she would be obliged to go out along the high road with her governess, a dreary lady who said that it made her teeth ache to talk while out of doors. Blanche paced mournfully along, watching the fields where the plough was tracing furrows or where the sheep were being driven from fold to fold. Soon the little girl almost loved these lonely roads marked with milestones, but little else, and where in the cold weather, some old shepherd might be seen, his face and chin muffled up, crook in hand, his dog beside him as he stood silently watching his sheep through the quiet day. Hannah did not see these things thus. She took prosaic constitutionals along the Wiltshire roads, counting her walk by the milestones, and when she had accomplished two miles she would promptly turn her face homewards.

Blanche would generally accompany her father to church on Sunday when he was at Everleigh for week-ends. The congregation of the church was altogether bucolic, and the rector's sermons had to be fitted to his audience. This congregation consisted of old men in elaborately embroidered smock-frocks, old women in traditional red cloaks and black poke bonnets, and the schoolboys who on week-days sat contentedly on gates and plied rattles to keep away the birds. These behaved so noisily in church that the severe schoolmaster bestowed much corporal punishment on them during the service. The sound thereof on the clean washed smock-frocks made a mighty noise and the quiet tenor of the sermon was often interrupted by loud whackings proceeding from the school benches.

Blanche rode many times with her father. She had learnt to ride some three years before, chiefly from her father himself, though on a few occasions she had lessons in a riding school, but there she had made little progress, having no interest in riding for its own sake. The truth was that it tired her, and her one aim in sitting on a horse was to have her father's company and, if possible, his conversation. FitzRoy was such a fine horseman that he was by no means easily satisfied with her riding. According to him, few women rode well, but when they did he expressed great admiration for them.

It was here that Blanche first learnt to leap, beginning over quite small obstacles. This rather pleased her, though the spirit in which she undertook her leaps was curious, for when the moment arrived for her pony to clear the fence she would shut her eyes and try to think hard how much she loved her father. Then, as the pony landed safely, she would heave a long sigh of relief.

Hannah was extremely nervous during these rides, remembering Arthur's terrible accident. Blanche was given a pretty, dark chestnut which, though spirited, was quiet. Its name was Violet, and Blanche had taught it to place a hoof affectionately in her palm when she said the magic words: "Shake hands!" One day, when Blanche and her father were riding on Salisbury Plain, they came upon a whole colony of mushrooms. FitzRoy dismounted to investigate, leaving his horse's bridle loosely over its neck. This horse, called Brown Stout, was so trustworthy an animal that FitzRoy had done this many times before. Sambo, the old retriever, who had been following closely behind, lay down, his long red tongue hanging out and his whole appearance indicating that he considered a short rest to be timely and wise, whilst his young mistress sat contentedly on her pony, scarcely holding a loose rein and eagerly pointing out the mushrooms to her father.

Quite suddenly something startled Brown Stout. The horse must have trodden on its bridle, for it started off at a tangent, the broken bridle reins streaming in the wind. FitzRoy turned round and seeing his horse disappear tried to win it back by cajoling and coaxing, but though he followed quite slowly at first, calling it gently by name, Brown Stout quickened its pace and Sambo, after rousing himself indolently, suddenly joined in. Blanche, knowing that her pony was no match for the big horse and doubtful of what her father wished her to do, kept motionless until he returned. In a few minutes he was beside her saying: "Think of Mama: come, we must run."

He started, running at her side, but long hours in committees had weakened his heart and Blanche could hear him beginning to breathe very hard. She knew that he could easily do himself harm. In front of them, Brown Stout was galloping on, but the distance between them became increasingly large. Blanche quaked as she thought of the scene that might possibly greet her mother's eyes—a riderless horse with a broken bridle rein! She turned swiftly to look into her father's face. It was white and drawn but firmly set. He was still running beside her, his hand touching the pommel of her saddle, but she fancied that he was not running quite so fast, for the chase seemed well-nigh useless; the runaway horse was gaining ground so rapidly that it must soon become a mere speck in the distance. If only Brown Stout were not galloping homewards!

"Yes, go, go!" whispered her father at last in quick jerky breaths, reading her thoughts. "Quick, quick as you can!" He took his hand from her pommel, yet without perceptibly slackening his pace. Then Blanche started off at a gallop, urging Violet by voice and whip. On, on she flew, faster and yet faster. Whether Brown Stout was beginning to slow down she could not tell, but she was certainly nearing the big horse. If only the animal would not turn down by the open gate and so gallop up to the front of the house where Hannah might chance to be! No. Blanche's heart beat quickly in thankfulness. That danger was past. Brown

Stout, with a sudden spurt, gathered its flagging senses and made for the stable yard. Clatter, clatter in it went, slackening speed as it reached home and allowing the frightened stable lad to approach. Blanche was close behind, but she was horrified to see her mother, whose eyes were fixed wide with terror on the riderless horse, standing in the archway of the stable wall. "Oh, Mama, Mama. It is all right!" cried the child, and thereupon she grew suddenly giddy, whilst her own voice, in what seemed to her to be an odd, far-away tone, repeated: "All right. It is all right, Mama!"

At the same moment the old coachman lifted her from her pony, while her father—yes, her father, pale and breathing hard was standing by, holding her mother's hand.

CHAPTER EIGHTEEN

SOMETHING momentous flashed through Arthur's brain as, on December 15th, he awoke to the anniversary of his fifteenth birthday. He had never quite given up the hope of a naval career, but now, as he reached the age limit for his cadetship, the bitter truth broke upon him. He would never be a midshipman.

He turned in his bed on this cold and foggy morning to look at the murky greyness that filtered into the room from the street, but even as he moved he felt the pain dig into his back. For years he had refused to believe the worst. Every old sailor at Brighton and at Folkestone knew and welcomed the boy with the serious face who lay in his spinal chair gazing lovingly out through his telescope at passing ships. The machinery that had driven him forward seemed of a sudden to stop. Not for him were the salt spray and the misty mornings out at sea!

For the first time in his life he felt utterly helpless. As he heard the whistling of an errand boy in the street he must have pictured the lad swinging along with a basket under his arm. At this rate he would not even know the joys of an ordinary school life, the crack of the cricket ball against the bat or the swish of the oar in the water.

He knew that his brain was as sharp as another boy's. In the class-room he would probably climb to the top. His Latin and Greek were far above the average. Long hours with Mr. Sims had taught him to read the classics fluently. For him the *Odyssey* was a human tale. He read *Cornelius Nepos* and loved the dream of Egeria in her laurel grove.

Hannah came quietly into his bedroom, raised the lace blinds and walking across to where he lay, bent over him and said: "A very happy birthday, Arthur dear."

"Thank you, Mama," said Arthur.

As he spoke he did not let go his mother's hand but held it in as tight a grip as he was able to command. Then a tear fell down his cheek and he whispered: "What will become of me, Mama?"

Hannah looked down at her son and answered: "Be brave, Arthur. You are growing to be a man."

She knew that her words were inadequate, but there was nothing that she could say. Her son smiled and answered: "You are right, Mama. I shall try and get well, if only for you."

The maid brought his breakfast and Blanche knocked at the door. She carried with her a Christmas tree with fifteen little candles. All this she had prepared entirely alone, covering it with things she had either bought herself or made with her own hands. There were little silk flags bordered at the edges and mounted on small flag-poles. She had planted each flag with small bunches of flowers—forget-me-nots and roses—and with a brush had written carefully between pencilled lines the words: "Many Happy Returns" and "*Gaudium et Felicitas*—God Bless Arthur." On a valentine was a picture of Violet, her horse, Lily, her tiny white dog, and the ship that Arthur had made for her at Brighton.

Also on the tree were a small scarlet comforter and a pair of muffetees that Blanche had knitted for her brother.

While Arthur was examining his gifts, the door opened again and his father came in. His arrival was not a surprise to anyone in the room. He had a habit of running up the stairs two or three at a time and on these occasions his family always heard him before they saw him. FitzRoy was still amazingly young. He had altered little since the miniature that Ross had made of him shortly after his marriage. He had a rich crop of curly black hair, thin black eyebrows, laughing blue eyes and fluffy whiskers. He was dressed to go out in a black coat cut rather tight at the waist but with extremely wide lapels. He wore a voluminous satin tie (with Blanche's first tooth mounted on a pin in it) and a deep blue velvet waistcoat.

"GOD BLESS ARTHUR."

Blanche FitzRoy paints a Valentine for her invalid brother on his fifteenth birthday and weaves into it her pony Violet, her dog Lily, and the ship he made for her.

CHAPTER NINETEEN

THERE was nothing particular to mark the New Year of 1858 in the minds of the FitzRoys. Possibly the head of the house stood at the top of the table as the clock chimed twelve and raised his glass to the health and prosperity of his small family. Arthur had just celebrated his fifteenth birthday. Blanche was little more than thirteen, with rather straight hair parted in the centre and two long pigtails hanging down her back.

The New Year had not grown old before big events took place. By the middle of February the Administration ran once more into stormy weather. It was not going to be a long pause in Palmerston's career. Nevertheless, on February 20th he and his colleagues resigned.

The night before, the Prime Minister had summoned his Cabinet together. They met in Downing Street at three o'clock in the afternoon. After an hour Palmerston, leaving the others behind, jumped into a hackney cab and told the driver to take him to Buckingham Palace. There he called on the Queen, who had cancelled a holiday trip to Osborne to be near at hand, and tendered his resignation. The curious thing was that though the Derbyites had occasioned the government's fall, yet they had won no laurels in the fight. They did not come in with drums beating or with colours flying. The Liberals just held the gates wide open and said: "This is the way in."

The Derby Administration did, however, witness an event of some interest. This was the last act of Lionel's fight to enter Parliament. One July day the Clerk announced to the Speaker that a member was waiting to take his seat. The Speaker directed that the member should advance and so Lionel once more walked up to the table. He was introduced this time by two tried friends,

Lord J. Russell and Mr. J. A. Smith. As soon as he reached the table, a Member of Parliament cried out: "I rise to order!"

The Speaker: "The question of a member taking his seat is a matter of privilege and should not be interrupted."

The Clerk started to administer the usual oath but Lionel having interrupted him, he went up to the Speaker and explained: "The hon. member says that he entertains conscientious objections to taking the oath in the form presented."

The Speaker: "Then the hon. member will please to withdraw."

Lionel accordingly withdrew to the space below the bar. Some time later Lord Russell moved a resolution to allow the Clerk to omit from the oath the words: "on the true faith of a Christian," to allow the new member to take the oath in a manner binding upon him. The House divided and the numbers were:

For the resolution	69
Against	37
Majority	32

The battle was won! A burst of cheering went up from friends and foes alike. Lord J. Russell and Mr. J. A. Smith flushed with pride, left the House and returned triumphantly with Lionel, whom they escorted to the table. Thus the curtain fell on the drama of Lionel de Rothschild. He had won after a long and bitter fight. On passing Disraeli, Lionel paused for a moment to shake him by the hand. Then he was conducted to the front opposition bench, below the gangway, where he took his seat not far from that of his brother-in-law, Henry FitzRoy.

*   *   *   *   *

That summer Blanche became delicate in health. There was nothing serious the matter, but she had been ill once or twice and was forbidden by her doctor to do any lessons. FitzRoy suggested that Hannah should take her to drink the waters at a

German spa called Schwalbach. As soon as Parliament rose he would come and spend a few weeks with his wife and daughter. Meanwhile Arthur would remain with his tutor at Everleigh.

Hannah and Blanche arrived in Paris one evening in July. They were accompanied by a maid and by Blanche's little white terrier, Lily. FitzRoy asked his wife to stay, if possible, at the Hôtel du Rhin, so that he could get in touch with her if necessary without waiting for an address. He requested her also to convey all his sympathy to Nathaniel, for a great tragedy had befallen this gay, cheerful fellow who only a few years ago seemed to have the world at his feet. One day Nathaniel had gone hunting. He was thrown from his horse and was taken home on a stretcher. The doctors came to look at him, just as they had looked at little Arthur, but they could do nothing. Gradually Nathaniel became paralysed and then blind. Now he lived entirely in Paris, watched over by his wife Charlotte, daughter of the Baron James. It was remarkable that, in spite of his great injuries, Nathaniel's intellect was never clouded and many members of his family as well as countless friends came to him for advice. He kept himself in close touch with the outside world, and had the French and English newspapers read to him each morning.

During the next few weeks, while FitzRoy's little family was scattered, many letters passed between London, Everleigh and Paris. Meanwhile the lease of Everleigh was coming to an end and FitzRoy was busy hunting for a new country house to take its place.

Blanche, to her father.

Hôtel Windsor,
Paris.

My dearest Papa,

We arrived at Paris last night and I hasten to write you a few particulars of our journey. We had only two fellow travellers— a lady and a little girl who was twelve years old. They had left their Pa behind them, too, and we saw them bid good-bye in the train. They were going on the continent and intended to reach Paris the same day. During the first half hour of our cross-Channel passage nobody was ill, but after that the sea was a little rougher and we were sick. Ma and I were both glad to get to Boulogne, where we slept at the Hôtel des Bains.

Yesterday morning we left Boulogne and travelled alone in a very nice coupé. To-day we have been out already to take a little walk along the Boulevards. We could not find any apartments at the Hôtel du Rhin except at the top of the house, or at the Hôtel Brighton, except those looking on the yard; so we have come here. These apartments look on the yard, but we are going to change them for others that look over the Tuileries.

Lily put her nose out of her basket yesterday as we came from the station to admire the Place Vendôme, though perhaps it was really to see what the little French dogs were like. Did you stay in bed as long as you wanted to to-day? I wish the House of Commons was always up the first of July and then you could be with us to walk and to look at the shops and the people.

Believe me, my dear Pa,
Your very affectionate daughter,
Blanche.

Henry FitzRoy to his wife, Hannah.
Upper Grosvenor Street.

My dearest wife,

I am indeed thankful to learn from your note from Boulogne that you had a good passage, for it blew enough here to make me fear that you might not cross. I never had so hard a day as yesterday since I was Chairman, and at last I was fairly done. I was so sound asleep this morning at half-past nine that they could hardly wake me. You are now on the road to Amiens, I suppose. I do not know what to do for a country place when you come back.

I think we had better take the Cedars. I hardly like leaving with nothing fixed.

The Speaker sent me twelve peaches and nectarines yesterday. I have cut off my whiskers and look so absurd that I cannot go anywhere; I lie in bed as long as I can and think of my wife.

Your very affectionate
Hub.

Arthur, to his father.

Everleigh.

My dear Pa,

I hope you are not very lonely to-day and found some nice place to dine at yesterday. I wish it were not so far and that you could pass two days with me. There is no fruit ripe or likely to be for a fortnight, except strawberries, so you need not fear my making myself ill. There are as many bunnies as ever. I have had several tries at them with my rifle and have succeeded amidst a host of failures in knocking over one unfortunate little brute about six inches long, which of course I had cooked for dinner.

My carriage is much more comfortable to lie in than the other, but it rolls rather roughly, not being on springs, and I am afraid that in winter it will be dreadfully cold from not having sides. I enclose a piece of Everleigh mignonette and a wood strawberry.

Your affectionate son,
Arthur.

Blanche, to her father.

Hôtel Windsor,
Rue de Rivoli,
Paris.

My dearest Pa,

Mama is not going to write to you to-day because she wrote to Arthur, so I will send my Pa a few lines instead. Ma received your letter this morning. She wishes me to ask you not to write on such thick paper because she has a great deal extra to pay, and to seal and close your letters more firmly as the last one had been opened when it arrived.

I am very sorry to hear that you are dull, my own Pa, and equally indignant at your cutting off the manly ornaments of your physiognomy, and Mama is of my opinion that you are very naughty to do so. We went to the Louvre this morning and so as not to tire me we went and came back in a fly. We have a delicious little apartment with a drawing-room and dining-room all to ourselves. Are we not grand? Paris is full of soldiers. The other morning we went to the little town of Boulogne to visit Uncle Nathaniel. There was a fair that is to last a week, and I saw people going round and round on wooden horses and in small armchairs, and everywhere there was a great quantity of gingerbread and toys, while men, principally soldiers, shot at small figures. I went with Bobby Rothschild and his nurse. The warlike young gentleman bought three pistols. As we walked home a Sergeant de Ville stopped us and wanted to know why my large and ferocious Lily was not muzzled. Just think of it! They go about stopping all the little unmuzzled dogs in Paris.

I will bid you good-bye and with a kiss remain, my dearest Papa,

Your affectionate,
Blanchy.

Henry FitzRoy to his wife, Hannah.

Upper Grosvenor Street.

My darling Woman,

I begin my letter to-day as I long to be talking to you before I start for church, where I hope to pray for you. Yesterday I went down to look at the Cedars. It was a dark, wet day, cold and dreary. When I drove up I found that it had been let and occupied for more than a fortnight. I had to walk about the station for two hours, which was not gay. I passed the evening at Brooks's Club, where there was literally not a soul. In a short time I shall learn to run away when I see anyone.

It is now midnight. After writing my last paragraph I went out for a solitary walk round Kensington Gardens, then to church at Quebec Chapel, then to see Mrs. 'Lionel' and then the evening service at Westminster Abbey, after which I dined at Brooks's on a slice of roast lamb. I hope this paper is thin enough.

Ever your affectionate,
Hub.

Henry FitzRoy to his daughter, Blanche.

House of Commons.

My darling little Pet,

I am indeed sorry that the Frenchmen are so alarmed at Lily. You should soothe them and assure them that she is not dangerous. She must look funny in her muzzle. I suppose I shall not write any more to Paris, as I fancy you must be even now on your way to Schwalbach. I hope the journey will not knock you up. When you are settled write me all your adventures and what you think of the splendid Rhine, of Strasbourg and all that you see.

We shall, I hope, ride donkeys together as soon as I can get over. I have not seen Violet since you left, but I think you will

want a larger and stronger pony when next you are in England.
I have only ridden once since you went. I live in the chair and
shall be very glad when I am out of it.

Believe me,
Your very affectionate,
Pa.

Arthur to his father, Henry FitzRoy.

Everleigh.

My dear Pa,

I am afraid I cannot say that I have improved since I have been
here. I was three whole days without eating so much as a green
pea in the way of vegetables and fruit, and I think I was worse
than ever. The doctor thinks it is much to do with the weather,
which has been very blighty and thundery. I enclose a little
piece of wheat to show you how fine it is. All along the Marl-
borough Road where there were turnips, there is now wheat and
that is where I got it.

I am sorry to say I have killed no more bunnies and my only
exploit has been to knock a few feathers out of a thrush which
I did not get; indeed, I have hardly had six shots with my rifle
since I wrote last, and those not at rabbits. That is because I have
to cross a field to get to them, which shakes me terribly so that
the two or three shots I have had have been out of the window
at thrushes.

I remain, dear Pa, your affectionate son,

Arthur.

Henry FitzRoy to his wife, Hannah.

The House of Commons.

My darling Wife,

I think your account of poor Nathaniel is, all things considered,
favourable. Pray give him my love and tell him how much I
would like to see him. I am just out of the chair and am going
in again, and am now waiting for my dinner. I cannot go out
and can go nowhere.

Believe me,
Your very affectionate,
Hub.

147

Blanche, to her father.   Hôtel Windsor,
                                                              Paris.

My dearest Pa,

My darling Lily is lost. I am so sorry about it. They stole her
on Friday. This is very badly written, dear Pa, but I cannot help
it. They have just come in to say that a gendarme knows a little
white dog, a bitch, with a black eye, only he does not know
whether it is Lily's kind. Mama's maid has gone to look, for
it is quite close. If it was Lily!

I shall be very glad, dear Pa, when you come to us. We are
not so gay at Paris as you think. For two or three days the rain
kept us indoors. Ma's maid has just come back. It is *not* Lily
but a dog with long hair and a black head; that is not my pet Lil.
As for Violet, I think she can last me quite well three years
longer, for she is not so very little nor I so very heavy. Yesterday
we passed the day with Uncle Nat and I played and walked in the
garden with Bobby.

The only muzzle poor Lily was to have known is a narrow
piece of sky-blue velvet I had made up and which looked so
pretty on her, but there it lies untouched on the table.

Dear Pa, this is rather a stupid letter, but I was so startled
about Lily that I could only think she might return.

                                      Your affectionate,
                                                    Blanchy.

P.S.—We have had bills printed and have offered a reward.

FitzRoy to his wife, Hannah.

                                      Upper Grosvenor Street.

My dearest Wife,

I am not sure that you will ever get this letter as you will be
en route, but it is some comfort to talk to you on paper, if I cannot
talk by word of mouth. I wonder where you are (probably just
getting into bed: 10 p.m.), but where? You do not tell me how
you go, but I hope, as it is so hot, that you have rested all day at
Strasbourg and amused yourselves. I think the journey will do
Blanchy as much good as the waters. I do not believe you will
manage it all in one day, but I shall follow you in imagination.
I shall have to get up at half-past six to go to Cologne, but the
next day will be Sunday and I shall be able to rest.

                          With best love to my duck,
                                      Your very affectionate,
                                                    Hub.

A CENTURY BETWEEN

From Henry FitzRoy to his son, Arthur.

House of Commons,
Midnight.

My darling Boy,

I am very thankful to hear that you are going on well. I was hoping to start to rejoin Ma this evening, but the best I can hope for is to leave at six o'clock in the morning and that will compel me to remain at Cologne all Sunday, as I do not like to travel on that day.

I think you will have to prepare for Paris for a few weeks, and I believe that an autumn there would not be by any means disagreeable. Only take care of yourself and get strong enough for the journey, and then it would do you good.

God bless you.

Your very affectionate,
Pa.

Meanwhile Lily turned up safe and sound and Blanche, with a much lighter heart, accompanied her mother to Schwalbach.

The Rhine was new to her and so was Cologne, and its cathedral and bridge of boats, the noisy steamers, the castles and the historic scenery. Blanche conscientiously sketched at every pause of the journey.

There were many unaccustomed things for Blanche at Schwalbach: the promenade with the smartly dressed people, the breakfast of rolls and coffee served out under the trees where the band played, the *table d'hôte* with the everlasting boiled veal and stewed prunes, and the Germans eating with their knives.

Real black Sedan chairs were used in wet weather to convey the ladies from their hotel to the baths and back again. One day a Sedan chair was provided for Blanche. She hopped easily enough into it, but when two stalwart men lifted it up and walked off with it, she felt sick and was thankful when the short journey came to an end.

FitzRoy joined his wife and daughter in early August. General Grey often came to the FitzRoys' apartment. He used constantly to carry in his pocket a volume of Don Quixote in Spanish, which he pulled out and read on every possible occasion.

Back at Everleigh one morning Arthur received an impressive envelope with an array of blue and yellow stamps—stamps that were cut out with a pair of scissors from a solid sheet. The writing paper on which Blanche had written to her brother was not less exciting. It bore on the top a fine coloured print of Schwalbach showing the avenue of trees, the baths and the people who walked up and down. She wrote to him:

Schwalbach,

August 10.

My dear Arthur,

Mama is gone to Frankfort for a day or two. I tasted the water people have to drink here and it is scalding hot, rather hotter than you would bear even to sip. People are not allowed to eat fruit here because of the steel in the water, but even if they might it would be no great advantage, for there is no fruit to be found here.

The country about here is hilly and these are all covered with woods. Schwalbach is entirely in a valley surrounded by green hills, and when you look down from one of them on the little town you see nothing but slate roofs.

Believe me, my dear Arthur,

Your affectionate sister,

Blanche.

Two days later, Hannah wrote to her son:

Schwalbach.

My dear Arthur,

I should like you to leave Everleigh two days before my return, which will be on the 25th or the 26th, and to find you quite rested at Grosvenor Street. I do not wish to be longer in London than to pay my bills and make arrangements to leave for Paris. I must try and send you some money for your journey from Everleigh up to Town and you must collect all the bills of your expenses in the country which I can send to pay by cheque from London. You must have a fly from Andover to take you to the station. Miles' carriage is not long enough. You can write to Mrs. Wolf at the Star Hotel, Andover, requesting her to send a large carriage with a pair of horses, the day you require it, and name also the time to be at your door.

DRINKING THE WATERS AT SCHWALBACH.

One morning in 1858 Blanche FitzRoy stepped
out of her black Sedan chair and wrote a letter to
her brother in England. "We're in a valley surrounded by green hills," she wrote, "and when
you look down from one of them you see nothing
but slate roofs."

I think you can also write a letter in my name to the station-master at Andover about the railway carriage particularly naming: "It will be required for an invalid to be tightly screwed so that it does not shake." The carriage with Charles, the footman, shall come to meet you in London. George, who will travel from Everleigh with you, and Charles, the footman, must both see you safely in the carriage when you arrive. George can follow immediately with some of the maids in a hack cab and Charles, the lad, can come in a light cart with the luggage to Grosvenor Street from the station, so that on arriving home both the men servants will be ready to take you out of the carriage and make you comfortable in the library, where you will find either dinner or tea according to the time you arrive.

Your very affectionate mother,
Hannah.

CHAPTER TWENTY

THE FitzRoys took a comfortable apartment in Paris for the coming winter. It was in the Avenue Gabriel and consisted of two floors with a private staircase, overlooking the Champs-Élysées and yet standing back from the main road behind a group of trees. This apartment solved the problem of looking for another house in the country to take the place of Everleigh. In many ways it was more convenient because Hannah had of late been suffering from ear trouble, and by remaining in Paris she was able to undergo treatment from a specialist. While Hannah and the children were settling down in their new quarters, FitzRoy returned for a short time to England to shoot partridges at Thetford in Norfolk. During his short stay in London he described the journey in a letter to his wife, thus: "I arrived here quite safely last evening about half-past eight. It was unbearably hot the first three hours, but then the wind got up and coming across it blew quite fresh. There was really no sea, but the way the people thought it necessary to vomit was quite wonderful. I did not feel sick myself. There was nobody I knew on the train, but there were loads of English in every carriage. It was very dark and heavy on approaching our shores. The air at Boulogne was as beautiful as ever, but here it is cooler than in Paris. The first thing I found on my arrival was the most wonderful bag. I kissed it for my darling wife, whose kindness had planned it. You say in your letter that I did not embrace my own, sweet wife before I left. I did not for fear of waking her up. I only dared to pat her and bless her because she had been so much disturbed lately."

FitzRoy's holiday at Thetford did him a lot of good and he planned to remain about a fortnight before returning to Paris. He sent a good many baskets of grouse not only to Hannah but also to Lionel, who happened at that time to be staying with Baron James. "I see in *The Times*," wrote FitzRoy, "that you have it hotter than ever in Paris. How funny it seems to read of the heat being overpowering now, for I am actually shivering here for want of a fire. Will you ascertain for me if I shall have any difficulty about bringing my guns? If there was much to pay I should not think it worth while. Alphonse promised to find out."

From his bedroom window little Arthur could look across the bare boughs of the trees towards the Champs-Élysées. On cold, brisk mornings when the sun came out, he could see the children playing on the grass, being pushed by their nurses on diminutive roundabouts. Along the gravel sidewalks old women sold coloured balloons and kept stalls where for a few sous children could buy sweets, pails, spades and windmills. The smallest rode on donkeys while their mothers or nurses walked slowly behind; others slithered in a sandy patch that gave them the illusion of being at the seaside. They could make mountains and castles or dig and irrigate rivers. There was a tang in the air on these autumn mornings, but by midday the sun burned with all its force. In the evenings Blanche and Arthur would often go out for drives in an open carriage constructed specially for the invalid to remain lying down on his couch. The two children followed the wide streets where women and gorgeously uniformed officers sauntered slowly. Blanche wrote to her father about the Parisian women in their voluminous crinolines of bright red and green, their bonnets and cashmere shawls. Officers rode proudly along the curb, their epaulettes shimmering and their dangling swords catching the last rays of the sun. Occasionally a diligence drawn by five horses rattled past, or a phaeton flew along on its way to the Bois. Gentlemen with pointed black beards and fine waving moustaches, white waistcoats, narrow trousers and high hats leaned back in their chairs outside the cafés reading the news from the papers. People argued, gesticulated and became heated about politics and the wars abroad.

The pavements were filled with passers-by who were in no particular hurry. Men would stop, raise their hats and bow when they passed a woman of their acquaintance. As the light faded and darkness fell, the shops would be lit to show silks and laces and bonnets through the windows. Blanche would draw a long breath and enjoy that smell so peculiar to Paris—a smell of perfumes and powders, of grass and damp trees. She would watch the lights going up outside the theatres, dream of the wonderful plays that must be given inside and yearn to be allowed to dine out like a grown-up in the smart cafés or the restaurants with famous names. For the two children, so accustomed to winters of fog and oppressive cold, this lovely feminine city sparkled like a diamond.

At times they would drive down the streets leading to the Bois and then through the avenues among the trees, where everything after dark was quiet and mysterious. As the carriage passed over the gravelled alleys, Arthur would explain to his sister all the great determinations he had made for the future. Since he had been constrained to abandon the idea of being a sailor, he had turned his thoughts to hopes of travel. He would shoot tigers and lions and lead expeditions to those parts of the world that remained unknown. Yet, again, he would charter a yacht and sail past the Grecian Archipelago, visit the site of Troy and retrace the journey of Ulysses homeward-bound for Ithaca. He knew Greek, but expressed a desire to master modern Greek and seven other languages! Only those who have known invalids suffering from long and incurable illnesses are acquainted with the fountain of hope they so ardently cherish. It is doubtful if Arthur ever looked upon his condition as being hopeless, nor consequently did Blanche, who took her views about his illness chiefly from him. One life was not sufficient for all the things that Arthur planned to do. Only when the horses stumbled and the carriage was brought up with a jolt, shaking his hard couch, did the stinging pain bring him face to face with reality.

Suddenly the great comet of 1858 would stream across the heavens and illumine the dark night with its weird brilliancy. People stood around marvelling and prophesying strange and terrible things. As the boy looked at this ball of white light with its long phosphorescent tail, he gripped his sister tightly by the hand. Perhaps he also read into it some disturbing presage. Then the coachman whipped up the horses and turned them towards the Champs-Élysées, with its cafés garlanded by coloured lamps, where singing and music were heard. Here was the Château des Fleurs, looking like a fairyland, where Hannah sometimes went to dine with her Rothschild cousins. As the children passed through the fashionable streets they doubtless noticed how house after house reflected lighted windows on the pavement. At this moment of the evening an incessant stream of carriages brought guests for dinner to the houses of the hostesses of the day. Paris was beginning to make itself the established centre of luxury and good taste. Baron Haussmann had already designed lawns and gardens all along the Champs-Élysées among which rose new places of amusement. The Palace of Industry reared its unfinished head on the site of the present Grand Palais. The boulevards that were spreading their fame throughout the civilised world were being enlarged and made more beautiful. The Emperor held a glamorous court, to which flocked Europe's most famous artists. Parisian women were known for their wit and their looks, and the crinoline, because it was so big, had the effect of making men more courteous and respectful. A few doors away from the apartment of the FitzRoys in the Avenue Gabriel was the home of the greediest man in Paris—Grimod de La Reynière, who said: "My only fear of being thirteen at table is that there should not be enough food to go round."

The first dressmakers were beginning to gain international reputation, although as a general rule women did not yet visit their dressmakers but received them at home. Many women of fashion, among them the Empress herself, not only chose dresses brought for their inspection, but also had girls working for them.

Blanche was extremely happy. She was an efficient little needle-woman and longed to copy the lovely things she saw. As she drove home with her brother they would stop before the shops filled with dolls. Blanche wrote often to her father in England. "We have just seen the comet again," she explained. "It is not necessary to use a telescope, for we can see it while we are driving or sometimes by just looking out of the window. I am so glad to have seen a comet, but I expected its tail to be longer. The weather is still fine and warm, and I am going this afternoon to the Parc Monceaux, which is very pleasant. I do so hope that you will bring Violet with you when you come, dear Papa. I should so much enjoy a ride with you in the Bois de Boulogne and to be able to use the new whip that Mama has given me. We have just come back from the Madeleine flower market."

During the weeks that followed, Blanche saw less of her brother than in the past. The days of childish games and stories and tin soldiers were over and gone and Arthur led the retired life of a student dwelling almost completely amongst his books, his pale little hands turning over the leaves of big Greek and Latin dictionaries morning, noon and night. FitzRoy arrived in Paris, having cut short his sporting holiday and previously written to Hannah: "I am already tired of it and would prefer you and Paris to not-you and Thetford!"

One evening Arthur sent for Blanche to come into his bedroom. It was getting late. Hannah was sitting near the fireside prepared to spend the night with him, by no means an unusual occurrence with her. Arthur did not speak much, but when he did his voice was husky, which struck his sister painfully and strangely. Hannah told her daughter she had better not stay or she might tire him, and then Arthur called her and said: "Kiss me, Blanchy" —a rare demand on his part, for he was extremely undemonstrative and cold in manner. Blanche kissed him with tears rising as she did so and then she left the room. A few minutes later Arthur asked his mother for the pair of knitted muffetees and the

small comforter made of red wool that Blanche had given him
for his birthday eleven months before. She had placed them on
the Christmas tree that she had arranged entirely herself. The boy
kept them on all night. He slept but little and occasionally
talked to his mother. In the morning the attendant brought in
his breakfast and it was then that, raising himself slightly in
bed, he suddenly drooped, sighed softly, and his spirit fled.
He was even then surrounded by the books he loved: a volume
of his favourite Thucydides lay beside his pillow. His end
was so peaceful that Hannah, who was in the room, was not even
aware of it.

There was a strange hush in the house, a terrible feeling that
something had happened. Blanche was troubled, but could get
no answers to her questions. She did not see her mother that
morning. FitzRoy—a very rare thing with him—had gone away
on a two days' visit to Ferrières. It was he who, having arrived
hurriedly (he had been instantly telegraphed for), told Blanche
of their loss. That is to say, he told her nothing. He came into
the room where she was and said: "I want to speak to you."
Then he looked at her and held out his arms and burst into a
passion of tears, the first she had ever seen him shed.

Hannah FitzRoy to her sister, Louisa.

Paris,
November 27th.

My dear Louisa,
   It is only within the last few days that I could bring my thoughts
together to enable me to write to my friends. I know that you
loved my poor departed son. I may for the sake of others appear
tranquil, but the best part of my existence is gone with my
beloved.
   The last few weeks of his life he seemed even more pensive
than before, and he wrote some lines which I will copy for you.
They describe feelings and thoughts that for his age were
wonderfully expressed. He wrote them in his bedroom and they
were intended to be given to me when re-copied—which, alas!
he never could from weakness:

"Hail, Silence! Queen of Night and soft repose,
    Thou welcome Refuge of a troubled breast,
Thou graceful solace of unuttered woes,
    Thou best of Friends, Giver of Peace and Rest.

Giver of Rest, rest from the din of words,
    Words without meaning, jarring on the ear,
Full of the pleasure that this world affords,
    Though to a Soul in pain, they vain appear.

But Silence! Oh, how hard thou art to find!
    Not e'en in Solitude's secluded bower
Is thy perpetual home, where anxious mind
    May find thee, seeking for a happier hour.

Though most 'tis there, that thou dost love to dwell,
    Still, oft a little inward voice intrudes,
Speaking of things we would not have it tell,
    And on past sins, woes and misfortunes brood.

But if not there, in Sleep's soft bosom hid,
    Thou com'st to renovate the weary heart,
And seated on the Slumberer's closèd lid
    Suff'rest him of his ills to feel but part.

For a small part we must e'en then endure
    In dreams renewing long-forgotten moil,
Recorders far too faultless, and too sure
    Of scenes from which, on waking, we recoil.

But yet, 'tis rest, for which we thankful feel,
    Until a Sleep more lasting shall release
The weary from his Toil, the sick shall heal
    And to the wretched bring unmingled bliss."

                Yours very affectionately,
                    Hannah Mayer F.

His head bowed and his whole body shaken, FitzRoy accompanied his son on the last journey home to England. All through the long night, with the exception of two hours when, worn out by fatigue, he fell into a dazed and troubled sleep, FitzRoy thought of his wife in Paris, praying that she might rest a little. His only comfort was to read again and again his son's verses and cry over them. Stunned and alone in his study in Upper Grosvenor Street, he wrote this grief-stricken letter:

My very dearest, blessed Wife,

I begin this to you as soon as I am arrived here. We got safe over by the boat, which left at three, and thanks to your brother Anthony brought our darling boy up with us in the train.

I am now waiting for Lionel, but as Anthony says that one day is the same as another to him, I have telegraphed to the Rev. Humphrey Allen and to Southampton that it will be to-morrow at ten. I shall return by Calais as I have too much recollection of Boulogne and Folkestone to choose that painful route. I shall go by the night boat, which arrives in Paris at 9 a.m. In any case I shall cross to Calais, so that having done that, I may as well come on as go to bed for four or five hours, and then be twice the time on the road.

I thought of you all night, except the two hours' passage, during which I slept, but I grudged the time, as I kept thinking what you were doing and praying to God that you might sleep. My only comfort now is reading his verses over and over and crying over them. I can read nothing else. I hope your weather has changed for Blanche's sake. Here it is very mild and now coming out lovely. It got mild about an hour before we reached Calais.

Noon. Your brother and my brother have just been here; I have no doubt they all thought me very callous for not crying, but I am fairly dry of tears and my heart is heavy. I have just been looking over all his letters, but though many, none contain any verses. I still think I have some somewhere, but I had no idea that I had so many from both children since their babyhood. Yours, I have preserved, including notes written before our marriage. How thankful I am to have destroyed none and what a pleasure, when left a withered stick, quite alone, to read again such words of love as some of yours contain.

I only think of you and him all day—but I feel stunned and stupefied, perhaps partly from excitement and no wine or meat, but my head feels like a stone and I am miserable! I now know the bitterest pang *but one* that can be felt on earth. When I have gone through that, will reason still remain?

Give my best fondest love to our only pet and with love as deep as ever was felt,

Believe me,

Your really devoted

F.

CHAPTER TWENTY-ONE

IT was a June day in 1859. The weather was hot and Londoners sought the shade of the trees in Hyde Park. The country was buzzing with rumours about the war in Southern Europe and some said that England might be dragged in. France had gone to help eject the Austrians from Italy and the employees in Mr. Reuter's London office were receiving the first authentic news of the Battle of Magenta, from which it was clear that the Austrians were everywhere in flight.

At this same moment there was great excitement in the London clubs. Lord Palmerston, once more Prime Minister, had been posting the names of his new Cabinet. Lord John Russell became Foreign Secretary and FitzRoy First Commissioner of Works. FitzRoy felt only a mild satisfaction. He was getting over the initial shock of his son's death, but he found that his health was broken. Those long hours in the Chair had made a wreck of him. When Hannah looked at her husband she noticed that deep lines now marked his features and his hair was turning grey. Committee work had, of course, kept his mind off other things, but a new interest might mean a renewal of vigour. He walked across the Green Park to Upper Grosvenor Street, where Charles, the footman, handed him a note. He broke the seal and saw that it was from Sir Evelyn Denison, the Speaker. "This intelligence gives me great pleasure," he read. "Though we must regret you as Chairman, we shall rejoice to think that both our business and our pleasure—the Houses of Parliament and Rotten Row—will be under your charge."

Meanwhile Palmerston was anxious to make Britain's position clear to the world. His government would pursue a policy of strict neutrality while doing everything possible to restore peace on the Continent.

As the days passed, the electric telegraph brought news of fresh victories for the allies, but suddenly the Emperor Napoleon drew back. He had decided that it was dangerous to tie up his money and his soldiers in Italy while Prussia was heavily arming. The Emperor did not even wait to consult his ally, Victor Emmanuel, but arranged with the Austrians for an armistice. Londoners read the news blazoned across their newspapers one morning at breakfast. People stepped back to consider what this war had proved. It was a long time since the Battle of Waterloo and Nathan's fast sailing ships and carrier pigeons. The railroad train now hurried reserves to the front, the telegraph had signalled each flank movement of the enemy, chemistry had doubled the strength of gunpowder, cannons and rifles carried twice as far and killed with double the precision.

As usual after a major war, thinking men looked into the future. One commentator wrote: "Wonderful suffocating agencies are invented for ships and fortresses. Inextinguishable liquid fire is to consume fleets. How long is mankind to endure the fearful waste, how long to suffer the sin of war? Over the heads of kings, let nations form a league and in the panoply of reason say that this may be no longer."

By the beginning of August, FitzRoy's nerves were on edge. In a way the Office of Works had proved a change, but he had come to it after long weeks in the Chair, and it was clear that he was on the verge of a breakdown. At home Blanche still showed some weakness and the doctors were worrying Hannah to take her to Trouville for the bathing. As it seemed tolerably certain that Parliament would go on for another fortnight, FitzRoy agreed, saying that he would come and join them at the first possible moment.

As soon as they had left he felt strangely sad. All that day he watched the sky and clouds, praying that they would have a safe crossing. In the evening he invited a few of his colleagues to dinner and beforehand carefully set out seven bottles of claret, but he and his guests were dull and the dinner a failure. They did not quite drink two bottles of the wine. Trouville was a mirage in FitzRoy's mind. He suddenly longed to go there and pictured a villa, golden sands and cool sea waves. But each day something happened to make that holiday appear more remote. It poured with rain, most of the people who could had left London, but still the session dragged on. Each morning FitzRoy went to the House until midday. He would then lunch at his club, afterwards spending from 3 p.m. to 6 p.m. at the Office of Works, receiving delegations against Sunday bands in Hyde Park or planning a fountain for Trafalgar Square. He spent all night at the Commons, seldom returning home before 2 a.m., but he found it almost impossible to sleep and generally put on a dressing-gown at daybreak and started work in bed. One morning the Queen announced her intention of going to Scotland at the end of August, and this meant that FitzRoy would have to precede her by a few hours. This gave him barely nineteen days, and he saw no chance of being able to leave London for Trouville before the end of the week. Hannah did not hide her annoyance. She blamed her husband for wearing himself out in politics when she was in need of him herself, but as the week drew to a close another difficulty arose. FitzRoy was suddenly abused in Parliament about a scheme to cleanse the Serpentine. Even a year before, he would have taken this sort of heckling in the right spirit. Now he saw that it would delay his journey indefinitely because there were all the specifications to be got ready and the engineer who was to be consulted was out of town until the following week. FitzRoy wrote to his wife every day, sometimes twice a day. For example:

"You say that surely I can find time to write you one line. If you knew what a comfort it is to sit down and throw off my hateful work and relieve myself by talking to you, even in this unsatisfactory manner, you would be sure that I shall not lose an opportunity of doing it. I have just received your letter. You are getting an excellent sailor. I am delighted in the hope that you are getting near Trouville. Pray write at once how you like it and if you are comfortable. I have already sent you four letters."

Aug. 9, 1859.
Office of Works.

I suppose that this will never reach you, but I take the chance of its doing so. This is my second to-day. I am going down to the House at 6 p.m. I have been here the whole blessed day and now, I suppose, I must go down to that vile place for the night, and then you say that because I lead this stupid, wearing life, that I cannot miss you. I am ready to hang myself and do not go home when I can, as this evening, for instance. If you were here, I should so enjoy my quiet evening with you. I think Blanchy might have written to me more than that one short letter. Do look at the dates of mine and see how long they take coming to you, for I cannot make out from yours. It is so cold and dismal to-day, pouring with rain. You say I never told you about my party; I told you how much they ate, what they drank and all about it. Did you ever get that? I am so sorry you do not like Trouville. I hoped it would just suit you. I do hope that Blanchy has begun to bathe for you might as well have stayed here as far as sea bathing goes, and she has now lost a whole year. I shall only be able to write once more to Trouville, I suppose. Let me know.

Tuesday.
Office of Works.

What a stupid post it must be at Trouville. I have written every day since Wednesday and twice last Friday. This is the ninth I have sent you. It is too bad—only one on Sunday when three were due! Your letters seem to take sometimes two days and sometimes only one. Surely Blanche could bathe by this time? The most we can hope for now is that the Scotch air will do her good. You see how I am abused about the Serpentine! Now, I hate the whole thing. I feel so low and out of sorts that I can scarcely write. I did not get home till more than half-past two, but I wake so early that I get up at 8 a.m. I am trying to do some of the pressing work before I leave or I shall get no holiday.

Thursday.
Office of Works.

Oh, how I hate it! If I could but get out, how happy I should be. I have, at last, done my estimates and have been shot at from all sides. I almost wish they had beaten me because then I should have washed my hands of this Serpentine, not in it! Now I must get all the specifications before I get away. I do not care about all this, but what I care for and cannot stand is my absence all the year round from those I love. My nerves will not now stand it and I am wretched. I almost hope I may start on Saturday. Tell me the way to come.

Friday.
Office of Works.

I have got your letter, from which it appears that you mean to remain at Trouville. In that case I suppose I must go through Paris. I do not care two straws about the place as long as I can be with you and see you both well. You do not say how Blanchy is. I shall not have an answer to this if I get away this week-end, but I am half afraid, and if I am to have another Sunday away from you my stay will be so very short. If I cannot come I shall lie down and die. I am so much out of heart and have a good deal to do before I go away. A dip would do me a deal of good, for I am as weak as a cat. If you knew what a comfort it is, worried and baited as I am, to receive a letter from you, it would please you.

Trouville was not an easy place to get to and FitzRoy had an idea that his best method was to cross by Dieppe. Each day the wind seemed to blow harder and the rain was incessant. He began to wonder if he was not taking a grave risk by attempting the Dieppe passage, but it was the shortest and if he went to Paris first and then took the train to Trouville, he would spend most of his short holiday travelling.

As the days went by it became obvious that he must abandon the scheme. He wrote to say that he would come and pick them up at Calais and that they would all go to Scotland together.

Blanche was getting stronger and she enjoyed the journey north. She burdened herself with a volume of Scott's poems which she carried everywhere and a pencil and a large sketch book in which she drew little barefooted boys in kilts. FitzRoy took his family from Edinburgh to Stirling, where they saw the Duc de Richelieu driving his large coloured boat upon wheels. It was a twilight afternoon—that long northern twilight—when they crossed the Firth from Burntisland to Granton on their way back to England. Blanche stood on the deck beside her father as he pointed eastward and said: "Now, that is where I should like to have a country house!"

Back in London FitzRoy spent his evening quietly at home and, with the exception of an occasional game of bagatelle with friends, he would generally read aloud to Hannah after dinner. Often he chose the lectures of Carlyle, who, like himself, longed to find satisfaction in spiritual belief. The religious strain in him was now definitely taking shape. He put the searchlight on his soul and cried with Coleridge: "You do not believe, you only believe that you believe." This hunger for spiritual truth drove him to listen with attention to the sermons at St. George's in Hanover Square, where twice he had been elected a Warden. He would be accompanied by Hannah, except when she was tired or not well. Were she unable to come he would take notes so that later in the day he would not forget the sermon, for he took pride in reciting to her the pastor's words from start to finish. What he read aloud in the evening, he invariably discussed with her afterwards. There were such works as the *Poetry of Science*, by Hunt, that referred to the immensity of space. For the first time he thought seriously about death. He asked himself whether he was prepared and decided that it was a matter of urgent importance to make himself ready. When he was unable to reconcile the things he read with his Christian belief, he would call upon his minister in order to ask for advice, and until such queries were answered to his satisfaction, a heavy load weighed on his mind. At times he would wake up in the middle of the night, sweat pouring from his feverish forehead, and would exclaim: "Lord, prepare me by a change of heart." These things he noted carefully in his diary.

His tall figure, slightly stooping now, was familiar outside St. George's Church. He wore a long square-cut frock-coat, a double-breasted white waistcoat, a shining black satin tie and a stove-pipe silk hat. The vicar and churchwardens were frequent guests at the house in Upper Grosvenor Street. He would sit in an armchair and listen carefully to what was said. If it was a question of money he would take careful note. Then, a few days later, his carriage would stop outside the vicarage door and he would leave a sealed envelope with the servant, saying: "I think this is what the vicar wants."

FitzRoy did not stay in London for long. The previous autumn he had noted that the air of Norfolk had done him a lot of good and he felt that a shooting holiday might give him just that tonic that he needed. One September evening, therefore, he arrived at the "Bell" at Thetford, but the journey tired him and he felt sick. The next morning, at about 10 o'clock, he went out shooting, but he was uncomfortable and his head ached so much that he could not bear the noise of his gun. After wading for about an hour in rain-sodden turnip fields, standing with water in his boots, he sent for his carriage and drove back to his hotel, where he called for a doctor, who gave him a draught to take every four hours and told him to drink a pint of sherry a day. He said he had been ruining his stomach by drinking soda-water.

The next day he felt slightly better and shot till half-past twelve, but he developed a cough that tore him to pieces. He wrote to Hannah, imploring her to go to Brighton and find a house where they could all spend the winter. If she could make arrangements sufficiently soon, he would be able to spend a full fortnight's holiday at Brighton and then, when Parliament was once more in session, he could come down for long week-ends.

His holiday at Thetford was a purgatory. He made valiant efforts to carry on, but after an hour or so he would be worn out and would sit on a gate in his great-coat in the drenching rain while his companions shot partridges. His throat became parched and he was always thirsty, but the doctor denied him his soda-water and told him to eat some solid food. FitzRoy tried in vain. He spent more than half an hour one evening seated before a miserable piece of mutton in the dreary dining-room of the inn. The good-natured old English waiter looked at the sick man with compassion and proposed half a glass of bitter beer. Well done, waiter! He did more than all the doctors. FitzRoy, after this, actually succeeded in eating a piece of meat the size of a half-crown and felt better for it. Hánnah, little realising how ill was her husband in this rain-swept country inn, told him he was fanciful and urged him to get young again. FitzRoy took this to heart. He might, for instance, have given up the Chair two years ago. Those long hours had certainly contributed to his breakdown. He was ready to do anything to meet her views, but he felt an old, old man and those around him let him see how much they found him altered.

Each evening at sunset the nasty, low, nervous fever crept over his limbs. The house at Brighton worried him. He felt that Hannah was not quick enough to take possession of the one in Lewes Crescent that had been offered them. He was frightened that it would slip through her fingers and he was looking forward to the day when he would be reunited with his family.

In London, one morning, Blanche received a letter in a well-known hand with the Thetford postmark. It was September 18th and she read:

So my little girl is grown into a young woman of fifteen. I was in no hurry to lose my playfellow, but I suppose it must be. The only thing in which I wish her to be a woman is in self-control and an effort to keep down temper when tempted. She cannot do it in her own strength, but I know she will pray for power to do it for her old Pa's sake. The doctor says I should go out to-morrow for two or three hours, but I am sure I could not do it, and it does not amuse me any more. I had reckoned upon buying you some miserable little thing here just to show you that I had not forgotten you till I came home, but I could never have got across the street yesterday to save my life. My third retriever came to-day, but poor old Sam is like his master—quite done in.

THE ART OF PHOTOGRAPHY.

The fold of the curtain was cunningly nailed to the wall, but this picture
shows a tired Henry FitzRoy, broken by the death of his son. "I feel
an old, old man and those around me let me know how much they find
me altered," he wrote to his wife soon after this was taken.

The following Sunday the end of his holiday was drawing near. FitzRoy wrote to his wife:

I indeed most heartily wish myself at home, but as I look forward to my sojourn with you at Brighton with delight, I shall stay out my time here till Friday. I do not pretend to say I am well. I am far from it, being very weak. I sleep with only one blanket and no counterpane, but the sweat literally runs in streams from me all night, and that, of course, makes me weaker than weak. Have you arranged for our house at Brighton? I shall not go up to Town more than twice a week during the first fortnight. I shall ride with Blanchy every day and walk with my darling wife and be happy. You think I am fanciful and tell me to get young again. You do not guess how ill I have been or how weak I am. But you will soon set me up, and the moment I can eat I shall get right. Indeed, it is not fancy! Home on Friday! Hurrah!

Tuesday.
Thetford.

I write a line to tell you that I am quite well, though, if I were not, I think I would never dare tell you again after the terrible hard sermon you wrote me this morning. You were a little too hard on me, were you not? What have I done to bring on an attack of fever? We went out to-day and it was lovely, but I did not stay out very long.

Thursday.
Thetford.

I only long for Lewes Crescent; yes, long for it, almost as much as to be out of office. Pray close with No. 14 as soon as you receive this. A really comfortable house is not a thing to let slip. Doctor gave me quinine, but I cannot bear it. I leave by the day train to-morrow so that I hope to be in town by 3.30. I must try and shoot Blanchy a young pheasant.

On his way through London, FitzRoy took a cab to the Office of Works in order to make contact with his department. There he heard that Big Ben had struck for the last time. This was already the second bell of that name. The first had been broken up and recast.

Big Ben's deep voice was already famous. The bell was a public character and a mishap of this kind would draw immediate attention to FitzRoy's department. The newspapers would doubt less cover him with ridicule, for there had been nothing whatever wrong with the bell. By some inconceivable error it had been firmly bolted to the beam from which it hung, so that it had been as rigid as the walls of the tower!

With some misgiving, FitzRoy travelled down to Brighton where the sea air did him good. He was able to take short walks along the front and he liked to visit the pier and call at those shops where tradesmen remembered the little boy with the flaxen hair. Before long, however, the fever came on again and in mid-October he wrote to the Prime Minister:

Dear Lord Palmerston,

I wish to place myself entirely in your hands. I have been, unfortunately, for some weeks laid up with fever. They now tell me that my only chance is to remain in bed for some days. In the meantime official business will now begin to be more abundant. As I wish entirely to consult the interests of your government and as I know you have plenty of candidates for office, I am quite ready at once to resign the office to which you kindly appointed me this summer, or if you think that the public service will no suffer by my taking the chance of what a week in bed may do for me, I might delay perhaps taking any final steps until that time. Pray, do not scruple to express to me frankly your wishes on the subject. Whatever your decision may be, I shall not cease to be grateful to you for the kind manner in which you appointed me to my present office and shall continue to feel the same interest in the future success of your government.

Believe me, dear Lord Palmerston, yours ever truly
Henry FitzRoy.

Lord Palmerston to Henry FitzRoy.

My dear FitzRoy,

I am very sorry to hear you have been so unwell, but I hope that with care and rest you will soon recover your health.

It is very handsome of you to offer to resign your office but when I have got a good man in an office which requires a good man, I do not easily part with him. Therefore take your time as well as your physician's prescriptions; and do not let anxiety about the business of your office interfere with and retard the progress of your recovery. I conclude that the staff of your office can carry on the ordinary details of your business for a while, with only occasional reference to you, and if there should be from time to time anything they may not be competent to deal with, and which would require more time and attention than your medical attendant would allow you to bestow upon it, tell your people to bring it to me, and I will deal with any such matters for you, so as to give your medical men fair play in their treatment of you.

There is nothing particular that I am aware of that need be brought under your cognizance at the present moment, and as to Big Ben nobody will complain of his prolonged silence except those who took a pride in inflicting such an evil upon the inhabitants of London.

Yours sincerely,
Palmerston.

FitzRoy received this mark of affection with gratitude. He also made slight progress in health until, some days later, he opened *The Times* and found all the details of the Serpentine and Big Ben raked up again. "Quarrel not with us, gentle FitzRoy, if we seem impatient," wrote the paper. "We are naturally anxious about arrears of public work. . . . A long parliamentary vacation is no excuse for a total cessation of work."

Tortured with fever, too ill to hold a pen, FitzRoy felt this cruel attack like cold steel between his ribs. The weeks went by, but there was no improvement in his health. FitzRoy considered it imperative that Palmerston should take steps to appoint a successor. One day, sitting up in bed, he dictated to his wife a letter for the Prime Minister. Under his direction, Hannah wrote:

Dear Lord Palmerston,

Circumstances are entirely changed since I received from you some weeks ago that very kind and friendly answer to my proposal of resigning from office. It was then a question that lay between the chief of the government and the head of a subordinate department—a question involving rather the convenience of the government than any matter of great importance. Loth as any man who has had the advantage of serving under you must be to quit a government over which you preside I accepted with pleasure the prospect you held out to me of still remaining attached to your forces, the more especially as I could not but receive with equal pride and gratitude the very kind terms in which you conveyed me your wishes. I then hoped that the delay of three or four weeks at the utmost would have enabled me to resume my work at the office and that the public service would sustain no loss by such a delay; but the circumstances are now entirely changed. After four weeks of confinement to my bed I see no chance of leaving it during probably as long a period. The business now to be done in the office can be transacted only under the personal inspection of the first commissioner. The whole preparation for the estimates must now be made and it is impossible that this can be done unless the first commissioner himself visits every spot and carefully examines the requirements that are sent in. Under these circumstances I should be lacking in what is due to myself as a gentleman did I continue to hold an office in your hard-working government, the duties of which it has pleased Providence to prevent my performing. It would be unjust to my successor so long to delay my resignation as not to give him time to make himself acquainted with the duties of the office before the meeting of Parliament. I therefore, with feelings of deepest regret, accompanied with sentiments of affection and gratitude towards you for all the kindness you have shown me, beg now unreservedly after the most careful consideration, to resign into your hands the office which I had hoped to fill during the duration of your government but which under existing circumstances it would no longer be compatible with my honour to retain.

Believe me, dear Lord Palmerston,
Yours ever gratefully and sincerely,
Henry FitzRoy.

A few mornings later Hannah, drawing the curtains in the bedroom, noticed that thick snow covered the ground. All through the night the wind had howled and whistled, the temperature falling to eight degrees below freezing-point. FitzRoy had slept badly. He woke with a high fever but asked what day it was, and when he was told that it was December 15 his eyes met those of his wife and he appeared too overcome with emotion to speak, but Hannah understood, for it was the anniversary of Arthur's birthday. The doctor, summoned to the bedside, diagnosed a combination of fever and ague and prescribed perfect quiet and warmth. All that night and the following day a raging snowstorm covered the town with a mantle of white. The sea beat against the front with a low, hammering sound and spray broke on the Marine Parade and there became frozen. Carriers' carts were unable to move. Horses fell because of the slippery state of the roads and pedestrians slithered along the pavements. People who with difficulty had travelled down from London told of three and a half inches of ice on the lake in Regent's Park. It was said that the south of England had not known such weather for thirty years.

Just before six o'clock on Saturday evening, FitzRoy asked Hannah to come and sit by his bedside and then, taking her hand in his, he recited the words of a hymn that runs:

> "Just as I am, without one plea
> But that Thy blood was shed for me,
> And that Thou bidst me come to Thee
> O Lamb of God, I come!"

As he finished the last words, Hannah looked at her husband with fear. Something warned her that he had spoken for the last time. She shook him almost violently as the appalling truth flashed into her brain. Her husband, her beloved husband, lay dead before her eyes. With a cry of anguish she threw herself over his prostrate body, clutching at his hands and arms until, convulsed with tears, she sank limply beside him, gently calling him by name.

CHAPTER TWENTY-TWO

FOR two or three years Hannah could not settle down. She carried her grief from place to place, trying to mitigate it by a change of scene. Blanche, turning into a little woman, her hair parted in the centre and brought down to form a frame over her rather wan features, was asked in marriage during this period. It happened about a year after FitzRoy's death. She had accompanied her mother to the seaside, where a young nobleman fell in love with her, and spent each morning sitting on the steps of a bathing tent waiting for her to come down to the beach. Back in London one Sunday afternoon, Hannah received an envelope bearing on the flap a ducal crown in red and gold. Inside was a note from Blanche's suitor saying:

> Sunday afternoon, 4.30.
>
> My dear Mrs. FitzRoy,
> Will you as a very great kindness let me see you for five minutes' conversation alone, at any hour that may suit you either to-day or to-morrow. I had intended to ask this favour of you while at your house but had no opportunity.

Hannah granted the interview, but it led to nothing. Blanche intended to marry the man of her own choice. Almost immediately afterwards Hannah took her daughter abroad, for she could not stand herself any longer at home. They went to Germany, where, for a brief moment, Hannah thought of making a temporary home, but she changed her mind and started slowly to return to England along the banks of the Rhine. "The noise and bustle of travelling has been inexpressibly painful to me," she wrote to her sister-in-law, Louisa. "But now I am a little more accustomed to the constant turmoil and I dare say the journey has been so far of use to me as to make me think and occupy myself more with the daily requirements of life instead of dwelling on

174

my sad thoughts. The weather has been trying. During the first few weeks we had rain and cold followed by the most intense heat, but since we have been near the Rhine it has changed to rain and the only cold days were those we had on the water. Blanchy feels these changes and is not so strong as when we left. I prefer returning to England instead of making a temporary home at some German town. Another fortnight will probably see us in Grosvenor Street."

Hannah did not go out much in London. Sometimes when it was particularly fine she would accompany her daughter for a drive in the carriage after lunch. Brown Stout was generally harnessed for these occasions, for FitzRoy's favourite bay now lived in the lap of luxury, there being no one to ride him. During these rare drives when the tyrannical old family coachman felt cold or when he thought it was time to get home for dinner, he would pull up and send the footman to the carriage door with a message to Hannah: "If you please, Ma'am, the coachman thinks Brown Stout ought to go home." Hannah, of course, always complied. She intended to cherish Brown Stout until the end of his days, for she remembered how fond her husband had been of him. As it was, she had nearly lost the animal by an excess of courtesy, for shortly after FitzRoy's death she had written to the Rev. Humphrey Allen asking if there was anything belonging to her husband that he would like to have as a little recollection. Mr. Allen answered promptly. He said he wanted that fine powerful bay, Brown Stout. This was more than Hannah could do. After fretting over the difficulty for some time, she purchased another bay horse as like Brown Stout as possible, and in order not to stint anything appertaining to the gift, she chose a picturesque horse-cloth and travelling wrap for the animal which was duly despatched to Clifton. Three days later the horse, travelling costume and all, was returned to Grosvenor Street with a bitter note from Mr. Allen in which he stated that an animal, hitherto unknown to him, had thrown him on the first opportunity, for it was a determined kicker!

One day, when Blanche was seventeen, Hannah said to her: "Blanchy, you grow so tall and thin and you loll about in every direction. I fancy that a few dancing lessons would do you a world of good. What do you think?" "Oh yes," Blanche answered vaguely. Her thoughts suddenly went back to the dancing class she attended once a week when Arthur was still alive. It was the nearest thing to school she had ever known. She recalled arriving at the class with Mademoiselle and retiring behind a high screen to take off her walking shoes, to lace on her pale grey dancing boots with the flexible soles. She would step out, her head erect and her eyes smiling, while her governess in the far distance, a volume of Corneille in her hand, sat among the nurses and mothers that encircled the room intent on their worsted work or crochet. Blanche was a good dancer, and in those days had but one rival, a girl called Helen, as robust as she was delicate. Blanche was a lonely child; her friend was the youngest of six. While Blanche's experience was chiefly bounded by Hyde Park and Piccadilly, a slight smattering of the latest political news and anecdotes of convent life gleaned from her French governess, Helen's talk was redolent of the moors, the long summer twilight on the loch, the exploits of her brother's ponies, and the old gardener down at the manse. One day when the two girls were sitting together Madame, who had been conversing with an elegant stranger, called upon Blanche to come into the middle of the room and perform alone a newly taught step. "This is Blanche FitzRoy, one of my best pupils," Madame had said graciously. The pianist, whose gaunt, knobbly hands performed marches and quadrilles with great decision, turned her pale face with its long pink nose in the direction of the mistress and came down with a tremendous crash on the long-suffering piano. Madame beat time with her jewelled fingers and the stately stranger smiled, but Blanche was nervous, and after acquitting herself badly stood ashamed as two big tears rolled down her cheeks. "You are not well, Miss FitzRoy," said Madame gravely. "Go back to your seat, my love."

It was then Helen's turn to perform the step. There was no hesitation in her manner, nothing but self-reliance. When she had come to the end, there was loud applause. "My dear girl," said Madame, stretching out her hands with emotion, "you have indeed done me credit." "I am glad it was right," answered Helen, making a bow that was something between a bend and a curtsy, "but Blanche FitzRoy can do the steps much better when she is not nervous." "Young ladies," said Madame: "take your places for the Lancers."

Blanche remembered this episode and looked forward with some interest to see the dancing class again. Madame received her former pupil with joy, and soon Blanche's tall, slender figure, clad in a plain black woollen gown half covered with crêpe, became well known in the room. One afternoon, as she was going through the figures of a quadrille, her attention was drawn to a young girl who had just entered the room and who, dressed in a walking costume, was standing near the door talking to Madame.

"Helen!" shouted Blanche. "I am so glad to see you."

"I have just come to say good-bye to Madame," said the girl.

"And I shall not see you again?"

"Not unless you come out to Melbourne."

Blanche was silent. She knew how short-lived her happiness had been. It was not always gay at home, and she had never wished so much for a friend.

It was not until the winter of 1862 that Hannah took her daughter abroad again. They went to Nice, where Blanche, wearing a black velvet bodice and striped crinoline, became one of the choir in the English church, though she had little voice to boast of. Here she met Lord Rokeby's daughter, who made a sensation at Nice because she was said to be strong-minded, though intelligent. It was rumoured that she played the fiddle, and that she had photographed a wrecked train immediately after she herself had been shaken up by the accident!

The next spring found England in a festive mood. A youthful princess had come from across the sea to wed Albert Edward,

Prince of Wales. There was something of the fairy tale in this romance, for he was twenty-one years old and she was eighteen!

The nation was in a state of unity, and the Throne was free from all those disputes that had assailed it in the past. The Prince of Wales was the successor to an uncontested Throne, and limited monarchy now satisfied even the boldest Liberals. The voice of congratulation was the language of gratitude for the best reign in English history. Reforms had succeeded one another with notable speed. Nearly seventy years had passed since the people of England had welcomed the arrival of a bride for the eldest son of their Monarch. Tender and true, loving and strong, England welcomed Princess Alexandra with wreaths of flowers as she came up the river to Gravesend.

Her drive through London was triumphal. As her carriage passed through the narrow streets of the City under the shadow of the Bank and of the Exchange, the words of Spenser's *Bride Song* came to the lips of the people:

> "Tell me, ye merchants' daughters, did ye see,
> So fair a creature in your town before?
> So sweet, so lovely and so mild as she?"

The Royal wedding took place at Windsor on March 10. That same day at Copenhagen people went mad with joy. The poor of the Danish capital were regaled and a splendid dress ball took place at the Casino. The King gave a court banquet at the Castle of Christiansborg. Flags were hoisted and ships in the harbour were decorated with bunting. Military bands played during the evening in all the public squares, and the entire city was brilliantly illuminated. During the evening's State banquet just as the King was proposing the health of the happy couple, a telegram was received from Prince Christian announcing the conclusion of the marriage ceremony at Windsor.

Meanwhile the big house in Upper Grosvenor street was a sombre place. Since her return to London from Nice, Hannah remained for long hours by herself and appeared to shun the

A FASHION IN THE 'SIXTIES.

In the winter of 1862 Blanche FitzRoy went to Nice. Since her father's
death she had lost her best playmate.

company of others. For some weeks also her health had been failing. Blanche was now eighteen, and, because she had little opportunity to go out, spent most of her time painting or playing the violin. She continued from time to time to write poetry. While the crowds were shouting in the streets for the wedding, she sat down at her escritoire, took a sheet of writing-paper with her name embossed in mauve at the top and wrote out in a clear hand, these lines to her mother:

> "If I have nothing to give thee,
>   'Tis because I have given my all;
> My life, my love, my strength are thine,
> And my love is strong, tho' my strength be small.
>   Daily, hourly, mother
> Would I show thee my heart's fond glow.
> But the gifts a mother cares to have
>   Were they not thine long ago?"

She wrote the date at the bottom: March 10, 1863.

Hannah was doubtless touched by her daughter's sentiments, but she had drunk deep of the cup of bitterness. She closed the blinds when the sun shone and banished flowers from her room, for daffodils and primroses reminded her too strongly of that sunny April day when, after her marriage, she drove with her husband to Petersham, to find, waiting at the door, a cart laden with spring flowers that were to bring joy and fragrance to every corner of her new home.

From the time of the Royal wedding, the Prince and Princess of Wales were prominently before the country. While Queen Victoria remained for a moment in retirement, the young couple filled her place at public functions. It was announced that, by command of the Queen, the Princess of Wales would hold a Drawing-room at St. James's Palace at which over five hundred women would be presented. These presentations were to be equivalent to presentations to the Queen. Hannah decided that Blanche should be present at this Drawing-room to effect what was known as her "coming out." The date fixed was Saturday, May 16. On the Friday, Queen Victoria, who had been at Windsor, came in from her morning walk in the Castle grounds to take leave of the Prince and Princess of Wales, who were returning to London for the Court. The Queen planned to leave for Balmoral the following morning.

Blanche looked forward to her presentation with some excitement. It was the beginning of a new life for her. She was growing wings. Sunshine streamed through her bedroom window that morning. She could not wait for breakfast but ran up to her maid to make another inspection of her Court dress and the feathers and lace she was to place in her hair. The Court was at two in the afternoon. Hannah, who was to present her, had ordered their carriage an hour and a half before.

It was an opportune moment for such a function. Popular opinion was still under the spell of the new princess. Europe was enjoying an interval of comparative peace. It is true that across the Atlantic America was engaged in civil war. News reached London that morning that General Grant was moving on Natchez, and a naval engagement was reported to have taken place at Grand Gulf, Mississippi. The Confederates under Marmaduke were said to have crossed Whitewater River and to have escaped out of Missouri, burning the bridges behind them. In New York young Pierpont Morgan, sitting in his Wall Street office, the first to have a private telegraph wire to the front, kept in touch with both North and South and prophesied: "The Union will win and with hard work we shall soon be the richest country in the world." As Blanche was trying on her dress and fixing the lace lappets on her hair, the people of Liverpool were giving a rousing send-off to the Atlantic liner *Great Eastern*, which, under the command of Captain Paxton, was leaving the Mersey for New York. The ship carried six hundred passengers of which eighty were travelling first-class. In London the Princess of Wales, accompanied by Princess Louis of Hesse, had taken an early morning drive in an open carriage. This delicate attention to the London crowds was rewarded by admiring glances and enthusiastic cheering. A few hours later these same Londoners would be making lines five deep to watch the arrival of the Prince and Princess of Wales at St. James's Palace.

By midday Blanche was decked in all the glory of her dress, with feathers and diamonds in her hair. Hannah insisted on an early departure, after a lunch that had been a trifle sad. In the Mall, traffic had come to a standstill. The lines of carriages stretched for nearly a mile in length from every direction. The crowds were immense. The Drawing-room was a magnificent affair. The Prince and Princess of Wales, escorted by a party of Life Guards in shining cuirasses, arrived at the Palace shortly after two o'clock and were received by the Mistress of the Robes and the great officers of State of the Queen's household. The Prince, youthful, clean-shaven with a slight wave in his curly hair, wore the uniform of the 10th Hussars, of which he was the Colonel. Princess Alexandra, little more than a girl, her finely chiselled features having an air of radiant happiness, wore a long train of rich white silk trimmed with wreaths of white lilac and priceless Honiton lace. Her petticoat was trimmed to match the train, and on her head she wore a diamond tiara together with feathers and a tulle veil.

Diamonds and opals flashed from her neck and arms. The Princess of Wales passed slowly through the ranks of the Yeomen of the Guard to her station in front of the Throne. At her side stood her husband. Just behind her were those women who bore the greatest names in the land—the Duchess of Wellington, Mistress of the Robes; the Countess of Gainsborough, Viscountess Jocelyn, Countess of Desart, the Marchioness of Ely and Lady Churchill, Ladies of the Bedchamber to the Queen. Moving forward in a mass of brilliant uniforms came the foreign ambassadors and ministers. In gorgeous apparel came the representative of the Czar of all the Russias. These were the days when kings and princes ruled over the states of Europe and ambassadors wore famous names as well as scarlet tunics. Prussia sent its ambassador in the person of Count Bernstorff, and Bavaria, Hanover and Saxony still had their accredited representatives at the Court of St. James.

The Princess of Wales smilingly received them all, and, as she bowed, her long ear-rings of diamonds flashed in the rays of a strong May sun that streamed into the throne-room. A moment later a sudden hush fell over the crowded room as the Archbishops of Canterbury, York and Armagh approached the Throne with measured steps. Then came Lord Palmerston, Prime Minister, heading his administration, in which was one new member—Her Majesty's First Commissioner of Works! Hannah, standing erect in her sombre dress of black moire, the long train trimmed with satin and black lace, saw through her tear-dimmed eyes the affectionate greeting that Palmerston gave her as he passed to the Throne. But the knowledge that another stood in her husband's place was almost more than she could bear.

Blanche looked with admiration at the rich dresses. When Princess Louis of Hesse gave a twist to her long train the warm velvet shimmered with silver bullion with which it was trimmed. Diamond tiaras and tulle veils studded with black and white pearls caught the rays of the afternoon light as it streamed through the windows. The trains of many women looked like peacock fans on the thick carpet. Some were of velvet bordered with ermine, others were of white silk with bouquets of the rose, shamrock and thistle tied with golden cord.

Rumour had it that the Prince and Princess would that night attend a play at the Lyceum. Invitations passed in low murmurs for coming balls. Blanche FitzRoy had grown up!

CHAPTER TWENTY-THREE

HANNAH made a great effort to take her daughter out that summer. She knew that her own strength was waning and that she must lose no time in getting her married. The first dance to which she took her was at Londonderry House, to which invitations were sparing. The Lady Londonderry of that time had a great regard for FitzRoy's widow, and during the evening took pains to find partners for her daughter. Although Blanche had travelled rather more than most young people of her age, she was, in point of fact, scarcely out of the schoolroom. That evening she went about with a heavy heart and red eyes, and her grief was so noticeable that a young man with whom she was slowly pacing through a quadrille asked her the reason. He was a perfect stranger, but as Blanche looked up at him she caught a sympathetic expression and confided to him that she had sat up the greater part of the night nursing a dying bullfinch! He laughed and from that time she took a dislike to him, for whenever they met he would ask her if she had been nursing any more bullfinches.

Lady Palmerston was particularly kind to Hannah, and a few days after Blanche had been presented at Court she came to say that both would be welcome at all her parties, whether she sent invitations or not. She probably bore in mind Hannah's retiring nature, for she sent invitations written in her own hand for every party she gave during the short remainder of her life. The other ball that Hannah took her daughter to was one given by Countess Apponyi, wife of the Austrian Ambassador. Blanche's first dance was with Count Wimpffen, attaché to the Embassy, her second with Viscount Hood. After these dances so many young people were introduced to her that she retained no recollection of any of their faces and on subsequent occasions found herself entirely

183

partnerless, the more so as Hannah's memory proved no better than her own.

Blanche discovered that dancing, at which she had been so proficient at Madame's class, did not particularly amuse her in society. She seldom did more than join in what were then known as 'square' dances. Her tastes were definitely Bohemian and whenever she had the opportunity she sought the company of painters and writers. Music gave her great pleasure. At the only ball that Hannah actually gave for her daughter in Upper Grosvenor Street, there were some good singers, among them Madame Trebelli, while Piatti played the violoncello. It was the first time that Blanche had heard him, and she fell into trouble for neglecting her duty towards tardily arriving guests in her eagerness to listen.

As the weeks passed, Hannah found that the strain was beyond her. She gradually retired to a secluded life and her strength began to ebb. In this way Blanche was left much to her own resources. She once went to visit the studio of an artist who was then painting the frescoes of Dorchester House. This artist was Sir Coutts Lindsay, son of a general who had been severely wounded in the disastrous storming of Bergen-op-Zoom. He was a big, good-looking man with hair that had already turned silver.

Blanche went back to her mother and described that visit in detail. Her features were flushed, and it was obvious that she was in love. Hannah said little. In principle she was delighted that Blanche should be thinking of marriage.

Before long it was clear that the romance was serious. Sir Coutts asked Hannah for her daughter's hand. He was of a fine family, and he was the eldest son. At the end of the Crimean war all London had turned out to welcome his younger brother, Robert, who had carried the colours with such gallantry during the Battle of Alma that the Queen had later pinned the Victoria Cross on his breast. Hannah did not feel justified in making any objection. Nevertheless, though he was good-looking, witty and

BLANCHE LINDSAY.
This picture was painted by her husband Sir Coutts Lindsay, founder of
the Grosvenor Gallery.

fascinating, Sir Coutts was twenty years older than Blanche. This in itself was a disadvantage.

Before long, Hannah's family put forward objections. They brought to light certain facts that neither Hannah nor her daughter was aware of. From that time Hannah set her mind against the marriage, but she lacked frankness with her daughter.

The result might have been foreseen. The more Blanche heard her suitor criticised, the more eager she became to champion his cause. Already her own parents had given proof of a certain tenacity in the matter of love. Blanche showed that she could be just as stubborn.

It was arranged that the wedding should take place at the end of June, little more than a year after Blanche had been presented at Court.

Meanwhile, the young girl blossomed out into a beautiful woman. A short time ago she had passed her days in school-room occupations. Now she was to be a bride. There were visions of Rome, where Sir Coutts had lived as a younger man and where for some time he had been a pupil of the great French painter, Ary Scheffer.

Up in Scotland also the grey turrets of an ancient castle rose above a rocky sea coast. The mist-covered sea rolled over the long sands towards dark crags and caverns and low white houses of Fifeshire fishermen where strings of herrings hung in the wind to dry.

Here was the ancestral home of Balcarres where Sir Coutts would soon be taking her.

At the moment, Hannah's health gave rise to great anxiety. Sir Coutts suggested that the wedding should take place by special licence in the drawing-room of his bride's home in Upper Grosvenor Street. He himself lived in a house a stone's throw away in Grosvenor Square.

On the last of June, while a hot sun streamed into the drawing-room, Blanche FitzRoy took her lover's hand and tiptoed into the room above where Hannah lay sick unto death. There she found

N

her mother's faithful maidservant moving noiselessly. Here also was the Rev. Evan Nepean, Canon of Westminster, Hannah's spiritual adviser and close friend, who in a few moments would be performing the wedding ceremony. Within this big and sombre house where so much human drama had taken place, where Cabinet ministers had met at FitzRoy's table to discuss the destinies of England, one life was drawing to a close; another was starting a new career.

Below in the drawing-room, not yet daring to disturb this intimate scene, waited Lord Southampton. During these few minutes of solitude a host of memories must have passed through his mind. It was now almost a quarter of a century ago that, embittered by a quarrel, he had remained cold and distantly hostile while his younger brother was wedded to the daughter of the banker, Nathan de Rothschild, at St. George's, in Hanover Square. His presence was thus doubly welcome to Hannah.

Blanche, clad in her wedding dress of white, scarcely knew how to control her emotions. In love, she felt ashamed of her happiness —hesitant to leave her mother. Was it fair that she should go for a radiant honeymoon while Hannah remained alone with a maidservant? Could she ever forgive herself if anything happened in her absence? Overcome, she knelt beside her mother in the darkened room and burst into tears.

The Rev. Evan Nepean placed his hand on her shoulder. She must brace herself up and face this situation with the courage that had been taught her in childhood days by her father. She longed now for his presence. She would give much for that look of his she knew so well, when, seeing her frightened to take a jump on horseback, he would fix her squarely and say: "Blanchy, you must do it for me!"

The little party went down to the drawing-room. It was refreshing to see the sun shining through the big windows and to catch a glimpse of the green leaves of the plane-trees in Grosvenor Square.

The Canon of Westminster, in his surplice and hood, intoned

the solemn service: "Dearly beloved, we are gathered together here in the sight of God . . ."

In the room above Hannah had opened the Prayer Book that her husband had given her when they were married, and her lips moved slightly as she followed the service. She desired but one thing—that this marriage should be a long and happy one. She would not live to see the result of this match. Nevertheless, the responsibility was hers. Blanche alone would now carry on the family that Henry FitzRoy had founded.

Downstairs Blanche FitzRoy and Coutts Lindsay knelt side by side: "I Blanche take thee Coutts to my wedded husband to have and to hold from this day forward, for better for worse, for richer for poorer, in sickness and in health, to love, cherish, and to obey, till death us do part, according to God's holy ordinance; and thereto I give thee my troth."

Blanche Lindsay looked up into her husband's eyes with as much joy and happiness as if she had been the first woman to discover the secret of love!

CHAPTER TWENTY-FOUR

Blanche Lindsay to her mother, Hannah FitzRoy.

Balcarres,
Fife.

My darling Mama,

You cannot tell how often I think of you now how tenderly and lovingly. I feel I have made a happy choice, and one which I do not think I shall ever have cause to regret, at least so far as human eyes can see and I cannot help thinking that this must be a comfort to you, and that the peace of mind of my present life will be some consolation to you. My only trouble is about yourself. I cannot help fretting about your health and wishing that you might be better.

Should you desire me at any time to return to London do not hesitate to say so; not only if you are ill, I do not mean that; but if you want me, and think that your recovery would be quicker were I in London for a few days.

The people here welcome me and seem to be glad to see me. The place certainly wants furnishing and doing up, but not so much as you think. The grounds could hardly be improved and the view is wild and desolate. We paid two visits yesterday, and you are right when you fancy my pony carriage dashing. It is both dashing and comfortable—dark blue picked out with red; and red and blue rosettes on the horses' heads. I set out dressed in my blue silk dress with white stripes, made by Madam Leblond, my silk jacket with tails, and my little hat with the peacocks' feathers; Poole's railway wrapper with its white embroideries on a dark blue ground looked admirable.

We went first to Sir John and Lady Bethune, our nearest neighbours, who have a place something like Balcarres in architecture. Lady Bethune was at home and we were shown into a drawing room much like any drawing room in London. She came in—a small, round, dark-haired Frenchwoman about thirty, dressed in muslin with a blue belt, one curl on one shoulder and a household basket of keys and letters in her hand. She told me she had been married six years and could not get used to the thick leather boots and wool dresses worn by the country ladies. I sympathised for I hate heavy soles an inch thick and clinging woollen dresses. She laughed and said I must come to that however I might struggle against it.

Our next visit was to Sir Robert and Lady Anstruther who were also at home. They are very different people; he is the Member and a Liberal. A bright, gay young man, shewing excellent teeth. They have five children all of whom seemed to have an ardent desire to break their necks, running into all sorts of holes and corners. We went to the Scotch church, which is only two miles from here. It is a strange service and I had great difficulty in making out what the clergyman said. One needs no Prayer Book; the minister prays what he pleases, and the people stand! They never kneel at all and sing sitting, listen to the Bible and the sermon sitting and stand during all the prayers.

We were obliged to return the visit of some amiable but peculiarly homely people whose name is Christie. I thought I should have been bored and should not have known what to do, but it turned out the reverse. The father is an old man who is proud of his garden and took us there. We ate some fruit. There were three daughters, one a widow, two unmarried and neither young nor beautiful, dressed astonishingly in pale cottons and brown holland! There was a piano, a harp and an organ in the drawing room. One of the daughters played the organ by heart and well. They brought in some tea and pound cake and the tea, as in the story books, was served in large, old-fashioned cups with thick cream.

I see the gardener's wife every day. She went to Edinburgh to consult a surgeon who took her into a large room with students all round. They stared at her and then pronounced her fate, telling her to return in a fortnight. She won my heart by saying that she knew what an only child was: she was one herself and she was sure that you and I must miss each other.

After lunch, the other day, instead of driving straight home we went to Elie and leaving our pony carriage, took a walk among the rocks, and on the sands, where it was sheltered. I sat down on Coutts' coat and watched the little waves lapping on the shore. There was not a soul to be seen anywhere; it is totally solitary and I do not know what you will say to me when I relate that I actually took my shoes and stockings off and holding my petticoats up (my tail and crinoline) in a most rustic way, danced about for a minute or two in the little wee waves at the edge of the sea!

We went to the dairy this morning. It is a clean room though the building is not picturesque. I mean it is not a poetical dairy but I lapped a little cream, of which there were some large flat dishes all round. The laundry is pleasant; there are excellent presses and drying grounds.

I had a note last night from Lady Bethune asking us to dinner. We hired the one available fly in the neighbourhood, having nothing of our own but an open pony carriage. I arrayed myself in what I considered to be a most appropriate costume; a pale blue silk dress, low at the neck, with short sleeves and a long train. In my hair a couple of bunches of crimson carnations. As a bride I was taken in with due ceremony by the host who carved the turbot and mutton himself, according to Scottish custom.

I have spent the greater part of the morning in the village of Colinsburgh. The air is fresh and pleasant and by a short cut through the park I can reach Colinsburgh in five minutes. There has been a great haul of herrings and the poor people buy two or three for a penny and hang them up in rows outside their doors to dry, which looks picturesque and northern. Many of the men are whalers and on the road to church there is a cottage with two huge teeth of a whale forming a fierce-looking arch. We met a regular Scotch girl; she was a milkmaid, I think, and wore good clothes with a tidy straw bonnet but she was barefoot, and you don't know how funny that looks!

Coutts has been trying to fish in the pond which is called a lake but after a while he gave it up, finding absolutely nothing, and rowed me about in a little boat called the *Kingfisher*.

Your loving daughter,
Blanche Lindsay.

On many of her visits to Colinsburgh, Blanche was accompanied by Mr. Briggs, Inspector of the Poor. He was a strange character who would answer most of her remarks with: "Hootakins, ma Leddy," which turned out to be equivalent to the German: "So," and to Blanche's southern ears were about the most intelligible words in his vocabulary. Old Briggs had a fund of humour and good sense and in an emergency resorted to canny expedients. When there was a slight escape of gas between the house and the village where the gasometer was, Mr. Briggs summoned all the villagers and despatched them to scour the park on all fours in order to ascertain by means of their smell where there was an injury to one of the pipes. He introduced Blanche to such famous characters as Molly Campbell, the old henwife, who used to hatch eggs by carrying them in the bosom of her dress and old David Mackay, the shepherd—a picturesque gaunt old figure with his collie dog at his heels. There was an old woman also who could hardly be said to keep a shop but who had three biscuits and two bottles of acidulated drops in her window. She had always lived in Colinsburgh, and when Blanche one day asked her if she had been away, answered that she had once been as far as Kilconquhar, one and a half miles distant, but she had never troubled to walk as far as the sea! The oldest inhabitant of all had but one eye left and that one was bleared. She wore a pointed frilled white cap tied round her head with a broad black ribbon not unlike old fairy godmothers in story-books. She used to speak of Sir Coutts's grandfather as 'young Mr. Robert,' and the first time she saw Blanche she wept and stroked her hands and cried out: "Eh, ma bonnie! Ye're just a flower, a bonnie flower!"

There were so many aged villagers in Colinsburgh that Blanche decided to give a tea party for them. Mr. Briggs was consulted, and a number of long tables were placed in the schoolroom laden with bread and butter, jam, cakes and strawberries. The old women arrived in plaid shawls of soft wool, and the old men in coloured comforters. Though many could do little more than mumble, Mr. Briggs kept up a running conversation and Blanche had spent the morning picking large quantities of roses to be distributed later to the guests. After tea everybody partook of a drink made of ginger wine and whisky, and Blanche's health was drunk with a great deal of feeble rapping on the table. The young hostess was called upon by Mr. Briggs to make a speech and Blanche, losing all presence of mind, could say nothing but: "I hope you will all live till next year!" Of course, what she meant was that she hoped they might all meet on a similar occasion the following summer. But her words cast a slight gloom over the party.

There was one old man at this gathering for whom Blanche had felt particularly sorry. He was stout and suffered from an affliction of the wind-pipe. He sat day and night in the same upright chair. When first Blanche made his acquaintance in Colinsburgh his wife and children wept profusely, saying that the doctor had ordered him to drink a great deal of whisky. Blanche promised to send him a bottle every fortnight and it was only later when Mr. Briggs came along that she discovered that the old man was drinking himself to death!

The guests at the party did not by any means represent all the aged folk of Colinsburgh. Most of these were quite unable to leave their homes. One old couple lived for countless years in a tumble-down cottage that had lately been declared unsafe. Mr. Briggs arranged that these people should move to a larger and more comfortable home. The change broke their hearts and when they took to their beds, Blanche hastened to visit them. They looked like two old people in a fairy tale, clean and tidy, tended by a neighbour, the old man's head covered with a pointed white cotton night-cap, the old woman's face framed in a frilled mutch. The hostess of Balcarres took them pudding which they ate with wooden spoons sitting up in bed. The old woman was deaf, and sad, but her husband kept up his spirits.

"Ay, she's an auld body, she is," he said, pointing at his wife contemptuously.

"And how old are you?" asked Blanche. "You're a long age, too, are you not?"

"Ay, ay, I'm getting on," he answered with a funny twinkle in his beady eyes. "I'm near upon forty year, that I am; but she's auld, she is."

He had a son who was close on sixty, and who lived, so he said, in China. Blanche asked if the son ever wrote to him.

"Whiles," he answered, "but the wauld's lairge, very lairge," as though the size of the globe added to the difficulties of letter-writing.

Blanche found each day brought her a new conception of Scottish life. She tried to understand the etiquette of these villages, the cold, bare front of the houses which compose too uniform a street to be called cottages, but which are nevertheless graced at the back by well-kept gardens each divided from the other by a high stone wall. As she walked down these streets, the good folks who happened to be standing about disappeared quickly into their homes. The more anxious they seemed to make acquaintance, the quicker they scurried inside their houses, considering this proper and polite.

Then the street would become empty save for the little bare-legged children playing in the gutter, and not a soul would look out of the windows. Blanche was required to keep up a good heart and feel that she was welcome after all. Then when she had knocked or rung at a door it would be opened a few inches, a hand would stealthily be put out to grasp hers and she would be drawn into the narrow passage where, when the door was firmly secured again, she would be warmly and effusively greeted.

She learnt many things about these homes. Often each house would contain two or three sets of lodgers. One would lodge to the left as she went in, one on her right and the third upstairs. There was one woman who had been bedridden for many years. All the members of her own family had died. She lay quite happily in her solitude in a kind of cupboard-bed in the wall. A neighbour used to come down from her own room upstairs every morning to light the fire and give the old woman some porridge and generally to "redd her up," as the saying was. Then the good neighbour went out to work in the fields all day.

At times Blanche would visit the village school, where boys and girls were taught together. While the dour Scotch master was teaching in one part of the room, most of the older boys were receiving their instruction from a little boy of nine years of age.

"He is a monitor, I imagine?" asked Blanche somewhat surprised. "He is very young for the post."

"He's young, that's true," answered the master: "but he's a severe boy, a varra severe boy!"

Blanche decided to build a school of her own for girls to learn needlework. Then she started a library for the village folk in a wing of the castle. The committee consisted of the chief lights of Colinsburgh, under the chairmanship of the local grocer. The colliers of the neighbourhood proved her keenest readers. There was a pitman who once came to visit her and brought with him two violins which he desired her to see and which he had made with his own hands when he was not busy working in the mine. One was a copy of a Stradivarius, and the other appeared to be a copy of an Amati. Both proved good instruments, and one especially had a fine mellow tone. The pitworker said he had made quite a number of violins and had sent them to Glasgow, where they sold for six to eight guineas each. He could not play at all himself, and when asked what had made him take to such a hobby answered simply: "Just amusement."

Balcarres itself was full of surprises. Though there was no haunted room there was an attic known as the Brownie's Room. This room had been kept locked up for long years, and when Sir Coutts one day decided to break open the door, expecting, no doubt, to discover a Brownie, he found nothing but ten disused spinning-wheels! It was at that time that the change-over to mechanical spinning had caused great misery. Near Balcarres was the village of Earlsferry, so called because MacDuff, in his escape, is supposed to have crossed the Firth thereabouts and hidden himself in a cave, and another called Barnyards. Here were whole colonies of weavers who, by reason of the new inventions, had been thrown out of work altogether. Many of these poor souls sat, nearly starving, gazing sorrowfully at their useless looms.

At that time there was but little garden round Balcarres. According to old Scottish custom the house seemed to stand in the middle of the park on a veritable hill of sheep, as its name implies. The kitchen garden was a mixture of fruit, vegetables and flowers, but there was no shrubbery. Blanche and her husband decided to build terraces to form a garden. Some of these they designed themselves, the three largest and the lower garden were inspired from an old book of engravings called: *The Gardens of the King of Poland.* Blanche had, however, one idea of her own. She planned to plant a sweet-briar hedge all round.

She had seen such hedges at Whittlebury, Lord Southampton's home. FitzRoy's brother planted so much sweet-briar in his park and around the village that when, on Sunday, he walked to church it was all the way between sweet-briar hedges.

It was decided that the hollies and yews for the terrace gardens should be brought from a place called Balniel, where the farmer, Mr. Bogie, had reared and clipped them himself for forty years. Mr. Bogie was a good-natured brown-faced man.

Blanche had seen him the first day she had trudged up the hill to Balcarres from the village. This part of the road was called the 'Double Dykes.' As she made her way slowly along, feeling tired and dusty, Mr. Bogie, seated in his comfortable gig while his pony went at a foot's pace up the hill, eyed her with interest, not knowing who this stranger could be and shouted: "Let me give you a lift, my girl!" Instead of accepting the offer, Blanche grew red and shaking her head shyly refused. It was only later that she came to appreciate the kindness of the farmers around.

As autumn came on Blanche and her husband decided to return to London. During the last days of packing, when she was turning over a number of canvases in her husband's studio, Blanche came upon a sketch in oils that was evidently the beginning of a picture that was startlingly like her mother. She ran to fetch Sir Coutts and asked him what it might be. He told her that it was a Scheffer. After the death of the great French painter, Sir Coutts, who had long been his pupil, had decided to purchase from Ary Scheffer's Italian valet some example of his work. This was the canvas that Blanche had found.

Hannah often told her daughter of the famous trip to Paris in 1834, and how Scheffer was never able to finish his portrait of her because Nathan cut the journey short. This coincidence was almost unbelievable! Blanche now held in her hands a rough sketch of her mother at the age of nineteen, drawn on the very eve of that great ball at which Prince de Clary fell so desperately in love with her.

It was in early September that the Lindsays returned to London. Blanche found herself living in a house in Grosvenor Square almost overlooking her childhood home where Hannah lay gravely ill. Each day she spent long hours with her mother. She would describe a room at Balcarres where Cromwell was supposed to have stayed when he took the house from the Royalists, the jutting-out rock on the top of the craig hard by which was called the Trumpeter's Seat, and she confided in her mother her own secret—that she was hoping to have a child. Hannah showed profound joy at the news, but often now her mind would wander back to Arthur, and she clung to memories of her dead son. For some time she had felt the urge to make a memorial to him and she now dreamt of a lifeboat to be called the *Arthur Frederick*. This boat, sturdy and strong, would answer the call of ships in distress along the coast. Manned by a good crew it would carry out the indomitable will of the boy who in life had been unable to leave his wooden board. She saw in this the spirit of her son released.

One night in early December, Blanche awoke in her bed with a start. There in the room before her stood her mother. She saw her features clearly and remained fascinated by the deep expression in those limpid eyes. But even as she watched, the vision vanished.

Scarcely an hour later, as the clock struck two, Blanche was awakened by a loud knocking at her door. A servant had hurried across from Upper Grosvenor Street to say that Mrs. FitzRoy had just passed away.

CHAPTER TWENTY-FIVE

AS the lilac-trees broke into bloom Blanche gave birth to a daughter at her new home in Grosvenor Square.

Euphemia Lindsay was born on the fifteenth day of May, 1865, and before she was three weeks old was taken by train to Balcarres, where she made youthful contact with the bracing air of the Fifeshire coast.

Three years later, Effie was to have a sister, Anne Helen. Together they would spend many summers playing in the garden or scrambling over the rocks, but also they would have ample time to appreciate the rigours of a Scottish winter.

While Effie and Helen were growing up their parents became, in a sort of way, the pivot on which the artistic genius of the 'seventies was to turn. Painters such as Holman Hunt, Watts, Millais, Whistler, Rossetti, and Edward Burne-Jones, gathered around Sir Coutts and Lady Lindsay for a common purpose. The poet Browning became an intimate friend, Gilbert and Sullivan were later to take the Grosvenor Gallery, the Lindsays' greatest venture, and work it into the theme of the opera *Patience*.

Blanche was to be thrust to the top of London's social world. The Prince of Wales would lead her in to dinner and publicly pay tribute to her genius. Browning would seek her advice on his poems, Millais and Watts on their paintings. It fell to her to carry along the torch of the family founded by Henry FitzRoy and Hannah Mayer. She was determined that this torch should burn brightly.

Between the years 1862 and 1875 Sir Coutts exhibited ten pictures at the Royal Academy. During this period he perceived that many fine artists were not represented at Burlington House.

He made enquiries and discovered that there was a good deal of grumbling under the surface. Pictures were being hung carelessly and without any sequence. Academicians who had prior rights were said to be crowding out the few brilliant but unusual painters who stood apart from their fellows in method and conviction.

Sir Coutts took counsel with his wife and together they decided to build a place that, though not necessarily a rival to the Royal Academy, might accommodate the younger school of painters.

At that time a man called Samuel Pratt owned an old curiosity shop at the corner of Maddox Street and Bond Street. Pratt was courteous but insinuating. He was known to all buyers of furniture, silks and armour and no man could give a better opinion on articles of virtu.

Sir Coutts was in the habit of turning into Pratt's place, and one day as he was following him down into the basement, the old man turned and said: "If you're looking for a site to build a gallery, I know of a fine piece of ground."

"Where?" asked Sir Coutts.

"Here in Bond Street," answered Pratt. "If you're interested I'll take you along."

That was the start of the Grosvenor Gallery. Blanche threw all her talent into the decoration of the new building that was to rise in the heart of London's smartest shopping centre at a cost of £120,000.

Sir Francis Grant, President of the Royal Academy, made the spontaneous statement that he would be delighted to exhibit at the new place. His action eased any tension that might have existed between the Royal Academy and the Grosvenor Gallery. Further, it allowed such artists as Leighton, Millais, G. F. Watts, Alma Tadema and Poynter, all academicians or associates, to rally round the Lindsays without giving the appearance of deserting Burlington House.

An architect called Sams was brought in to design the building. His eyes fell on a doorway made by the great Andrea Palladio, pupil of Michelangelo, for the church of Santa Lucia at Venice, which Sir Coutts had brought back from Italy. Sams asked that this masterpiece should be the entrance to the new building and thereafter he took it as the key-note to his design. What he really did was to put the sixteenth-century doorway in the middle and then build round it. Thus the stone façade was of Italian Renaissance and even the inside of the building came under the influence of that period.

Green marble was brought from Genoa to make the columns in the entrance hall. A staircase with pedestals for statues on either side led to the principal gallery, the ceiling of which was painted blue with gold stars. The wall panels were divided by Ionic pilasters, fluted and gilt, from the old Italian Opera House in Paris. The walls were entirely covered with deep crimson silk damask. The idea was that such a background would provide an ideal setting for the pictures and give them just such an atmosphere as would be found in a quiet and richly furnished room. Attention was even paid to the parquet floor, the tone of which was subdued so as not to attract the eye. Chairs and tables of old Italian design were to be placed here and there—the tables to have statuettes or works of art upon them. Each artist was to have a small portion of the gallery to himself; his pictures to be arranged under his own direction with ample space between and in such a way that one did not clash with another. Thus the visitor would be able to draw up a chair and concentrate upon some particular painting without having his mind distracted by others alongside.

*   *   *   *   *

It soon became evident that the Grosvenor Gallery would become the home of that group of artists known as the Pre-Raphaelites. This movement, of which Holman Hunt was the founder, had been launched some years earlier against the academic standards of the day.

Back in the 'forties, William Holman Hunt, then a student little more than eighteen years of age, began looking closely into the history of painting. He noticed that every time the pupils of a particular school began to follow dogmas instead of working direct from nature, that school came to an end. He took as an example the later work of Raphael. He was convinced that this showed less purity of style than did the works of earlier painters.

The young student examined the problem for himself. He decided that he would disregard the arbitrary rules of the moment. Instead, he started to study diligently those fundamentals that had made the success of all great painters.

One day he talked the matter over with a youth two years younger than himself—John Everett Millais. Then another artist came along in the person of Dante Gabriel Rossetti, who shared a studio with Holman Hunt in Cleveland Street. These three exhibited a few pictures in the summer of 1849. They were soon to attract considerable attention.

By the time the Grosvenor Gallery was ready to open its doors, each painter was interpreting the movement according to his own ideas. Holman Hunt and Millais, for instance, were realists, while Rossetti headed the school of romanticism. Brilliant colouring and a minute attention to detail, however, were common to all.

A short time before this, Rossetti had been giving friendly instruction to a young artist who was showing talent for just that romantic style of painting that was after his own heart. This new-comer was Edward Burne-Jones. His name figured on the lists of the Water Colour Society at some time in the late 'sixties, but by 1870 he had resigned because of a misunderstanding.

Sir Coutts Lindsay went to Rossetti's studio and asked the artist how much space he wanted at the Grosvenor Gallery.

"I am sorry," Rossetti answered, "I have been ill and cannot show anything. But go to Burne-Jones. He has been working for just seven years in his studio and by now should be able to cover a whole wall of your gallery."

He added: "A few years ago that young man was working under my guidance. Now I cannot teach him anything more. His work will take London by storm."

Sir Coutts went along to see the artist. Burne-Jones showed

"THE PICTURE I'VE BEEN WAITING FOR."

G. F. Watts said these words when he called at the Lindsays' home
one day and found Blanche playing the violin. This portrait is in the
Tate Gallery.

him three huge pictures: "The Days of Creation," "The Beguiling of Merlin," and "The Mirror of Venus."

"How do you like them?" Burne-Jones asked.

Sir Coutts looked at the canvases and knew that Rossetti was right. Only Burne-Jones himself succeeded in describing his own work: "I mean by a 'picture' a beautiful romantic dream of something that never was, never will be—in a light better than any light that ever shone—in a land no one can define or remember . . ."

"I will give you all the space you want," said Sir Coutts: "the opening of the Grosvenor Gallery will be your day of recognition."

*   *   *   *   *

Blanche Lindsay spent long hours in her studio painting a number of pictures for the great opening.

G. F. Watts called one morning. Blanche went to a corner of the room and, taking her violin, started to play softly.

Watts jumped up.

"There is the very picture I've been waiting for!" he explained. "It shall be a half-length portrait of Lady Lindsay playing on the violin."

To-day that picture hangs in the Tate Gallery.

Great activity went on behind the scenes. When Watts heard that Edward Burne-Jones was going to be introduced to the public, he took a cab to the young artist's studio and said: "They will want to know what sort of men painted all these angels."

He decided to add a portrait of Burne-Jones to that of Blanche Lindsay.

*   *   *   *   *

By this time the great building was virtually completed. Under Sams' guidance a façade of stone after the manner of the Italian Renaissance had already taken shape on either side of Palladio's masterpiece. The decorators were busy in the various galleries, where gorgeous hangings, tapestries and gilt Florentine consoles were already being put into place.

As Sir Coutts looked upon this combination of bright crimson, blue and green, he began to wonder how the public would take this dose of fifteenth-century art. He had shouldered a considerable responsibility. Though he had given each artist complete liberty, it was clear that he personally had chosen the artists. By the Quattrocentisti decoration of his building and by the introduction of such allegorical painters as Edward Burne-Jones, he was unconsciously leading away from the strict principles of the original Pre-Raphaelites.

He looked around the galleries and made a rough calculation where the pictures of the artists would hang. Burne-Jones would have an entire wall. His main picture was in six panels. It was this school that would find its highest expression in the Grosvenor Galleries. There would be plenty of ridicule heaped on this newcomer who pretended to make an English Renaissance by thinking, seeing and painting in a mediæval period of Italian mysticism. People would ask how far an artist can turn his mind to the past and yet keep his art alive and growing.

Nevertheless, Holman Hunt could be counted on to remain faithful to that absolute realism that typified the first Pre-Raphaelites. There was, for instance, a remarkable picture of this master showing a most lovable, dark-haired little girl. John Millais had promised two portraits together with a study called "Stitch, stitch, stitch" that Watts had insisted on buying. This had a slightly social vein because of the contrast between a number of fair creatures nursed in luxury and the hard-worked seamstress at their feet. Alma Tadema had gone to Greek skies for his inspiration of the sculptor Phidias showing some of his work to a friend. Nobody could paint stone like Alma Tadema.

Sir Coutts cast a critical eye over the engineering details of the building. Though he did not know it, there were two points about this place that were half a century before their time. One was a tolerably efficient forerunner of our present air conditioning.

BEDTIME STORY.

John Millais went up to the nursery and painted
a picture of Effie and her nurse. "There's no
fellow living who knows better than I what
paint can do and I don't care who knows that
I say so!"

I

By means of a steam engine cool, fresh and properly moist air was drawn through metal skirtings in the galleries. In hot weather the air could be cooled by means of a spray of water. The second thing of interest was that for the first time in London a picture gallery was being installed with a system of indirect lighting.

This place must be typical of an age.

*   *   *   *   *

Meanwhile, there hung in Blanche Lindsay's study at home a water colour that would not be shown in public. It was of a little girl with fair hair and a white frock kneeling at the feet of an aged nurse with a lace cap on her head, who was pointing to a page of a picture-book laid open on the apron of her comfortably large lap. One afternoon some years earlier, John Millais called at the Lindsays' home at tea-time. Blanche showed him up to the nursery where four-years-old Effie was playing with her nurse, Mrs. Baillie. Millais was delighted by the homely scene. He sketched it rapidly and in due time presented Effie's mother with the finished work.

There is something real in this nursery picture. The arm-chair that this good old nurse is sitting in is upholstered in a gay material with bright pink stripes. This is a pencil drawing covered over with water colour. It is full of detail. There is a doll lying on its back beside the arm-chair. The inference is clear. It was thrown hastily away when nurse announced her intention of opening the picture-book.

Blanche would look at this picture with affection. Millais had captured that rather serious expression on Effie's face. He had placed it on paper as if to defy the march of time. Many thoughts would pass through Blanche's mind as she looked at it. She would remember those scenes at Euston when she would bid farewell to her children (Anne Helen was then still a baby in arms) before their departure with a nurse for Balcarres. It was that very same nurse whose placid face was bending down over the picture-book in the drawing. Mrs. Baillie had a habit of hanging a rug across the centre of the reserved compartment in order to make two improvised sleepers—one for herself in which she read by the light of a candle, the other darkened, for the children.

How quickly the girls had grown! Effie was now nearly twelve years old. She would be celebrating her birthday a few days after the official opening of the Grosvenor Gallery. Anne Helen was eight and a half. The Lindsays' new studio home in Cromwell Place was filled with childish laughter.

*　　　*　　　*　　　*　　　*

It was a miracle that the gallery was ready in time.

The night before, Blanche, Sir Coutts and two artists called Halle and Carr, worked incessantly. Somebody noticed that gas was not laid on in the water-colour room. The Lindsays' private carriage plied between Cromwell Place and Bond Street to bring every available oil lamp to the rescue. Rugs had to be chosen to go under the console tables. The green silk brocade for one of the walls did not arrive until late. This brocade was brought by a little Frenchman with a happy smile and long curling moustaches. He looked around and inspected the pictures with care.

"Do you like pictures?" asked Sir Coutts amiably.

"Pictures?" echoed the little man. "No, sir, I do not, but I respect them."

By ten o'clock the next morning the first guests streamed up the stairs. Whistler arrived with the one white lock in his dark hair, prefacing every remark with the words: "Don't you know, eh? don't you know?" Watts advanced slowly in his long sealskin coat with a wisp of red ribbon showing at the neck, surrounded by the prettiest and youngest women in town. Browning walked up with Augustus Sala, whose beaming face and world-famed white waistcoat gave him an air of dignity. There was Miss Elizabeth Philp, the song composer, who had a rough manner, a tolerable moustache on her upper lip but a warm, womanly heart; the Duke and Duchess of Somerset, a kindly old couple, who walked arm-in-arm followed by the admiring actor Hare, who never could get over the fact that the Duke invariably dressed as a yeoman farmer of fifty years before. Edward Burne-Jones let himself be seen in this place where his work was to unleash a torrent of abuse because he had the gift never to read or listen to a single word of criticism.

On the evening of May 7, the Grosvenor Gallery was the scene of one of the most spectacular banquets of the time. Forty-eight hours beforehand, Gounard, the Lindsays' great French chef, worked to prepare the meal.

Four of Queen Victoria's children were present at this banquet: Edward, Prince of Wales, who was later to be King Edward VII; Princess Louise, who was to become the Duchess of Argyll; Prince Leopold, the future Duke of Albany, and the Duke of Connaught, whom Blanche had seen smacked by his Royal mother twenty-five years before. Arthur Sullivan and Halle were detailed to figure out who should take in who at this dinner. They had the most thankless job of all, for there were so many royalties and high-resounding names of every kind, that it was pretty well past the wit of man not to make a blunder. The Rothschilds sent cartfuls of flowers from their estates at Gunnersbury and Mentmore, while Blanche arranged that her own gardener at Balcarres should do his best to send as many as he could. It was late when she arrived home to change for the banquet and she found countless notes requesting last-moment invitations. Her maid was frantic. Blanche was obliged to take her jewels in a heap and put them on as best she could in the carriage. The drive from Cromwell Place to Bond Street is a tolerable distance. As she neared Piccadilly her teeth chattered and she turned cold. She was late and a long string of carriages blocked her way. She had visions of her Royal guests pacing up and down the doorstep. The police, on hearing her name, cut the string of traffic and ten minutes later she flew up the stairs of the exhibition, to be told that her system of numbering had proved too much for Arthur Sullivan! The great musician had hardly begun to explain all the trouble when the Prince of Wales arrived.

The Prince took Blanche in to dinner, Sir Coutts took in Princess Louise, the Duke of Connaught escorted the Duchess of Teck. Fortunately for Sullivan and Halle, guests sorted themselves out and all was well. Nevertheless, Blanche sat trembling with nervousness until the Prince of Wales accidentally upset a glassful of champagne over her shoulder and sleeve, wetting her considerably and causing a good deal of laughter. This dinner proved a turning-point in painting. It was the start of that æsthetic movement that was later to be turned into ridicule and become the butt of W. S. Gilbert in the opera *Patience* when he wrote:

> "A pallid and thin young man—
> A haggard and lank young man,
> A greenery-yallery, Grosvenor Gallery,
> Foot-in-the-grave young man!"

But by that time it was the public and not the founders who had gone too far.

CHAPTER TWENTY-SIX

THAT August Blanche and her husband decided to spend a short holiday abroad. They were bound for Cadenabbia on Lake Como, but they mapped out their route by way of the old German city of Treves on the Moselle. Arthur Sullivan went with them.

The cathedral at Treves is beautiful inside and out.

"Here," said the old sacristan in his funny English, "here on this him stone, you will come and stand." Then, pointing with his arm to the arches of the aisle, "Pleaze," he said, "it is peautiful the style of these columns. We have the Roman style, the Corinthian style, the Gothic style and the Johnny style."

"The Johnny style?"

"Of course. The English Inigo Johnny style!"

On leaving Treves they drove for some miles and then took a boat and floated down the river to Coblenz. Blanche set out with a store of sketch-books and drawing materials and had been pressed by her husband to engage Wyatt, a dignified English courier.

"How long will it take us to float down the Moselle, Wyatt?"

"Not long, ma'am, if no time is wasted in drawing."

The country was green and undulating, the hills dumpling-like in shape. A couple of hours later the sky became overcast, and for the remainder of the journey they were enwrapped in a shroud of drizzling rain. Sir Coutts and Sullivan rigged up a sort of canvas roof to the boat through which the rain soaked and dripped but did not actually pour, and under this shelter crouched the courier with an expression of desperate resignation on his face, holding on his knees a tall box wherein lay his cherished Sunday silk hat. As they neared Coblenz the rain-clouds lightened and the sky grew clear. They determined to land and allow the courier and Blanche's maid to go on to the town to engage rooms.

They lunched on hot cabbage soup at a small inn on the river bank. Sir Coutts enquired if a carriage could be hired to drive them to the Castle of Els.

"Well," answered the hostess smiling, "we have, of course, a *Wagen*."

The good lady returned with the news that the carriage was at the door. It was a large open wooden cart with a big bundle of straw to do duty for seats and cushions. The coachman wore a blue cotton blouse. The party crossed the village slowly and proceeded by the castle road up the hillside. This road was the almost dried-up bed of a river. Blanche, after holding on to her straw bolster for some time, much shaken by jolts and laughter, decided to climb down and walk, hopping from boulder to boulder whilst the phlegmatic driver of the Albert Dürer cart and his stolid Teutonic horse went calmly on. The woman at the inn warned the visitors that, though the Castle of Els was a fine one, strangers were not admitted, because foreigners persistently carved their names on tables, chairs and walls. Sir Coutts was sanguine that a little politeness combined with some silver might gain them admission.

The castle lay just below them in a green hollow surrounded by trees. Its high red-and-green roof made it look something like a picture from a fairy-tale book; a peasant was working among the cabbages in the kitchen garden. Blanche went eagerly up to him and asked if she might see the castle, but he pointed over his shoulder with his finger and thumb and never said a word.

Sullivan tackled the driver of the wagon, asking if he thought there was any chance of getting inside the castle. The driver smiled and shook his head and smiled again, saying that the party could go and try if it pleased, but he would wait in the cart! All three therefore walked valiantly up to the castle door and rang an iron bell that resounded and reverberated through the whole building, re-echoing from every hillside.

Above their heads great painted weathercocks went swinging round and round, which, if it had been midnight, might have suggested ghosts in torment. They rang again. After much delay came the sound of footsteps . . . wooden pattens along a stone floor . . . until at last a rough countrywoman unfastened the door and opened it a few inches. Blanche, in her best and most courteous German, expressed her desire to see the interior of the castle. The old woman took one look at the three strangers, and for answer shut the door loudly in their faces! There was nothing more to be done. They returned to the inn by the high road—a flat and uninteresting ribbon of white, bordered by apple-trees, where country damsels with red cheeks nodded as they passed, wishing the strangers a smiling "*guten Abend*." There was no hurrying the driver. He was very different from the one who earlier had driven Blanche at Aix-la-Chapelle. This one flourished his whip, taking his hackney coach over fields and ditches, crying out triumphantly: "So goes the Prussian artillery!"

At Dresden Blanche sent Wyatt to bring the luggage while they went to the post-office to collect any mail. There was no mail. "Are you sure?" asked Sir Coutts. "I will spell the name carefully, for I am expecting some letters."

The clerk listened, bowed and repeated his denial.

"Never mind," said Coutts, turning to his wife. "I will send the courier Wyatt to-morrow morning."

"Oh, it is *die Familie* Wyatt!" exclaimed the clerk. "You should have said you belonged to him!" He then produced a huge bundle of letters from a pigeon-hole marked "W".

The next day Arthur Sullivan, who knew Dresden well, took the Lindsays to a number of old curiosity shops.

Wyatt was furious. He turned to Blanche's maid and shouted: "It is unfair the way that man Sullivan takes them around. He will get my commission!"

A week later they took a diligence near the Swiss border and crossed the frontier into Italy by way of the Splügen Pass.

At the Customs House the Italian officers looked with suspicion at the easels and painting umbrellas packed on the top of the diligence.

"Is it for shooting?" they asked.

"No, these are . . ."

"Are you surveyors?"

"No; I tell you, they are . . ."

"Are you photographers?"

"No. No."

"Well, then, you are acrobats."

That evening they arrived at Chiavenna with its green chestnut woods. It was *festa* and all the village folks were sitting out under the trees eating chestnuts and brown bread and drinking the rough, bluish-red wine of the country out of big bottles. Even the children sat on the grass and drank generously. The weather was so hot that they dined in the courtyard of the inn where lemon-trees and myrtles grew; just across the road stood the ancient castle of the De Salis, and while they ate there came the sound of singing and chanting as a procession of priests and choir-boys came slowly into view.

From here they travelled first by road and then by steamer, reaching Cadenabbia one broiling afternoon, glad to leave the boat and enter the cool hotel, where they were given rooms with broad, shady verandahs overlooking the lake. For the next ten days the temperature was seldom less than ninety-six in the shade. There was nothing to do but laze the time away.

Arthur Sullivan was then vaguely intending to write a Primer of Music. Partly owing to the heat of the weather, partly because of his disinclination for the task, he never got beyond the first page.

He used persistently to ask:

"What is an interval?" or "How would you define a sound?"

Each morning, lazily reclining in a rocking chair, dressed in a light suit hastily made by a tailor of Cadenabbia, he would smoke innumerable local cigarettes and repeat to Blanche:

"You see, it is necessary to begin at the very beginning: it is no use to talk of a note or a stave. What is a note? What is a stave?"

To change his conversation Blanche would beg him to exercise his Italian, which consisted of three sentences: "*Portate una grande bottiglia di limonata fresca.*" "*Avete ancora del ghiaccio? Molto ghiaccio.*" Then, having accumulated large bottles of lemonade and more and more ice, Sullivan would temporarily forget all about his Primer.

As evening fell there would be sleepy music on the lake as a party of peasants would drift down twanging guitars and playing mandolines. Then silence would reign and there would be nothing to do but dream as the stars shone down in all their splendour. What starlit nights these hot days produced! Only once was there a storm and that was on their last evening at Cadenabbia. The thunder pealed and rolled among the mountains and never ceased to echo and re-echo. The lightning was so vivid that every corner of the room where they sat was illuminated. Frightened birds flew on to the carpet. This was Sullivan's first visit to Italy. He saw the country at its best, the gardens full of great pink oleanders, heavy white magnolias, scarlet pomegranates and groves of lemons.

On their return Blanche spent a day alone at Verona. She noticed a particularly lovely Italian girl selling fruit in the market and she was anxious to make a sketch of her. Blanche's Italian was as limited as that of Arthur Sullivan, with the result that she was unable to make her request intelligible. She retraced her steps to the hotel and invoked the aid of her host, who sallied forth with her and speedily induced the girl to leave her pears and grapes to the care of a friend and follow them back to the hotel.

As soon as Blanche secured her victim she discovered that she had left her paint-brushes behind. She again sought the innkeeper, who took her to a shop filled with large cruses of oil, blacking, dried fruit, candles and a couple of brushes for painting the sides of a house.

After a lengthy search she found one tiny brush of camel's hair with neither point nor handle.

All that afternoon Blanche worked at the portrait. She managed to carry on a somewhat halting conversation with the model. Her name was Speranza and she was seventeen. She said she had sold pears and grapes all her life; sometimes she sold few, sometimes many. "Did she ever eat any herself?" "Oh no!" whereupon she laughed and showed two rows of strong white teeth. "Would she ever marry?" "Certainly, she would marry, and the sooner the better." "And what would she do then?" "Why, sell pears and grapes."

Just as Blanche was deluding herself into the belief that her model was going to remain quiet, a swift and terrible transformation came over her beautiful face. She rushed to the window and closed the shutters with a violent bang, growling fiercely in an unintelligible patois, shaking her fist and leaving Blanche in darkness and bewilderment.

Two or three gentlemen of Verona, young peasants of her acquaintance, had followed her back to the inn and stood making faces at her through the open window. That was more than Speranza could bear.

"But I must have light to paint you by!" expostulated Blanche.

A compromise was effected. The shutters were opened to give some light and yet to afford protection from inquisitive eyes.

*   *   *   *   *

The Lindsays returned to England that September and almost immediately travelled north. Prince Leopold, Queen Victoria's youngest son, invited himself for a week's holiday at Balcarres.

Blanche quickly adjusted herself to the northern form of hospitality. She told her friends that they could come when they liked and stay for as long as they pleased. In this way she felt less responsible for their amusement and it was not her fault if it rained or hailed. One week there were fourteen men and only three women to keep them in countenance. Blanche considered that this was an exceptional case needing adjustment. She telegraphed for all her women friends to come to the rescue.

A week later the men all departed and a dozen women, eager to make themselves attractive, trooped in. It was too late. Impossible to find a single man!

The Prince was in great spirits. Blanche intended to give a ball in his honour, for his enthusiasm for dancing was great and he would have gladly danced the night away, but Queen Victoria sent a telegram with strict orders that her son should not be allowed to do so. She was frightened that he would tire himself. Her fears were not vain. He died some years later from over-exertion at a ball! When, after dinner, Prince Leopold would ask to have the big oak table pushed aside so that they could dance, everybody pretended that it was much too heavy to move.

Some evenings they would all crowd into Arthur Sullivan's bedroom where he was composing his opera, *The Sorcerer*, in front of the schoolroom piano. A century earlier the ballad of "Auld Robin Gray" was written here, and this room had a touch of romance because of a mysterious door that opened from it on to a corkscrew staircase built within a tall, narrow tower.

On other nights they would have theatricals. There was a tableau in which Blanche figured as Henrietta Maria bidding farewell to Charles the First, who was Prince Leopold. As Blanche was kneeling on one knee uncomfortably tilted on her toe and unable to cling to his hand, which was her only support, she had some difficulty in keeping her balance. When the curtain was lowered, Charles the First hissed: "You rocked!" The audience overheard that whisper and had its best laugh of the evening. The next morning the guests appeared at breakfast in the costumes of the night before. The party gathered on the terrace, where Lord Charles Scott planned to photograph the various groups. They were suddenly startled by the sound of horses and hounds! A hunt was meeting at their very door. Hunting folk and fishwives were not a little surprised to see their Sovereign's son dressed up as Charles the First, attended by courtiers in broad-brimmed hats and plumes!

Christine Nilsson, the great Swedish singer, arrived that

evening, and so did Goschen, then a Lord of the Admiralty. Christine Nilsson said she had come to rest and not to sing, but immediately after dinner, while sitting in an armchair, she became tired of her restraint and filled the large room with her magnificent voice. Arthur Sullivan went softly up to the piano and accompanied her without any break in the melody. The next morning Nilsson insisted on going out shooting with the men. She wore high Russian boots, a short black leather petticoat, a tight cloth jacket and a Tyrolese hat perched on top of her fair hair. After an hour's work she blew an unfortunate rabbit to pieces from a distance of exactly three yards!

The Channel Fleet was then anchored in the Forth not far from Edinburgh. After lunch somebody brought the news that the ironclads were steaming out to sea and everybody ran to tell Mr. Goschen the news. The Admiralty Lord was so short-sighted that it was in vain that a dozen people took him to the highest tower of Balcarres to survey the Firth. Everybody but he could see the Fleet. Several guests tried to piece together an aged and broken telescope which had ornamented the library for many years so that the distinguished gentleman might improve his sight. "I prefer my eyeglass," he said.

Goschen left Balcarres a few days later and spent a dismal hour on a draughty platform of Ladybank Junction. He wrote, for distraction, a letter in rhyme to his hostess in which he said:

> Fresh from you, my mind is so aesthetic,
> That, even here, I'm forced to be poetic.
> Melons and models, melodies and mirth
> Still float before us on our way to Perth,
> Yet scarce I dare to sing in doggrel rhyme
> Our bright impressions of that handsome time.
> How shall I tell the zest with which we fell on
> Our luscious lumps of the nine-pounder melon?
> What rounder compliments, what pretty speeches
> Would do full justice to our feasts of peaches?
> Yet, hush! How ill these greedy thoughts become
> Guests who have basked in your aesthetic home,

A CENTURY BETWEEN

So steeped in art, that even every rose
Seems bent on blooming in a perfect pose.
Full many a day my memory will recall
The panelled chamber and the armoured hall !
The gems of art, the dazzling shell of roses
In which each day we bathed our happy noses.
Still in my thoughts I see your happy look
Glancing so bright above your music book,
While o'er the keys your gentle fingers stray
And waft around us Schubert's sweetest lay.
Yet there were moments when the mood in favour
Was somewhat spiced with a Bohemian flavour
And when, o'er fruit and wine, in merry session
We each in turn made terrible confession.
But hark! the distant locomotive's whistle
Warns me 'tis time to finish this epistle.

CHAPTER TWENTY-SEVEN

ONE October evening in 1879 Blanche went to her desk and, sitting down, opened a new diary at the first page. This is what she wrote:

"I carried my violin this afternoon to Watts, as I had promised. He thought I had improved and seemed delighted for me to play while he worked on one of his larger pictures. He has repainted 'Time and Death' since last year and also 'Love and Death.' I think he has improved the first of these and strengthened the colour, but I liked the other so well before that I did not wish to see it altered. 'So you think I have spoilt it?' he asked, turning quickly on me.

" 'No, not that, but it was good before.'

" 'It was foggy.'

" 'I liked it foggy; it suited the subject.'

" 'Then you do not like it now?'

" 'I wish you could have painted a second picture and compared the two, rather than repainted the first. I do like this picture, but I regret the first.'

" 'I had such a nice dream last night,' said Watts, laying down his brushes suddenly. 'I dreamt that Titian and Sir Joshua were both in the room talking about painting. They both gave me a lesson. I have learnt a great deal, I can assure you.'

"He then showed me a head of Mrs. Langtry, which I told him in good truth was excellent.

" 'I have been working at it all day,' he said, smiling. 'You like it? That is because Titian has been teaching me in my dream.' "

Blanche put down her pen and saw again the artist, looking much like Titian himself, as he talked to her. She saw his keen eyes and grey beard, a certain noble air, under his velvet skull cap.

A POET'S DREAM.

"Tennyson came to see me, wishing to look at a drawing I had done of a squirrel; but he was disappointed because the squirrel was seated on the dinner table, eating a nut on a white table-cloth and not on the branches of a forest tree. . . ."

That evening Blanche went to the St. James's Theatre, which had been redecorated by Mr. Hare and Mrs. Kendal. For some months to come she kept up her diary from time to time.

Thursday, October 30. "Tennyson came to see me, wishing to look at a drawing I had done of a squirrel; but he was disappointed because the squirrel was represented seated on the dinner table, eating a nut on a white tablecloth, and not on the branches of a forest tree. He wandered round my study, looking at everything. He wore a short cape and carried his black felt hat in his hand, restlessly. His son, Hallam, accompanied him. He told me that his disenchantment at my squirrel recalled to him a walk he once had with his grandson. The poet had pointed to some fairy rings on the grass, making an imaginative explanation relative to the midnight dances of elves and fairies. 'Oh no, grandpa,' said the boy, 'that is quite wrong. Those marks are due to the growth of a fungus.' "

Friday, October 31. "I have a cold and cannot go out. I wrote a line to Mr. Burne-Jones to come and chat if possible, but he is just off to Cambridge and writes: 'I am glad you are back in Town—the uncomfortable and absurd summer is over and let us hope the peaceful winter begun.' "

Tuesday, November 4. "I went last night to the first Monday Popular concert of the season. I sat where I have often sat before, beside Mr. and Mrs. Poynter—Mr. Halle behind us, rows of well-known Monday Popular faces in front of us, around us and about us. On the platform Madame Neruda, Piatti, Ries and Zerbini all looking just the same as ever, playing Haydn's familiar strains. They might have been sitting thus since this time last year. Maybe the hall with its artists, and audience, had been peacefully asleep throughout the summer and autumn, suddenly waking up to life when Arthur Chappell clapped his hands and turned on the gas. This sounds like the palace of the sleeping princess, and if a princess is needed there was Princess Louise sitting in a back seat, but she was by no means asleep. She had just come home on leave from Canada. I went to tell her how glad I was that she had returned and she kissed me affectionately on both cheeks. After the concert, I went as usual into the artists' room where everybody was shaking hands with everybody. A great deal of German was talked. Madame Neruda was being wrapped up in shawls, little Janotha was bustling about, Miss Bailey, the singer, was sitting perched up to have her fur shoes tied by her maid. 'Tiny,' Madame Neruda's white dog, was barking vociferously. Piatti was silently and carefully tucking away his fiddle into its case. Afterwards, as Pepys says, home to bed."

Sunday, November 9. "Last night Prescott Hewett, the surgeon, and Carl Haag came to dinner. Carl Haag was born at Nuremberg —a little man, clever, bright, with dark iron-grey hair and the keenest, quickest black eyes. *En revanche* his wife is fat, fair and a little over forty, serene, tranquil and comfortable. Haag and Hewett are great friends. At dinner Hewett told us a story of Carl Haag who was painting at Balmoral for the Queen. She had asked him to paint the picture of one of her horses. The sittings took place in the stables, where one of the head grooms anxious for a pipe but frightened of the royal dislike of tobacco, tried to get the artist to smoke first. 'I can't do that,' said Haag. 'The Queen might come. Who knows?'

" 'No chances of that,' said the other, and thereupon began to smoke.

"A couple of minutes later the Queen arrived to inspect the picture. The groom made a rapid exit by a side door. Queen Victoria sniffed the air, turned a little stiffly to Haag and said:

" 'This smacks somewhat of Germany, Mr. Haag!'

"As Hewett finished the story, the artist turned to the surgeon and said drily: 'Ah, my dear Hewedd, vat a good memory you hafe!'

"Carl Haag's studio is at the top of his Hampstead house. The place is called 'Ida Villa,' after his wife's Christian name. It is furnished with divans, decorated with portions of Moorish woodwork and elaborately carved Oriental windows with a balcony inside the room."

Friday, November 14. "Browning has just come in to see us. He is back from a visit to Italy with his old maiden sister. Robert Browning is one of those people who improve with friendship, for on mere acquaintance his loud and harsh voice, his incessant flow, not of conversation but of monologue, and his slightly aggressive manner are not in his favour. As a friend he is loyal and true, kind and warm-hearted. His mind is stored with curious anecdotes and his monologues are nearly always interesting. He is short, rather stout, with a fine head and grey hair and beard. He sat down to luncheon with us after his usual fashion, that is to say, a slice of roast mutton lay and cooled itself on the plate before him while he talked on energetically as the other guests plodded through the meal."

Monday, November 17. "I am writing this at Aston Clinton, the home of my aunt Louisa. She is now a widow, for my uncle, Sir Anthony Rothschild, died three years ago.

"I came here hoping to regain health and strength from two days in the country. Burne-Jones once told me that when he felt ill and lay down, he wanted to lie still lower down. That is how I feel.

"There are several other guests here. It did not take me long to see that the party was divided into two camps. The earnest-minded and æsthetic are at daggers drawn with the 'modern' and anti-æsthetic! So they all go up to London by different trains to-day.

"I sadly miss the portly figure and kindly face of my uncle and I remember his parties with pleasure. Once I was here when the Duke of Edinburgh and the Czarewitch came for a day's shooting. They arrived by an early train and we had a ceremonious breakfast in the large dining-room, having had an unceremonious one upstairs, in my bedroom, my cousins and I, some time before. Then the gentlemen all went out shooting, Sir Anthony, who was already out of health at that time, accompanying them on his piebald pony. We, the ladies, went out to join them at luncheon, which took place in an Oriental tent pitched for the purpose on a convenient spot not far from the village. After luncheon, all the little village schoolgirls, in their red cloaks, crowded round the railings that protected the tent from approach, and the Russian prince, a big, burly, good-humoured fellow, went out to them and amused himself by giving them slices of *pâté de foie gras*, laughing boisterously while the children in their shrill voices kept on shouting: 'Long live the Sarrywitz, long live the Sarrywitz!'

"After the shooting, when they went back to the house, the Russian princes and suite all went to bed. The house not being very large, my cousins had given up their own bedrooms for the day, and Annie, in her excitement forgetting this arrangement altogether, walked unceremoniously into her bedroom, where she found an elderly Russian, sitting up in her bed, placidly smoking his pipe!

"But the Duke of Edinburgh, having changed his things, came down, according to our English custom, to five o'clock tea, looking very spruce and tidy, and charming us all by his amiable manners. Then, as eager as ever for music, he seized upon my violin and fiddled away, accompanied by myself, till there remained but ten minutes before dinner-time. Everyone had gone to dress, but he and I, for, loyal though I am, I would not leave my beloved fiddle in his hands, yet each time I suggested that we should dress, the Duke answered: 'Oh no, not yet; let us play something else.' At last he allowed me to escape, and I rushed upstairs to slip on a white satin gown, my maid in a fever of agitation. Of course I was a minute or two late, and when I entered the drawing-room I found the Duke cool and composed, the centre of the group of guests. Being a sailor as well as a Prince, he is very punctual, and being a man instead of a woman, he does not take long to dress so I thought it very mischievous of him to turn towards me, smiling, and say aloud: 'How late you are, Lady Lindsay!' "

Wednesday, November 19. "I am now back in London after travelling from Aston Clinton in the company of Mr. Gladstone. As we entered the railway compartment, Mr. Gladstone turned to me and said: 'You won't mind if I don't talk, will you? Talking in the train tires my throat very much.'

" 'Oh no,' I answered meekly, conscious, however, of disappointment.

"We had scarcely gone a mile or two when Mr. Gladstone, forgetful of his throat, began to talk, and never ceased until we reached Euston Station. I do not remember what started him on the subject of Homer, but from Greek poetry he took a mental leap to Ireland, St. Patrick and the snakes which the saint is supposed to have expelled. Presently I spoke to him of the fear of death, and asked his opinion as to whether he thought it possible for many natures absolutely to overcome that fear. He answered: 'It is there, ever present, the fear, in the minds of most of us; yet, thank God, when the last moment comes, that dread which is physical disappears.' On this subject he talked for some time. I have always found him an interesting personality, with hawk-like eyes that look straight at one. Much of his fascination is, I think, due to his habit of throwing himself thoroughly into the interests of the man, woman or child with whom he is conversing. I remember a children's party given for me when I was about eight years old. In the midst of it my father and mother, with Mr. Gladstone, whose own children were among the guests, came into the room. He talked to all of us and his charm was immense.

"I have noticed that for the time being the person whom he addresses appears for Mr. Gladstone to be the centre of his thoughts. No subject is too trivial for him. His keen eyes glitter, his face lights up, and he shows an attention far greater than would be demanded by mere courtesy. On one occasion Mr. Gladstone and I talked through the whole of dinner on the two subjects of violin playing and neuralgia! When the ladies left the dinner table, I had a very bad fit of neuralgia, and I felt as though I had been conversing for the last hour with the most ardent violinist of my acquaintance.

"Disraeli, on the contrary, talks down to what he considers the level of women. Often as a child I saw Mr. and Mrs. Disraeli coming home from their walk in the park on Sunday afternoons. They lived at the other end of Upper Grosvenor Street to ourselves. Indeed, they were altogether on the opposite side from my father and mother, for party spirit in politics ran high in those days and Liberals and Conservatives were barely friendly.

"When I was eighteen my uncle and aunt used to give parties at Gunnersbury Park on Sundays. The guests would arrive in the afternoon and sit on the lawns under the trees, until dinner time. They went to dinner in the order they chose. After the coffee they would once more go out of doors until dusk. It was all very pleasant.

"One evening Dizzy came up to where I was sitting and began to converse. I was nothing loth and we talked for a long time. Then suddenly he said: 'I like to talk to you; do tell me who you are.' But I would not, and only laughed, and so we talked on till the party broke up, and then, when we went into the house, we were duly introduced to each other in the lamplight.

"The last time I met him was at a small dinner party at Kensington Palace. He was sadly changed. He sat between Prince Leopold and myself, and scarcely opened his lips during the whole of the dinner. He looked like a melancholy sphinx."

December 1. "The Alma Tademas dined to-night. Tadema is the image of a Dutch burgomaster. He talks the funniest possible

English, speaking rapidly on an upward rising scale of intonation and emphasizing all unemphasized syllables. Mrs. Tadema is also an artist and paints in a somewhat Pre-Raphaelite style. She and Tadema are great friends. She is usually dressed according to his taste, her reddish hair combed low on her forehead. She wears a severely classical gown, sandalled shoes and a big gold serpent bracelet a little below the shoulder according to classic custom. After dinner when we went up to my husband's studio the lay-figure, standing in the centre of the room with a towel around its waist, startled everyone. Tadema told us how a French friend of his, having gone to see an English painter of modern subjects, was asked to wait in the studio where such a figure stood clad in the deepest mourning—bonnet, cloak and crêpe veil. Hat in hand, he politely addressed the 'stranger' and, receiving no answer, ventured to speak to her again. At last, repelled by her continued silence, he turned away in anger and exclaimed: 'Heavens, how cold these Englishwomen can be!'

"The Lehmanns were here. I cannot see them without being reminded of the many pleasant evenings I have spent at their home. There was one party with the Leightons, Browning, Rubinstein, and George Eliot. The first time I saw George Eliot I asked who she was. An elderly woman, decidedly plain in face and features, dressed in a simple black silk skirt with a loose high jacket of the same material. Pinned on her head was a small knitted Shetland shawl, like a veil. She had shining eyes, a soft, low voice, and a gentle earnest manner. She was surrounded by several deferentially listening men.

"George Lewes, her husband, as he was called, positively adored her.

" 'Child!' he addressed her in tones of tenderest affection. She was one of those women who cannot possibly manage for or look after themselves. Now that he is dead, her health has given way and her own life is practically ended. Certainly his help and encouragement, his advice and sympathy, the strong manly arm on which she leaned, went far towards the nourishment and perfection of her genius. One evening when I met him at a party, I asked if Mrs. Lewes was also present. 'Yes,' he replied, pointing to where she sat conversing in low, eager tones with a friend. Ten minutes later he returned to me. 'She is free now,' he said, in a way that implied he was conferring a great honour. I saw that she was sitting alone and that I might have a short audience if I liked.

"George Lewes certainly was one of the ugliest men I ever saw. But he had a pleasant voice and a sympathetic manner. His conversation was amusing. The Leweses used to take a drive together, almost every afternoon, sitting side by side in a shabby open landau with one horse that plodded its way slowly and methodically round Hyde Park, where I had met them and was attracted by their appearance long before I knew who they were.

"On Sunday afternoons they used to receive at home, at the Priory, Regent's Park. The house stood in a moderate sized London garden, but there was nothing interesting or worthy of record in the rooms, all of which were scantily furnished. The hostess sat by the fireside and in the chair next to her sat the last comer, who invariably yielded his place when a fresh visitor entered. The guest who had been deposed would then join the circle of other guests who were probably talking to Mr. Lewes. Two or three celebrities were usually present, two or three shy-looking philosophers in embryo—young men of large foreheads, dreamy eyes, ill-fitting clothes and boots with thick soles. These would sit in a corner of the room, listening but hardly ever joining in the general conversation. Moreover, they were never introduced to the other guests. Five o'clock tea came—cake in a silver basket. Everything was handed to us by Mr. Lewes so that we had no occasion to leave the magic circle."

March 23, 1880. "I have just come from a visit to the Priory—my first since the death of Mr. Lewes. I found everything little changed. The hostess, looking paler and more worn, perhaps, and wearing a white cap—not an absolute widow's cap—received me in her accustomed corner. The room was the same. A few visitors sat in the old places. I missed George Lewes and his cheery voice.

"Tennyson came in. I had a long talk with him which pleased us both. He was full of the fact that Ruskin had abused him for saying that a crushed daisy blushes red—meaning that it then shows the lower side of the petals. Ruskin called this a sentimental fallacy. Tennyson averred that Ruskin had no knowledge of daisies. Then ensued a long conversation about flowers in which George Eliot joined, too learnedly as it appeared to me to please Tennyson who, I thought, was rather desirous to be amused than instructed. He probably found some difficulty in understanding George Eliot, for she scarcely raises her voice above a whisper and several times during his visit Tennyson barked abruptly: 'I am very deaf, very deaf.'

"Of course nobody talked about books, except indeed that the pamphlets of the day with caricatures of Gladstone were mentioned, and one of them was shown to Tennyson, who acknowledged himself a Liberal in creed but at the present moment, owing to the critical state of political affairs, inclined to Conservatism. It has often struck me that, whereas it is allowed to talk to an artist about his pictures (and artists among themselves seldom talk about anything else), whilst a musician loves to argue about music, provided he be not pestered to sing or play, it is considered the lowest depths of bad manners, when conversing with a writer or a poet, to allude to his works, past, present or future. Perhaps I should say present and future only, for a delicate allusion to past triumphs is allowed, nay, acceptable. But why on earth are we told that it would be an unpardonable offence to ask George Eliot if she has begun a new novel, when we may enquire of Rubinstein as to his new opera? Or why should not George Eliot ask Tennyson what is the subject of his new poem, when Watts may urge Millais to show him his unfinished picture?"

Wednesday, April 28. "Varnishing day at the Grosvenor Gallery. I went in for an hour in the afternoon and found a good many artists there, some at work finishing, touching up or varnishing their own pictures; some standing moodily—an expression of discontent upon their features. Others arguing and talking, gesticulating and gossiping mostly about the merits of the Grosvenor *versus* the Royal Academy. In one part of the room, Mrs. Jopling and Mrs. Perugini were arm-in-arm, looking at Collier's portrait of his wife, the said picture having been taken down from the wall and placed temporarily against the door, whilst Mrs. Collier herself, looking like a bright and mischievous Bacchante in nineteenth-century costume, was seated opposite her own portrait, engaged in making a pen-and-ink sketch of it for Blackburn's illustrated catalogue. There were many arguments for and against a crimson rose which the painter had placed in the white dress in the portrait. I happened to have a yellow rose in my hand which was seized upon by Mrs. Jopling and pinned up against the picture while the unhappy painter, quickly surrounded by an amused group of friends, was made then and there to alter the colour of the rose, in spite of his hesitating protestations, for he does stammer terribly!

"In another part of the room the Tademas were congregated in front of Holman Hunt's portrait of his son—a portrait representing a young man in boating costume of plum-coloured velvet with a magenta necktie. The young man's head was lost in some trees, a bridge and a stream, while one thumb, the only visible part of his hand, was holding a large round straw hat. The frame of this picture is perhaps the most marvellous part of it. It represents apples and apple blossom carved in wood and highly polished.

" 'Have you heard what Val Prinsep, he say?' asks Tadema in his comical ascending scale of speech. 'He says that if the painter have not succeeded in his picture, he have succeeded in his frame, very apple-y!' Roaring with laughter, Tadema goes off to the next comer to repeat the joke."

Friday, April 30. "Signor Piatti came to dine with us. After dinner he and I played duets, both of us at sight, he playing violin sonatas, I accompanying him on the piano. Piatti is simple-minded, sensitive and easily offended. His character is proud and retiring. He withdraws from the admiration that his genius deserves. We played a little piece called 'Chant Religieux.' 'I like this piece,' said Piatti, smiling in his grey beard. 'I wrote it when I was young. I had just come to Paris and I only had one hundred francs in the world.'

" 'What did you do?' I asked, naturally enough.

" 'Liszt had heard of me,' replied Piatti: 'he came to see me. He said I must give a concert. He lent me a violoncello. I had none and I played at my concert.'

" 'And after that?'

" 'Ah! After that . . . ! It was all right then. But I like this little piece.'

"Piatti tells me stories of other musicians. Travelling, he once spent the night in the same room as Sivori, the violinist. He was suddenly waked by hearing what he thought was the hum of a persistent bluebottle fly, but which turned out to be his enthu-siastic bedfellow, who had got up in order to practise trills with the mute upon the bridge of his violin to dull the sound. He often slept in the same room with other impecunious musicians. It was a simple-minded German fellow-musician who equally woke him one night with a request to pack and start immediately, because the landlord told him that there was a land route from England to Ireland to which they were about to proceed! Piatti is a determined violin purchaser. In his lodging there is a violin case on every chair, under every sofa. There are violins swathed in flannel or even pieces of brown paper in every available corner."

CHAPTER TWENTY-EIGHT

ONE July afternoon in 1884, Sir James Linton, then President of the Royal Institute of Painters in Water Colours, walked across Hans Place, a quiet London square, and knocked at the door of the house numbered forty-one.

Blanche, whose smile seemed now to have something sad in it, welcomed the artist. After a few years of brilliant happiness a shock had ended the dream of her marriage. She had now parted from her husband and was living alone with her two daughters. Helen, fifteen years old, who had been keeping her mother company, ran upstairs to the room on the second floor that she shared with her sister, but neither Effie nor Miss Starie, a governess-companion, was there. After a short time Blanche went up from the drawing-room to her studio in order to get a picture that she wished Sir James to see. There was an almost perpendicular staircase to this studio, and because Blanche planned to leave for the country, the carpet had been removed and the steps were bare.

Helen heard her mother fetch the picture and start on her return journey to the drawing-room. There was a startled cry and a crash. The young girl rushed out from her room to see her mother lying prone on the landing below, having fallen right through a frail gate at the top. Helen and Sir James rushed to the rescue. They found her still tightly clutching the unframed picture she had gone to fetch. It was a study of a flower garden at Milverton Cottage, where Blanche had intended to go the next day, and showed beds of brilliant Shirley poppies planted on what the children called, in fun, the Giant's Grave. Beside the poppies stood a little black-gowned ghost of a person that was Helen.

At first it did not appear as if the hurt was serious, for although Blanche's face was cut and bleeding, she was able to

LADY LINDSAY.

sit up and speak, but later the doctors diagnosed a crushed shoulder and contusion of the brain. These injuries had the effect not of dulling sensitiveness but of increasing it, so that the patient's powers of hearing became unusually acute and a ray of light would cause intense cerebral pain.

For a time Helen felt a childish pleasure at being installed as guardian and nurse with blue bottles of lead lotion and laudanum. These mixtures were to be dabbed on with cotton-wool at intervals. Soon this satisfaction gave place to long and weary months of trial. It was only a short time ago that Blanche had passed through the ruin of her married life, and to this was now added physical suffering and shock. One day, as Helen embroidered a velvet binding for her mother's Book of Greek Gospels (Blanche preferred to read the Testament in Greek), she looked up and asked: "What lettering shall I work upon it?" Blanche answered: "He restoreth my soul."

Hans Place and its neighbourhood were at that time being transformed from a quiet old-world backwater into part of a new estate. Houses were being built or modernised. Blanche sent her daughter sallying out to beseech foremen of works at least to mitigate the sound. All this was in vain; the three women removed first to a house in Lowndes Square and later to a more distant abode in the relative quiet of St. John's Wood. The patient was taken through the streets in the dead of night before the market carts made their appearance, and on the second occasion the journey was broken for a pause at Lady Leslie's house in Stratford Place. The owner was away and dust-sheets covered all the furniture save in one room, where blazed a warm fire next to which young Helen, exhausted, fell asleep.

The house at St. John's Wood was of the small old-fashioned villa type, with verandahs and back and front gardens. Even here it was found necessary to stuff mattresses into the windows to keep out the distant roar of traffic. This was a house of strange silences and continual shadows, for daylight was never allowed to enter except through thicknesses of black gauze. For long months the two girls lived in what seemed to them a mine. The only light in Blanche's room came from a candle stub within a metal case, and even the fire had to be closely screened.

Blanche's existence alternated between long sleeps, mostly in the daytime, and moments of abnormal mental activity during which she would call in her daughter, Helen, and dictate whatever passed through her brain—memories of her childhood, poems and even chords of music. These things Helen was obliged to write down with the stub of a quickly sharpened pencil beside what light happened to filter through the crack of a badly closed shutter. In the evening it was the fire flickering behind the high screen that gave her just enough ghost-like illumination to read aloud, for she tried to quieten her mother's brain by translating Grimm's *Fairy Tales* from the German. It was very early one morning that Blanche called her daughter to her side to dictate to her a dream that she was later to make the title-poem of one of her volumes, *The King's Last Vigil*.

Months elapsed and then one morning Blanche went into the garden, where the pain of daylight drove her frantic, but time brought summer roses and peace came slowly back. Birds were a source of delight, and her room generally harboured a tame bullfinch (as in little Arthur's days) and the bird was often liberated. The first years of convalescence were made easier by the faithfulness of friends. Sir Edward Burne-Jones caused one of his large new pictures to be brought by the vanmen to her on its way for exhibition. Ferdinand de Rothschild, her favourite cousin, sent her boxes of fairy-like orchids, whilst her aunt Louisa often welcomed her at Aston Clinton.

By the summer of 1887 Blanche was sufficiently recovered to give small dinner parties at Hans Place and to take a fairly active interest in the London season. She still painted, though less frequently, because it strained her eyes, and for some time she was unable to bear her beloved Stradivarius against her crushed shoulder, and took instead to playing an instrument known as a *machette*, while Helen played the guitar.

HELEN LINDSAY.
She went to her first ball at Lansdowne House when London was garlanded for Queen Victoria's Jubilee.

That season London was garlanded for Queen Victoria's Jubilee, and the streets were filled with flags and crimson cloth. Blanche felt well enough to watch the procession, and was invited to do so from her cousin Ferdinand's house in Piccadilly, while her daughter Helen was invited to that of Louisa, Lady Rothschild.

Helen left home that morning soon after seven o'clock. She stood looking down from the balcony of Lady Rothschild's home when she suddenly saw her mother's carriage wedged tightly in the traffic of Piccadilly. Mother and daughter smiled at one another and Helen was just thinking of hurrying down when, after speaking to a policeman, Blanche got out and started to walk the few steps to her destination. Helen could not see her walk because of the high paling in front of the house, but she could follow the little blue-grey feather in her mother's dainty bonnet.

Two days later Helen went to her first ball—that given by Lady Rosebery at Lansdowne House. Everyone was in Court dress, and the uniforms of the Royalty and of the Indian princes against the rose-covered walls of the brilliantly lit ballroom impressed the young girl. Helen saw a great many people whom she knew and was introduced to many whom she did not know. There was little dancing except among the Royalties, who danced with each other, and Helen found talking a more amusing occupation. She returned to Hans Place, where her mother was anxious to hear all her adventures, and the two women sat up talking until close on four o'clock.

CHAPTER TWENTY-NINE

IT was not until the dawn of the twentieth century that Blanche once more put her thoughts on paper. Millais and Burne-Jones had gone. Watts still rose at four o'clock each summer morning, not to be robbed of a moment's daylight. "I have nearly reached Titian's age," he said to Blanche. "I am in my eighty-seventh year!"

"And still at work?"

"Oh yes. What else could I do? I hope I have never to stop. When I cannot work any more I shall leave."

He smiled as he spoke. Blanche told him how, two months before, in the archives at Venice, she had seen a letter of Titian's, and how she had been struck by the resemblance in their writings.

Watts swung round. "Really? Do you mean that really?"

He still wore his old painting coat known affectionately as 'Squalid.' It was a friend of many years' standing. When he married, his wife was so shocked at the sight of its ragged lining that she persuaded the maid to reline it.

"It is squalid," said the maid. But she relined it. Later the outside became so disreputable that Watts surreptitiously persuaded the girl to make a new outside to fit the lining, so that his dear coat might go on.

These moments with Watts left a tinge of sadness. He was almost the last of the great Pre-Raphaelite school. Blanche's thoughts would go back to those afternoons that Sir Frederick Leighton used to give in his crowded studio, lit by one great window. What a host of celebrities gathered in that room! Tall camellia trees in full red bloom and saffron-tinted azaleas half hid the pictures that would be later shown at the Royal Academy. Closing her eyes, she could see again those pictures on their easels. Leighton's figures, when but half completed, were often

232

modelled in subdued monochrome, and this seemed to send them into a far-away and ghostly twilight. Madame Neruda and Joachim would play Bach's concerto for two violins. First the *motif* was taken up by one, then by the other, each performer merging in turn into a mere accompanist, only to rise again immediately and take the lead once more. Around the momentarily silent piano, in front of the fireplace, were grouped: Charles Hallé, who had probably played some of Chopin's waltzes; Piatti, one hand resting on the neck of his beloved 'cello, and tall, black-bearded De Soria, from whose liquid voice "Bonjour, Suzon" would shortly be demanded. A knot of painters stood hard by: Watts, Millais, Poynter, Burne-Jones, the Tademas, Val Prinsep and Holman Hunt, their picturesque heads in full relief against the dusky walls, where gilt patches of decoration shimmered obscurely and multitudinous sketches and studies were barely discernible amongst the lengthening shadows. Robert Browning was certain to be near, closely following each bar of music and just perceptibly beating time.

These things brought a host of other memories flowing back. Quickly she put them on paper, thus:

"There was a dinner party I remember during which the conversation turned upon rhyme.

" 'I'll bet you anything you like,' said Millais, taking a survey of the company and earnestly scanning each face: 'I'll bet you anything you like that everybody here to-night has scribbled some rhymes, good, bad or indifferent, in early youth. I plead guilty myself to begin with.'

"Every man present looked down at his plate in a sheepish, shamefaced way. The women laughed.

"It was at Millais's house that I met Lord Houghton for the last time. He and Robert Browning were dining at Palace Gate; there was no other guest but myself. After dinner we sat in the studio. It was bitterly cold and Lady Millais retired to another room, but bade me stay on with the men if I liked. I sat wrapped in a fur coat unwilling to withdraw. Millais smoked a short pipe, talking impetuously as usual; Browning's white hair and beard shone out in the firelight as he answered his host's remarks in a ponderous and reflective way; Lord Houghton, small and spare, wearing a black velvet skull-cap, was plunged in a deep arm-chair, mostly listening.

"Millais, during the last few years of his life, would ask me to come and see his unfinished pictures and offer my criticism. 'Consider it done,' was generally his curt remark when I had suggested some alteration.

"Once he wanted to introduce a rose into part of his picture without delay. 'Pink—just like the one in your hat,' he said, laughing. 'I could paint from that quite well.' I therefore unpinned the rose.

" 'As for paint,' said Millais to me in his joyous, debonair way, as he painted the rose, 'I will say this for myself—there's no fellow living who knows better than I what paint can do. I won't talk about anything else, but I do know how far paint will go and how to put it on the canvas, and I don't care who knows that I say so!'

"Suddenly he turned around and said to me: 'What do you think I've been doing? I have been writing poetry.' He then began talking of his intentions for future pictures. One composition was to represent the Saviour, as a Child, lying asleep on the steps of the Temple after His discussions with the doctors. The steps were to be of white marble, and the hand of the sleeping Jesus was to hold white lilies. Another intention of his was the vision of St. Hubert, which apparently he had wished all his life to express on canvas. He had fixed upon the exact spot in a dense forest of fir-trees in Scotland which was to form the background. I told him I had treated this same subject in blank verse. 'But it is unfinished and in the rough,' I said. 'Never mind,' said he, 'bring it, I implore you . . . bring it to-morrow.'

"That promise could not be fulfilled. He was taken seriously ill. When next I went to Palace Gate I found a piece of paper fastened to the house door announcing that he had passed away a few hours before.

"Sad indeed was the sight of the procession which some days later I saw on my way to the funeral at St. Paul's . . . the big palette and paint brushes swathed in crêpe. Sadder still the ceremony beneath the Cathedral dome—more cheerless, less beautiful than had it been at Westminster Abbey. The service was half finished when Sir Edward Burne-Jones came in and took a place at no great distance from where I was. After he had stood there a few minutes, during some solemn singing, I saw him grow deathly pale. He seemed to sway and I quietly left my seat and went to stand beside him. Tears were coursing slowly down his cheeks. 'It is terrible, terrible,' he murmured. 'I cannot bear it.' Then he added prophetically: 'Morris's turn next, and then mine.' A couple of years had not passed before those sad words came true.

"Lady Millais asked me to go and see her. She wept as she told me how it had been at the end. The terrible malady that killed him had for some time robbed him of speech. Shortly before his death, as she sat beside him, he wrote on his slate: 'I would like to have the little Spanish crucifix.' This crucifix was small and made of gold, with three or four drop pearls suspended from it. She had given it to him many years before. When she fetched it, he wrote again: 'Fasten it to my wrist,' and she tied it on with a piece of black ribbon. 'I want something to think of,' he wrote again. 'The hours are very long.' Then he took his wife in his arms and embraced her. After that, except for what was needful, he did not write upon his slate at all. But a very little while before his death, he wrote: 'You can take the crucifix off my wrist; I shall not want it now.'"

*   *   *   *   *

"At my elbow is a note from Sir Edward Burne-Jones. He wrote it one foggy November day. 'I have been at work ever since August began at one of the pictures of the sleeping palace—and this is now the fourteenth week and it looks as if it were

still the fourteenth day.' He made innumerable and careful
studies of every portion of his pictures, slurring (scamping, as it
is termed) nothing. If a piece of drapery, however unimportant,
did not please him, he would rearrange and re-draw it again and
again. The same with a hand, or arm, or foot, or flower. I sat
for him once for a couple of hours on the top of a high ladder
for the head of the angel in his painting of the Annunciation.
The sketch that he made was done with a raw-umber chalk pencil.

"His studios at The Grange were bare whitewashed rooms, full
of big easels and pictures in various stages of progress. On the
walls, sometimes on the floor, were written the addresses of
models. He often wore the cotton smock affected by French
painters. The Grange was an old house. For a long time no
jerry-built villas or subway stations dared to approach it. Then
some new houses rose up at the back of the countrified garden
and threatened to overlook his apple-trees and hawthorns. This
made him build a garden studio with a high roof capable of
accommodating his larger works as well as serving to shut out
the ugly row of bricks and mortar and prying windows.

"But at last arrived the great wheel of Earl's Court Exhibition
and that could not be shut out! It revolved against the grey sky
in the very face of the indignant artist, who was never brought
to view it with the merest toleration. One day Carr and Halle,
directors of the New Gallery, going their round of visits to
painters, looked in at The Grange. They bade the servant tell
Sir Edward that two gentlemen had called to ask if he would like
to take shares in the Great Wheel. Without waiting to put down
palette, brushes or mahlstick, out from his studio flew Burne-
Jones, dashing fiercely down the stairs, pale and speechless with
anger to meet—his friends!

"That Big Wheel really tortured him. He once sent me a little
note that began: 'Whit Tuesday—and to-morrow is Whit-
Wednesday—and it will go on being Whit all the week—noise,
drink, bits of paper, East Wind and the Big Wheel. How I hate
these feasts!'

"Burne-Jones and his wife were very kind to me when my marriage turned definitely unhappy. They allowed me to go and paint early in the morning at The Grange in a studio next to the one in which he worked and afterwards to stay to luncheon. In those days their daughter was still unmarried. I remember her vividly, particularly in the garden one summer afternoon. She sat swinging herself on the low branches of an apple-tree, the blossoms all above and around her. She was dressed in a cotton gown of that blue that her father liked so much, and she wore a big straw hat. I thought her one of the most beauteous beings I had ever seen, with her wonderful eyes and exquisite oval face.

"Then on Sunday I was invited to supper, a simple and informal meal, to which only a few close friends were admitted. No late hours were kept. Sometimes a bottle of some wonderful Cyprus wine was opened and Burne-Jones would exclaim: 'It is just what must have been drunk by Aphrodite, goddess of love, when she rose from the sea.'

"One day when he was painting, he said, laughingly: 'I never could show anyone how to paint. Now, watch carefully how I do this. If you were not looking, I should certainly do it in quite a different way!'

"Burne-Jones and the poet, William Morris, breakfasted together every Sunday morning. They never gave this habit up, even in illness, till the hand of death parted the poet and teller of sagas from the painter who was so much at one with him in thought."

CHAPTER THIRTY

EACH succeeding year of the new century robbed Blanche of more friends. "Pleasant it is in youth," she wrote at this time, "to enjoy friendship with those who are considerably older than ourselves; yet the penalty has to be paid. If we continue to live, they must needs pass on before us, and in after-years we become painfully conscious of many an empty place, and of the silence of many a kindly voice. Only memory remains."

There was the funeral of Cecil Rhodes and the death of Lord Kimberley. Strange, because Rhodes was called by the humorists Sir Cecil of Kimberley. Blanche met Cecil Rhodes several times. She got on well with him, though he was said to be a woman-hater. One evening at dinner she asked him for some of his views about women. "Their great fault," he answered, "is that they cannot apprehend the affairs of men."

She now received few guests, though she read considerably. The æsthetic craze was over. Oscar Wilde, who by his sunflowers and by his gross exaggeration had covered the movement with ridicule, was dead. How well Blanche remembered the day when Mr. Tom Taylor, at one of her parties in the Grosvenor Gallery, brought a friend to her, saying: "This young fellow has just won the Newdigate prize: I venture to introduce him to you." That was Oscar Wilde!

Blanche was not bitter. The Pre-Raphaelite movement had already served its purpose long before Wilde butted in. She had just been reading his *De Profundis* and was impressed by its beautiful English and its incomparable style. But the mind that dictated it was warped.

In the spring of 1905 Sir Lewes Morris came to see her. They talked of old friends. "People say," observed he, "that Tennyson and Browning were great friends. It was not so. Tennyson said to me one day: 'That fellow Browning writes himself down every day more and more.' "

At this time Lady Halle was staying with Blanche at Hans Place. One morning Queen Alexandra telegraphed for the great violinist to come to see her. The Queen was very fond of Lady Halle, and loved to talk Danish with her. She now showed her a letter she had received from her sister, the Dowager Empress of Russia. "We are all doomed," wrote the Czar's mother.

When Lady Halle came back to Hans Place, she and Blanche spent the evening quietly together. Lady Halle played magnificently on Blanche's violin for nearly two hours in her study. Standing in the middle of the room, she played piece after piece from her faultless memory: Bach first, and then several studies by Paganini which Blanche had never heard before. In a pause, Blanche wished she would play some part of the Mendelssohn concerto, but she did not say so. Suddenly Lady Halle struck up the last movement, the Allegro. A wave of thought had impelled her!

As they sat in the half-dark drawing-room, Lady Halle started talking about Hans Andersen. She had known him well both at Copenhagen and at Christiania. When she was quite a child Hans Andersen listened enrapt to her playing, and when she greeted him with a smile of recognition after the concert, he stood up quickly in his place and made her a low and ceremonious bow. He gave her a volume of his stories and wrote on the fly-leaf, together with her name:

"To you who understand the secret of legends."

He was vain and could not endure to be passed over. He lived alone and was poor and had a great dread of being buried alive. Every evening he would pin on his night-shirt a notice saying:

"I only appear to be dead!"

After Lady Halle retired for the night, Blanche took up a copy of Tennyson's *Enid and Geraint*. After a few minutes she put the book down: it brought too many poignant memories.

Closing her eyes, she saw herself a girl of fifteen listening to her mother reading these words aloud to her dying father at Brighton, whilst through the open windows came the monotonous stroke of waves upon the pebbly shore, beating time, as it seemed, to the metrical words of the legend, the picturesque fancy and magic colour of which would weave about her heart a thrall from which she had never altogether been freed.

She remembered an evening at Little Holland House when she was first introduced to the poet. In her youthful admiration she had followed Mrs. Prinsep and Tennyson as they walked across the lawn and she eagerly awaited the moment when the great man should speak. Her childish folly caused her a dreadful disappointment when she overheard the poet's words, spoken in a deep sonorous voice:

"Is there mutton for dinner?"

And as the book lay unread on her lap, and she mused on, she remembered how only a short time later she first met Sir Edwin Landseer—small of stature, with a face and head that somehow reminded her of a lion. She used to laugh at the way he would suddenly twist up his light grey hair, moustaches and beard, with a dexterous movement of the hand, and imitate the roar of a wild beast. One afternoon he discussed with her a novel called *The Woman in White*, and shortly afterwards she asked him what he was painting.

"The Woman in White," he answered; and would tell her no more, but at the next exhibition of the Royal Academy there appeared a picture by him representing a beautiful white mare.

These quiet evenings were a great satisfaction to Blanche. She would still meet Joachim and would then remind him of those days at Mentmore when he would play on his violin, wandering from room to room in the big house, while the few other guests present would follow him as though they were the children and he was the Pied Piper of Hamelin. He was a big man with a fine presence and a kindly heart, and the music he made was like himself, broad and deep in tone, devoid of fireworks, yet accomplishing difficult passages with a sort of grand and quiet ease, especially in his majestic chords and harmonies. One winter's day he had hired some skates and attempted for the first time to make his way on the ice. But he speedily came crashing down.

"Ah, sir!" said the vendor of skates, running to his assistance. "It ain't so easy as fiddling!"

Many years before, at Paris, on a bright sunshiny day during the International Exhibition, Blanche remembered seeing the dark procession of the funeral of the blind old King of Hanover crossing the Place de la Concorde. The King of Hanover had chosen to be godfather to Joachim.

The great violinist often played to her. She only once accompanied him. That was at Aston Clinton. They played Spohr's "Barcarolle." She said to him: "I am rather nervous."

"That doesn't matter," he answered, "as long as you don't play any wrong notes."

CHAPTER THIRTY-ONE

SHORTLY after she was presented at Court, Blanche's elder daughter, Effie, went to Mildmay in the north of London to become a deaconess.

From a parish in Brentford, once a famous coaching station, then a grimy bottle-neck on the road through Hounslow to the West, came a clergyman to Mildmay in search of a deaconess. Effie met this clergyman across the parlour table and agreed to look into the proposition. One fine summer day an older deaconess took her to Brentford, where the matter was settled. The two women refused tea for fear of inconveniencing the bachelor cleric and returned by river steamboat down the Thames from Kew Bridge. In due course Effie settled at Brentford to take up her duties and the Rev. T. Selby Henrey was more than satisfied with his new helper. A year later they were married quietly near Hull before leaving for Norway on their honeymoon.

*   *   *   *   *

I was born of that union on the fourteenth of August, 1901, at Brentford, in a room overlooking the Thames. Its fast-running tide swirled past the low wall at the bottom of our garden. When the tide was high, the yellow, troubled water would gently lap over the top of the wall and make puddles round the old mulberry tree, but when it was low tide, that arm of the river that was between the garden and the eyot shrank into thick, slimy mud and a beach of little pebbles.

That was doubtless my first view of the world. All day long the hammers of the barge-makers never ceased their monotonous, high-pitched tapping, for there was a great congregation of these barges at the extreme end of our garden wall, and if one of these should so much as stray from its moorings and bump up against our domain, my father would run out and make a great ado.

When evening fell and the barge-makers ceased their din, big white swans would sail majestically past and the kingfisher would perch on his accustomed tree-stump. Men would row across to the eyot and cut the osiers to twine them into baskets, and if lucky one of my father's more favoured parishioners would be allowed to come armed with a fishing-rod and throw his line over the side of our wall.

At night-time all this wide expanse between ourselves and the trees of Kew Gardens, on the opposite side, would glitter with a myriad coloured lights, for this was a highway for river traffic, and every tug whistled and shrieked as it started its journey downstream to the sea, with its load of barges behind. Then towards midnight from the top of the lilac-trees in our garden the two round eyes of a barn owl would look down upon our sleeping home and his sad cry would echo through the air.

Behind the house, or rather in front of it, at the top of the slope, ran the High Street, which was so narrow and so congested that it was known as the Brentford "bottle-neck." Tramways clanged their bells impatiently, the dray horses from the brewery up the street strained at their loads and over all this in summer the air reeked with the acrid smell from the gasworks.

But our home lay like a pearl in its river setting and in front of us was nothing but water and trees. It was an old house, so old that nobody could tell for certain its age. Without a doubt it had been a farmhouse in the days when stage coaches from the West of England changed their horses in the High Street. The kitchen was reminiscent of those where Royalists hid their menfolk in the chimney stacks, and indeed, King Charles is said to have stayed there. The walls were thick and some of them were panelled. Clanging chains and heavy locks bolted our doors, and iron shutters protected our windows at night.

Our house was covered in creeper that stretched its tentacles over every inch of mellow brick, and the roots of it were as fat as a man's fist. The foliage was so luxuriant that it came pushing through our schoolroom window together with the vine and the climbing fig, that never did more than produce sour and stunted fruit, but filled the house with a rich, aromatic scent.

The garden was not large, but the long view across the river to Kew gave it depth. Lilies of the valley grew like weeds, probably because in winter time there were days when the whole of the soil was under water, so that the goldfish in the pond that my father had made swam out into midstream and were replaced by minnows, and the cellar was turned into a lake. Whatever the reason, there was one big bed that stretched the whole length of the garden, where the lilies of the valley grew thick and the soil suited them so well that they had to be dug out of the gravel paths. Just under my father's study window was a quince-tree that produced great globes of furry gold and on the other side of the lawn a long trellis of loganberries that my mother would pick for us on occasion, placing the fruit on a fig-leaf that she would bring to the schoolroom after morning lessons.

There were small, white cherries difficult of access and apples in profusion, but the fruit that we liked best were the big black mulberries that as soon as they were ripe flopped off the branches and fell in little pools of juice on the grass underneath. There were roses and lavender and sweet-smelling verbena that my father would pinch between his forefinger and thumb and place under my nose. There were sunflowers up against our river wall, and, best of all, a whole line of evening primroses that would open as you watched them and make a hedge of gold in the setting sun.

My earliest recollection in this garden was marching behind Mr. Stamp, one of my father's churchwardens, who could tell stories of the South African War and who was a good amateur conjuror when necessity arose, for he was the first man I ever saw produce a rabbit from a hat and an egg from under his sleeve. His warfare was gentle and kind and my sister and I took turns to be the Boer spy hunted for amid the undergrowth of the lilac bushes.

My sister was three years older than I and wiser in everything. She wore printed cotton frocks and her hair fell in magnificent curls. We had a French governess, and nurses of different nationalities who changed with great frequency. Mostly, I think, they were German and they took us out for walks in the afternoon, whereas our governess came only in the morning.

Chance had played a strange hand in choosing Brentford for my mother's home. It was within easy walking distance of Gunnersbury Park. She herself had been there many times as a child, driving to visit Baron Lionel, by then an ageing man who propelled himself in a chair, and his wife, Charlotte. Gunnersbury was now the property of their youngest son Leopold. As children we were permitted to use this place just as often as we liked and we took full advantage of it.

To reach Gunnersbury Park one had to follow the High Street for half a mile between the brewery and the gasworks on one side, my father's church on the other, and a bit higher up, the waterworks with a couple of reservoirs and a tower that was taller and uglier than any other in the neighbourhood. Here was Kew Bridge. Then a sharp turn to the left just beyond the railroad and there was a lane with hawthorn bushes and dandelions. There were still market gardens and orchards around here resisting the factory invasion until the bitter end.

Gunnersbury Park was the most wonderful place I ever saw, but then it was all our own, for we seldom met a soul except Mr. Thomas, the lodge-keeper, or a stray gardener. Mr. Thomas's lodge was a stone building almost square where we were always welcome, and just beyond an avenue of chestnut-trees he had fixed us up a swing. After that came a sweeping view of trim flower-beds and the lake bordered by mounds that in spring turned yellow with primroses and an old boat-house in the depths of which were dark, damp caverns where the water lapped against the sides. We were not allowed on the lake, but there was nothing to stop us from sitting in the boat that rode the waves within this eerie place. Swans with long, fierce necks and black feathers wandered under the crab-apple-trees and gave vent to raucous and uncomely cries.

Every afternoon we could change our walks. There was the big field beyond the lake where the sheep grazed as peacefully as if they had been in the heart of the country, and the aviary where thousands of gaily coloured birds from every corner of the globe screeched and chirruped behind their wire netting. There were the stables and the Japanese garden that was filled with narrow rivulets and small stone bridges and bamboo canes that grew to twice our height. Here the palm-trees were covered with sacking in winter, and the flower-beds were made in the form of baskets with heliotrope round the edges and climbing rose-trees to form the handles.

There was another lake near the house with smooth, clean edges. Ducks gathered on its shores under the shadow of an old Greek temple, flanked by cedar-trees that in the evening would be silhouetted against the sky. This temple had cool, white walls and a mighty echo answered our voices—an echo so monstrous that we would flee from it in terror. On the other side was Princess Amelia's bath, half hidden from view by ivy and brush-wood. It had not changed since the days when Hannah stayed with her mother at Gunnersbury. Amelia's dressing-room was the best hiding-place in the whole park, with its walls of flint stones and shells.

My sister and I would return from these excursions to walk on either side of our nurse, who wheeled the new addition to the family—a one-year-old Blanche—in a perambulator. I remember clearly the day she was born, for she came into the world four years after me. Kitty, my elder sister, and I were left alone in the schoolroom and we had hit on the idea of producing a snow-storm by clambering on high chairs and spitting furiously into space. The 'snowstorm' came to an end with the news of Blanche's arrival. We argued for some time whether this must be con-strued as good or bad news. We were afraid the newcomer would take up too much of our mother's affection.

GUNNERSBURY PARK.

"An old Greek Temple flanked by cedar trees that in the evening would be silhouetted against the sky." A hundred years saw no change here.

Blanche was not yet of any useful age in the park. We would leave her with the nurse, who sat on a tree-stump reading a German novel while she gently rocked the perambulator. My sister and I had other things to do. We had built a Red Indian wigwam with dead branches and thatched it with newly mown hay.

Sometimes we ran into our cousin Leopold himself. He had a magnificent head, with laughing eyes and white moustaches.

He would take us back to the house and offer us chocolate cake, and four months ahead of time he would ask us what we would like for Christmas. This necessitated long conferences. The gifts were always princely; if we requested a book we would receive a library. I remember once asking for a fairy tale. I received twenty-four marvellously bound volumes—each in a different colour, and we read every single story many times over. I have one of these volumes at my elbow as I write. I once asked for a cactus—I cannot imagine why—and received a greenhouse so large that it took two men to carry it. I proceeded to heat this greenhouse that I thought ought to be a hothouse, by pouring boiling water into old coffee cans with holes punched in the lids. This system of central heating was not successful. Most of the rarer species of prickly plants shrivelled up and died.

We wheeled our hoops in the park and wore round hats of panama, fastened under the chin by elastic that we chewed to bits. Our German nurses were mostly good-natured and, anyway, we did not fear them. But our French governess was not to be trifled with. We took all our lessons in French and she taught us remarkably well. She came from Falaise in Normandy, home of William the Conqueror, and she made me love that land like my second country. She was to have been called Mademoiselle, but that was too much for me at the tender age when first I came under her spell. The best I could do was to call her 'Mallalal,' and that was the name she was evermore known by. We came under her jurisdiction almost immediately after breakfast. We took this meal alone, although we occasionally looked into the dining-room while my father and mother were breakfasting. This room was on the ground floor. It overlooked the garden and had three big windows of which one, near the kitchen garden, was entirely hidden by creepers that turned copper colour in autumn. The walls were papered with green. I believe there was some fine panelling behind, but nobody ever took the trouble to bring it to light. Anyway, the green wallpaper proved an excellent background for a whole number of paintings that my grand-mother had copied from Old Masters during her journeys to Munich and to Venice. There was a piano and a low table on which stood the little model frigate that Arthur had made at Brighton in the fifties. My father was always the last down to breakfast. He would present his cheek to my mother to show her the perfection of his shave and then he would cut off a small square of toast and marmalade and hand me this delicacy as I stood with my head just reaching the top of the table.

Mallalal arrived—I never quite knew from where—at nine o'clock. Her ring at the front-door bell was short and peremptory. She would walk up the stairs under the cuckoo clock that my father had brought back from Switzerland and arrive on our landing just as the cuckoo came out to sing the hour. My sister and I would be seated on either side of the schoolroom table, with pencils and books all arranged on the green cloth, and as Mallalal opened the little gate that my mother had fixed across the top steps so that we should not fall down the stairs, our eyes would become grave and expectant. Then the schoolroom door would be pushed wide and Mallalal would say:

"*Bonjour, mes enfants.*"

Without wasting time she would take her seat between us— that is to say, at the top of the table, and we would read, alter-nately, a few verses from the New Testament in French.

That was the start of the lesson.

Our schoolroom also looked across the river. We ended by not hearing the tapping of the barge-makers, and the noise certainly did not inconvenience our lessons. Our schoolroom was plainly decorated with half a wall filled with books, a piano that was seldom used and a big coal fire guarded by an immense fender, higher than ourselves, because my father was always frightened we should fall in.

Blanche did not come to these lessons, because she was four years younger and still very small. I slipped out to see her one morning and found her hugging a sixpence. I offered her a penny for the sixpence, pointing out that my coin was much larger than hers and, because it was new, the burnished brass flashed in the sun. She accepted the deal and thanked me for my kindness, until she was asked later by my mother what had happened to her sixpence, and then my fraud was exposed!

At midday we closed our school books and went out for a walk. Quite often Mallalal would walk one mile along the High Street in the direction of Gunnersbury and then come back.

She liked Kew Gardens. It meant turning sharply to the left by our gate and walking past a soap-works to the ferry. That soap-works had a devastating smell. The ferry was at the spot where the ancient Britons are supposed to have defended the north banks of the Thames from the assault of the Romans under Julius Cæsar. Every now and then Roman spear-heads and daggers were fished out of the mud at the bottom of the river. An old Charon used to stand beside a heavy oar-boat ready to row us over to the other side for a few pence. At low tide the water went down and the mud came up and this necessitated Charon putting long planks from the landing-stage to his boat across which we walked gingerly, as the weight of our bodies sent the slime oozing up on either side of the wood. When we had reached the other side of the river we were in Surrey, somewhere half-way between Kew and Richmond, and the country was lovely.

Mallalal timed our walks to perfection, as, indeed, she timed her own arrival in the morning. We would be back at the top of our slope at five minutes before one exactly. We would troop up to the bathroom in order to wash our hands and brush our hair before the gong went. We all lunched together. My father would ask if we had received any ducks' eggs that morning or whether, on the contrary, we had been deserving of any good mark. When the pudding came along, my mother asked us if we wanted a second helping, but we had an idea that our governess did not approve of this manifestation of greed and I think we generally refused. She watched our manners closely, and we were never allowed to accept the last cutlet or the last pancake on the dish.

After lunch Mallalal went home and we were handed into the care of our nurse. This is the time when we made a bee-line for Gunnersbury Park. I remember one of these German nurses, in particular, who received at Christmas large parcels of marzipan and black sausage that she distributed with generosity.

It was in the evening that we saw most of our parents. My father's study was down three or four steps leading from the hall. It was a relatively new wing to the old farm-house and a big, pleasant room with a door that led straight into the garden. My father owned a big roll-top bureau and a large schoolmaster's chair and desk combined, at which he never sat but stood. The space between the stool and that part on which he wrote made an excellent hiding-place. My mother would sit on a sofa drawn up near the chair and either knit or read my father's letters back to him. I do not think that he ever sent a letter that she had not first read. He would then say: "Have you put the tick?" And she would put a little tick with her pencil to show that she had taken cognisance of that particular letter and passed it as being correct.

My father had a safe in his study next to the garden door. I do not think he ever kept more in this than papers and a few pounds' worth of silver, but each night, before we left, he would lock the safe and then make great efforts to test the handle by pulling it forward. At times we would be called in to give him a hand, but the safe was much bigger than ourselves.

In summer my father and mother would sometimes give parties in our garden. There were those at which most of the guests turned out to be dear, good souls in black-beaded bonnets. At others members of the local Conservative club would arrive escorted by my father. These festivities generally took place after I had been dismissed for the night, but happily my window overlooked the garden and from my bed I enjoyed a privileged view. There would be masses of strawberries and cream and buns and a loud brass band, and Mr. Stamp would arrive with his conjuring apparatus. Then as night fell the little coloured lamps that we had all helped to fix in the loganberry bushes were lit and the place was a real enchantment.

I was sometimes taken to London to call on my grandmother. She still lived in Hans Place. Her study was filled with old books and fine pictures, but I was generally called upon to recite a poem that Mallalal had specially taught me some days beforehand. I would then be told to sit on the Persian carpet and keep still. Sometimes she would send me out to the big store at the back of Hans Place with her secretary, who would be authorised to buy me whatever I liked best. I once fell in love with a trumpet and, blowing this instrument with gusto, I returned to my grandmother's study. She must have had a real affection for me not to rise horror-stricken at the appalling row I made and her beloved Stradivarius must have shivered in its case in the corner of the room! At times she would ask me what I had learnt and would recall her own lessons with Arthur's tutor. She would also question me about Gunnersbury, which she had so often visited.

I remember my grandmother most clearly at Froyle, where she had a home in the country. I recall going down in the train with my mother and my aunt and how they both spent the whole of the journey trying to make me memorise that French tongue-twister: "*Ton thé t'a-t-il ôté ta toux.*" I could not fathom this sentence and was unable to memorise it. The idea was that I should recite it to my grandmother. Much later I realised the reason. These words would have reminded her of that journey to Pau with her brother, Arthur, just after he had fallen from his pony and injured his spine. It was on Twelfth Night, I think, that her mother had also tried to make her memorise these words, but she had been quite unable to do so and was carried off to bed crying. I do not know whether I wept about my own failure, but I know that for a long time I wondered what it had all been about and why my mother and my aunt should have wanted me to repeat this gibberish to my grandmother.

I ran fairly wild at Froyle. It was a beautiful house and an absolute museum of lovely things. My grandmother's personality filled any room, but her quick mind was apt to frighten me as a child. Nevertheless, I was happy in her company and only once incurred her wrath.

She had taken me in her carriage to visit some friends for tea. It was a large house, and because the weather was fine tea was served on a wide terrace from which one had a long view across country. I soon left my grandmother's side and inspected the guests with interest. The terrace was fairly crowded, but in a corner, leaning slightly over the balustrade, was a young man taking stray shots with an air-gun into the wood beyond.

I approached him with interest. It was the first time I had ever seen a man shooting. He looked down at me and said: "Would you like to have a shot?"

"I certainly would," I answered.

He put his gun in my hand. I rested the barrel on the balustrade while he held the butt with his hand and when everything was set I pulled the trigger.

At that very moment my grandmother arrived on the scene.

We drove back to Froyle in her carriage. I knew from her face that I was in for it. She held her sunshade over her head, remained quite dignified, and, for some reason or other, gave me a severe dressing down!

* * * * *

At the beginning of every August we went to Rottingdean for our holidays. The journey started from the platform of Kew Bridge station that was the nearest to our house My father would line us all up in front of the luggage and count first us and then trunks, the wicker baskets, the hold-alls and the bundles of walking-sticks and umbrellas. We took a slow train from here to Clapham Junction, where we waited for the fast train to Brighton. But while we waited we would all be counted again!

In those days there was a horse omnibus from Brighton to Rottingdean. It carried the letters as well as passengers, and had the coat of arms emblazoned upon it with the words: "Royal Mail." Its entry into the village was heralded by the guard, who would blow his bugle, and whenever we heard this we ran out to its stopping-place outside Mr. Coe's chemist shop. Before returning to Brighton the omnibus would make a sort of processional tour round the pond. We made friends with the guard and were often allowed to ride round with him during this performance. Everybody would come out to see the four horses swing round the corner. We would stop at the church and outside Lady Burne-Jones's house, where as children we were always welcome.

This journey took only a few minutes and we would not have missed it for anything.

Our house was in the main street and still stands with its white bow windows. There was a large garden behind filled with lavender bushes and apple-trees and there was a little arbour seat. At this time my mother had been advised to make me drink sour milk and every morning she would hand me a glass full of this nauseous stuff. I told her that I could perhaps drink it better if I were left alone in the garden, but the more I looked at it, the less I liked it. It struck me that I could empty my glass behind the arbour without much fear of detection, and after I had done this I came back to be greeted with effusion. This went on for the best part of a month, until one day my father and mother took it into their heads to spend five minutes in the arbour. The sun was shining and there arose the most appalling stench from behind the rose bushes. My mother made a closer inspection and found the burying ground of her sour milk and I was duly punished.

It was at Rottingdean that my father decided to cut off his moustache. The day he cut this manly appendage I met him walking solemnly down the stairs before breakfast and rushed up to my mother with the news that there was a strange man in the house! I was truly sorry that he had cut it off. They were long moustaches of the period that suited him admirably.

In the morning we sat on the sands and watched my father swim. He stayed in the water for nearly an hour each day.

Rottingdean was a real village then. No trippers ever came to mar its peace. The omnibus that carried the mail to Brighton was the only link with urban life. The road to Newhaven was deserted. There were no signs of life but a couple of coast-guards' cottages under the shadow of a flagpole at Telescombe. There was a cove where we used to walk occasionally and take dips in the water, sure of never seeing a living soul. On the other side of the dusty chalk road the undulating downs were covered with blackberry bushes laden with fruit.

My father always offered us a drive to Newhaven for my birth-day, that fell during the holidays. I was taken to a toyshop near the harbour, where I was allowed to choose my own present, but my greatest thrill of all was the drive back with the coachman on his box seat. When I was allowed to hold the reins, life held no greater joys.

Only once did we not go to Rottingdean for our holidays and then, for some reason, we went to Folkestone. That summer my father took a house overlooking the harbour. It was a tall, rambling place commanding a magnificent view. My father and mother took an instant dislike to it, but we found enjoyment in watching the cross-Channel ships that lay just below our window, and we regulated our bedtime each evening by the siren of the out-going Ostend packet. We took with us to Folkestone my mother's Pekinese dog—a fierce and beautiful creature who adored her. He fought anybody who came near her, and during meal-times rushed under the table to bite the maid's shins each time she made her round with the dishes.

We crossed the Channel several times with my father, and he bought us dolls made to represent the fishwives of Boulogne. My youngest sister stayed at home. At that time she showed an ardent desire to throw herself out of her nursery window five storeys high, and this left my parents in continual alarm, although they erected a suitable barrier.

In London my grandmother lay seriously ill. For some years she had written four times each year a short, chatty letter which she then had printed and distributed to her personal friends. She called these missives: "Green Leaves." Even as she took to her bed her latest was written. It was on the art of learning to grow old and she said: "To those who have owned happy youth, beauty, riches and all the good things of this world, it is indeed hard to grow old, to lose admiration, enjoyment, strength, and lust of life, to part with old friends and be passed over by new acquaintances, above all, to bid farewell to what is called beyond all else love, warm human love and yearning; to stand by, physically and mentally colourless and unsought, whilst others, newcomers, and surely inferior souls, are praised and lauded— this surely is old age, and we are not well learned in the art of it. Certainly as we grow old we must keep our eyes more fixed on Heaven and less on earth!"

One night very late there was a great commotion in our house at Folkestone. My mother, looking white, came in to see me, for I was then ill with appendicitis. She looked worried and was off to the station to catch a train back to London.

A few days later we learnt that my grandmother had died.

CHAPTER THIRTY-TWO

OUR holiday at Folkestone was a sad memory for my mother and father, and it was natural that in subsequent years they should turn to Rottingdean. The village was changed very little since we were first there. A few cars now stood parked in the courtyard opposite the inn and motor omnibuses replaced the horse-driven Royal Mail. The big white cliffs had somewhat crumbled and a house that a few years earlier stood on the extreme edge had lost a portion of its parlour and was condemned as unsafe. Mr. Volk's sea railway that once travelled above the waves all the way from Brighton stopped short at Black Rock and the high steel structure built to carry the track stood covered with shells and seaweed.

There was Mr. Stamford's big school half-way down the street. My father had sent me there for a short while and on the whole I enjoyed it, but the winter walks on those wind-swept downs did not suit me and I was brought away. Mr. Coe, the chemist, stood benevolently outside his shop and we bought bananas and plums, as usual, from the greengrocer, on our way down to the sands at midday. The big windmill towered above the sleepy village and I rediscovered an old chalk pit where I often dug for fossils. We went back to the same house and our pink-cheeked cook took up again the thread of her last talk with the village policeman at the kitchen door. Every evening my father gave me a penny to run down to the old lady who kept the toyshop, because she received the latest papers from Brighton and he liked to know the news. That is how, in 1914, I brought him tidings of the outbreak of war!

I made friends with the youthful lieutenant of a Sussex regiment and attended the concert his men gave in the village hall before marching off to France. I thought that concert was the most wonderful thing I had ever heard, and wept with emotion when the chorus struck up "Sussex by the sea!" Then I ran around with the local Boy Scouts, gave the salute to every youth I met in the village and kept a notebook with all the potential good turns that I could do each day. Before we left, my mother handed me some gold coins and told me to pay the tradesmen's bills. I was growing up, but the war was a vague and distant thing which I understood but little.

We returned to Brentford and my mother threw herself into a life of devotion to the men of the parish who had gone to France. She looked after their families, wrote to them personally and knitted them thick woollen scarves a yard in length. The tugs continued their journeys down to the sea, calling to one another at night with their peculiar hooting, but the lights on the river were quenched and from the Surrey bank rose a network of milky searchlights that swept and reswept the sky, making queer reflections in the dark and murky water.

One evening my father and mother took me in a train bound for Windsor. We sat in the ill-lit compartment and looked at one another with damp eyes. I was going to school. It was my father who planned that I should go to Eton.

That night I found myself in a small square room with a bed in one corner, a large box covered over with cretonne, known as an ottoman, in another; a bath-tub leant against the wall with a big towel folded above it, a little desk revealed a new pad of writing-paper, bearing the arms of Eton in light blue and the name of my house tutor below. The maid with whom my father had already made friends looked in and asked if I was comfortable. She said to me: "I have given you the best face towels because I am sure you do not shave yet."

"Oh," I said, "and what difference does that make?"

"The older boys wipe their razor-blades on the towels and cut them," she explained.

She told me there were no bathrooms but that I could take a

tub, and that I would have to go and draw the water myself. "You'll learn about it to-morrow," she said. "Each boy must take a hip-bath so many times a week."

She closed the door and I looked out of my window. It was a narrow stone window with a bar in front, but there was sufficient width to lean out comfortably. Underneath was my tutor's garden discernible in the moonlight—a real English garden with rose-trees, an arbour and a small tool-house in front of which was a half-cut tree and an axe. Beyond the garden wall stretched the grass playing field called 'Sixpenny,' a small stream and some willow trees. Most of my neighbours had left their bedroom doors half-open. I could hear these returning boys exchanging holiday news. They discussed the theatres and arrived with gramophone records under their arms. A few minutes later a slow measured tread came along the passage and a tall, grey-haired man put his head into my room.

"Good evening to you."

My tutor had an old-world courtesy. It was never: "Good morning," or "Good evening," but "Good morning to you!" and "Good evening to you!" He was so tall that his big, slim figure was rather stooping. He told me that I must get to bed because within half an hour he would be switching off the lights. I undressed and went to bed. A new world was opening before me.

The next morning I struggled with a hard and large white collar and black tie. My new Eton jacket and trousers were neatly folded over the back of a chair. I expected that these first days at school would produce hard knocks. Instead I was taken for a walk down the High Street and told that I must walk on one side only, although I could cross to shop on the other. My tailor treated me with the utmost respect and told me what was the latest fashion in flannels. Old Solomon, with his wizened face and paper cap perched on the top of his head, looked up at me when I entered my hosier's and offered to pass the iron over my silk hat, though it was the first time I had ever worn it. The bootmaker bowed and explained that most of his clients had their shoes made of box calf made specially to their order, and the newsagent opposite asked me if I had yet bought my copy of *The Times*, and whether he was to send it down daily to my house.

My first class-room was in School Yard opposite the Founder's statue, and the pillars and rafters of oak were so old and gnarled that the names of boys throughout the centuries before were carved on every available inch of space. Brinton, who limped into the room in cap and gown to take us through our first lesson, spoke with an enforced harshness that was quite out of keeping with his heart of gold. I was lucky in my first class master. He was one of the best I ever had.

At midday we walked back to our houses and the first to get there found biscuits and milk. It was summer, and from each housemaster's garden came the perfume of roses and wistaria. It was incredible that this was school!

My housemaster was anxious that I should row during the summer term rather than play cricket and I was in full agreement. Before we were allowed to go to the boat-house we were obliged to pass a swimming test and as I had only floundered rather feebly in the sea at Rottingdean with my father, I had to set about learning to swim in soft water. The bathing place was rather more than a mile away across the fields, and it provided me with an excuse to take the whole of that summer in a leisurely fashion, for I took longer to learn than most people in spite of the fact that my house tutor himself was one of those who each week held the swimming trials, and would certainly have passed me if I had shown the slightest aptitude.

Nevertheless, I enjoyed these bathes, and afterwards would seek out the shade of a willow tree and read a book until dusk. The war seemed a long way from our lives. We knew of it only because of the lights that were dimmed at night, the scarcity of meat and sugar and the knowledge that as each term ended those who left went to Sandhurst instead of the university.

It was one morning during the summer half of 1916, if I remember rightly, that my house tutor said to me: "I want you to go over to Mr. Eric Underwood's study after twelve to-day. I shall be busy." Mr. Underwood was an assistant master who lived in a small house in Weston's Yard. The front of it had a pleasant old English garden and looked across to the Provost's quarters, while the back was on the main Slough to Eton road and faced the entrance to my own tutor's house. Mr. Underwood's study was a pleasing change from the severity of an ordinary class-room. It was a bright and sunny room with white woodwork and chintz curtains. He was expounding Russian grammar to a boy in one corner and, looking over his shoulder, said to me as I entered: "You had better go and join Leopold over there by the window."

The boy by the window was fairly tall and slim, with wavy hair cut straight across his forehead. I nodded to him and asked him what he was doing. "Reading Racine," he said. Then Eric Underwood, looking over towards us, said: "You can take turns and read aloud to each other."

We read the best part of an act without much enthusiasm.

"What house are you in?" I asked.

"Lubbock's," he answered, "and you, what's your name?"

I was interested because Prince Leopold was probably the only boy amongst us who had visited the trenches. When the Belgian G.H.Q. evacuated the town of Furnes and established itself at Houthem, King Albert took a house at La Panne, on the coast and there Queen Elizabeth joined him. It was to La Panne, therefore, that Leopold went for his holidays. King Albert would leave his home each day to visit G.H.Q., occasionally taking his twelve years old son with him.

It was at this time that I was prepared for my first Communion in Upper Chapel and I was singularly impressed. I still consider this chapel one of the finest I have ever seen, and when on Sunday evening Dr. Alington, in his surplice and red hood, rose from his stall to give the blessing, I felt genuinely moved.

As we trooped out into school-yard, someone would start

whistling: "K-k-k-katie, beautiful Katie!" or "Irish eyes are smiling." It was the time of *Chu Chin Chow* and *The Bing Boys*. As the summer term came to an end we would visit the hosier's to have silk shirts made to measure, and order gloves and a walking stick for the day we were released from our Eton clothes. I would choose a new soft hat and probably shoes, and the tradesmen would smile obsequiously and make no mention of the price, for the bills were sent home at the same time as the school reports. These moments brought me to grips with Prince Henry, only later to become the Duke of Gloucester, who was continually receiving my parcels at Lubbock's while I was receiving his. There was one more 'e' in my name than in his, but the confusion continually arose.

As the special train pulled out from Slough, I felt the first thrill of liberty. I spent the whole journey making plans. At Paddington I dived into the underground and took a ticket to Hammersmith, where I found an omnibus for Brentford. The Broadway was crowded and a woman conductor gave me my ticket. Men in uniform crowded the pavements. Women carried baskets of hard-come-by provisions while their features were tired and anxious. Through Turnham Green and Gunnersbury long queues of people waited outside the butchers' shops, while the streets were in half-darkness. Brentford High Street seemed narrower and more dismal than ever, while the fumes from the gasworks permeated the air.

I pushed the green gate and ran down the slope. Every window was barred and shuttered. In the kitchen I found our cook, Mary, reading the paper under the light of her flickering oil-lamp. My mother greeted me and we sat down to a meal in our old dining-room, where my grandmother's old masters looked down on us from their gilt frames. I ran out into our garden, but nothing was changed except that the river looked darker than ever, and from behind the trees on the Surrey bank there were now countless batteries of searchlights slowly sweeping the sky with monotonous regularity. Then I found that Mary had gone out and that my mother was busy doing the washing-up of our supper, so that I took off my coat, put a dishcloth round my waist and did the wiping-up as she handed me the wet crockery. At ten o'clock she put half a dozen candlesticks on the kitchen table, each with its box of matches. As far as lighting was concerned, our old farm-house was still as primitive as two hundred years before. The walls were supposed to be too old for electric light wires. Now that I think of it, our bedtime would have made any stranger smile. We each took our candle and walked up the staircase in Indian file, while my father always paused lovingly in front of his cuckoo clock to pull the long chains and check up on the hour.

I had changed my bedroom since the old days. The room that looked out over the garden was now used by my father as a dressing-room. I had taken up my quarters in a much smaller one overlooking the slope, which had been used before by our various German nurses. It was not uncomfortable though bitterly cold, and late at night and early in the morning the tramcars clanged and rumbled in the High Street, using the top of our gate as a stopping-place.

Eton gave me just enough idea of the outside world for me to chafe at the restrictions that this life at Brentford necessarily imposed. I really knew nothing about London and decided that my first step during the holidays would be to explore it. Wisely my parents did not give me too much pocket money, but a great deal of it went in fares. It took about forty minutes to get into the heart of the West End from Brentford. The best way was to ride in a tramcar to Turnham Green and then take the underground to Hammersmith, where I would change into the Piccadilly tube. I spent each day walking round, arriving home much later than I should have done. Neither then nor later did my father agree to give me a latch-key. I began returning home later and later, and as I knocked at our front door, I would be filled with remorse to see my mother, tired and reproachful, standing before me in a dressing-gown, holding a dripping candle in her hand.

As time went on I no longer felt any pang at returning to Eton. I had gone up to see several friends in London and one of these asked his parents to invite me to see *Madame Butterfly* at the opera. I went to see part of it, though I was obliged to leave after the first act. I had the best part of an hour's journey home, and I did not dare keep my mother up too late.

At heart I was somewhat ashamed of living between a gasworks and a brewery. These young people took too much pride in talking about their first nights and their fox-hunting.

"Where do you live?" I was asked one evening.

"In Regent Street," I answered without a moment to consider the question.

"Bah, nobody lives in Regent Street."

"Well, I do," I answered heatedly.

These days at Eton followed one another with admirable smoothness. I played games as little as was humanly possible, and it was doubtless for this reason that I found this life pleasant though unsatisfactory. I had been shielded enough in life and wanted to see what was happening in the outside world. I was just ready to leave for Sandhurst when one day the old woman who sold papers on Barnes Pool Bridge shouted out in her cracked voice the news of the armistice. That evening our house-master climbed down into his cellar and brought up a dozen bottles of hock. He placed them on the long tables at supper and, lifting his glass, bade us drink to our victory.

The war had passed over my head without so much as a ripple!

CHAPTER THIRTY-THREE

MY father's church bore the name of St. George. It was a gloomy brick edifice with a peal of bells given to it by an old gentleman called Leyton who lived at the corner of Kew Bridge, and who towards the end of his life passed as an eccentric, turning day into night, and starting for his walks when his neighbours were retiring to bed. He had a long age and a prodigious memory going back to the days when highwaymen robbed passers-by on the road to Gunnersbury. He could remember when there had been toll-houses on either side of the old bridge over the Thames.

The name of the Bohemian painter, Zoffany, was closely connected with our church. Zoffany was born in 1735, and after a study of historical portraiture came to England as a young man, being elected one of the original members of the Royal Academy. He painted several portraits of George III, who became his patron, and he subsequently settled down at Strand-on-the-Green. It was then that he made his picture called "The Lord's Supper," which he presented to the Church of St. George. The most prominent figures in this work are a negro, said to be Zoffany's slave, and a cherub sitting in a ridiculous position astride the Cross. All the heads, with the exception of those of Christ and of St. Peter, were the portraits of Brentford fishermen who lived in the Thames-side cottages, and the portrait of St. Peter is commonly accepted as that of Zoffany himself.

The church stands behind iron railings in the High Street, and faces the main entrance to the gasworks, where a dozen grimy stokers were generally to be found seated on the curb with their peculiar sackcloth headgears. My father was a fine preacher, and was anxious as soon as I left Eton that I should read the lessons in a determined voice on Sunday mornings. I did this several times, but my oratory left much to be desired.

I was still undetermined about my future career. After considerable difficulty I succeeded in passing whatever examinations are necessary for Oxford and was received at Magdalen by Sir Herbert Warren, an old friend of my father's, who was then President of the college. Now that the war was over a great many men came back from France to seek their university degrees. The usual restrictions placed on undergraduates were temporarily lifted, and we led a life of complete freedom. There were neither roll-calls nor compulsory chapel, and our Dean was generous with his week-end leave.

I was given rooms overlooking the Deer Park in the new buildings. They were great, big rooms with high ceilings and almost impossible to heat in winter except by coal fires that immediately rendered one drowsy. But in summer the Cherwell flowed lazily past the shadow of Magdalen tower, and we drifted down-stream in canoes or punts beneath the branches of heavily laden may-trees and nosed our crafts into the soft banks covered with bluebells and buttercups.

Europe was seething with great events, and I was anxious to take some active interest in what was going on. My room at Brentford during the holidays that followed my summer term became a mere place to sleep. My unstable bookcase had become stuffed with French yellow-backs that described in novel form the maelstrom of the post-war period. Diplomats moved from country to country in the beginning of that fever of international conference that was to continue for the next fifteen years.

One evening I walked down Ludgate Hill and stopped to buy a paper from a news-stand. I was about to leave it when it suddenly struck me that I might be in front of a solution to my problems. I cast my eye down a list of morning papers and decided that one of these was going to give me my first job.

After ten minutes in a whitewashed waiting-room, somebody came in to see me.

"Have you any experience?"

"No, none at all."

"Most men start on a provincial paper and only come to London when they're trained."

"Possibly, but I don't want to be paid. I'd like to stay for a week on trial."

"Whose house were you in at Eton?"

"Kindersley's."

"If you like to go on the copy desk for a week, I don't see that you'll be doing any harm."

I could have jumped through the roof with joy.

"Would you like to start now?"

"Why, of course, the sooner the better."

I followed through a vast pillared room to the horseshoe table at the far end. Reporters were drumming out their stories on well-worn typewriters. The men on the desk were bending over copy with thick black pencils.

For a week I sub-edited little six-line paragraphs. Most of the headings I put on were changed, but when the first got into the page proof as I had written it, I would not have given up my triumph for a thousand pounds.

One of the greatest editors of his day had pasted up a list of DO's and DON'T's on a pillar by our desk. I learnt that a split infinitive was worth the sack and that the word 'very' was banned. At the end of that week I was handed over to the News Editor and sent off on my first news story as a reporter. And the next morning in my bedroom at Brentford I read that interview in print. No other story has ever given me the same thrill!

Early in the new year the allies were already squabbling over their prey. M. Briand arrived in Cannes for a meeting of leading statesmen from Great Britain, France, Italy, Japan and Belgium. They were to discuss German reparations and a future conference on the reconstruction of Europe. The two allied Premiers, Mr. Lloyd George and M. Briand, were trying to harmonise the British and French viewpoints.

Ten days later, home news was squeezed off the front page,

when Briand was overthrown and the Cannes conference was torpedoed before it had even started. Lloyd George left Cannes for Paris, where he interviewed the new Premier, Raymond Poincaré, who was being accused of thinking in superlatives—a superlative army, a superlative navy and a superlative indemnity.

In London I was put on to a night shift, starting at four o'clock in the afternoon and ending at midnight. We used to eat at night with the taxi-drivers in a narrow 'sausage-and-mash' bar on high stools. It was here that I cashed my first pay-cheque between minor assignments in town. By the end of July there appeared signs that the wheels of industry were restarting and City men were of the opinion that, if people could be made to spend, confidence would return.

Money, however, was needed for commerce and not for armaments. The War Office saw itself accused of extravagance, and it was stated that this department could save at least fifteen millions a year. It was already forecast that 2,000 officers of the Regular army at home and in India would be asked to resign their commissions in the near future.

A fortnight later a quarrel about the Ulster boundary began to take an ugly turn. North and South, not satisfied with the terms of the Treaty, decided to settle the problem among themselves. Representatives of Southern Ireland were now claiming large transfers of land, and Sir James Craig, Prime Minister of Ulster, hurried to London in order to consult with Mr. Winston Churchill and other members of the Irish committee of the Cabinet. Sir James had been willing to consider some rectification of the border-line for the sake of convenience. Mr. Michael Collins, Premier of the Irish Free State, was claiming the whole of Fermanagh and Tyrone, large parts of Armagh and Down, Derry City, Enniskillen and Newry.

A few days later a new session of Parliament opened and Mr. Lloyd George made it clear that this boundary problem must be relegated to the comparatively distant future. Germany was on the verge of revolution. The railroad strike had thrown the country into chaos, disorder had begun in the factories and Berlin found itself without water, coal or electricity.

Suddenly the ticker announced that Sinn Fein raiders, during the early morning, had attacked the border counties of Fermanagh and Tyrone, kidnapping a hundred unionists, Orange leaders and magistrates. Ireland sprang back into the news, and Michael Collins came out with a statement that these raids were probably reprisals because some Sinn Feiners were to have been executed in Ulster that morning.

By evening the situation approached the state of civil war.

In the office it was decided to send a couple of men to Ireland. At that moment I walked in from my fish and chips and because it was late and the man who generally made these trips preferred not to run into any more shooting, the choice fell on me. I was sent over as the assistant to a good, hard-boiled reporter who never even troubled to go home for his tooth-brush.

We crossed over to Dublin and slept in an otherwise empty third-class compartment all the way to Belfast. We arrived in time for a cold dinner and a lugubrious, though quite unexciting, walk through the ill-lit city. The civil war looked tame and I went to bed disappointed.

The next morning was a Saturday. We looked for something to cable home, but there was really nothing. Only a few pickings from the local papers that might presumably be rehashed. There had been a spot of bother at Monaghan. A party of special constables had been driving towards Enniskillen in an ambulance when they lost their way. Some civilians offered to guide them. The ambulance was brought into the town of Monaghan, where it was commandeered, and the constables were taken off to an unknown destination.

I offered to ride down in the day train and see what was happening. It struck me as a more interesting way of spending the week-end than waiting around the hotel.

I took the 'Belfast to Cavan' and enjoyed my first leisurely view of the Irish countryside. We arrived at Clones at half-past five in the evening, where we were to change engines. At the rear of the train were two carriages of 'B' Specials, armed with rifles, and as the first men trooped out on the platform they were told by members of the Republican army who were in possession of the station to surrender. Somebody opened fire and in the mêlée a Republican officer was killed. Seeing this, his men started to shoot indiscriminately. A hail of bullets swept through the carriages and with a shattering of glass four of the constabulary who remained inside were shot dead in their seats.

This was my baptism of fire, and I was wise enough, instead of running out on the platform, to open the opposite door and dive out on the permanent way, where I lay on the centre track until the trouble was over. I had seen all I wanted. At that moment a train came along on the Cavan–Belfast line. As it came to a stand-still a post-office official opened his van and threw a couple of mailbags on the ballast.

"Hi!" I shouted, "is this the border-line?"

"It is," he answered.

"Where are you going now?"

"Belfast," he answered.

"Then I'm coming with you," I announced, and scrambled up into his mail-van.

I was not particularly keen on returning to the city. It was now about six o'clock, and it struck me that if I could get to a telegraph office before seven, I should be able to front-page for our Sunday edition. This story was a gift.

After a short run our train came to a standstill. I looked out and saw the name of the station. It was Monaghan!

I had timed our run by my watch and tried to translate the result into miles. My argument ran something like this: If Clones was the border and we had been travelling for twenty minutes we must be at least seven miles inside Northern territory. I bade good-bye to my postman, swung down the dark slope from the station into the town and meditated on the story I was going to write.

My luck held out. There was a telegraph office on the way down and I hastily scribbled half a column as the hands of the clock approached seven.

"Do you want to send this?" asked the girl behind the counter.

"Why, certainly," I answered.

"Well, it's your business," she said.

There was a commercial hotel opposite. I walked across to it, wondering just why she had given me such a strange look. I booked my room and put a call through to Belfast where I spoke to my colleague. "I am at the hotel at Monaghan," I said. "There was some shooting at Clones and I've just filed a story."

Suddenly the local telephone operator's voice cut in:

"Your message to London was not correct. The 'B' Specials shot first."

This sounded odd. Why was she so keen to put the blame on the constabulary? Four of them had been murdered before they could take up their rifles.

Then I understood. The ever-changing border-line had made a curve and my train had been taking me right into Sinn Fein territory. Monaghan was the headquarters of those Republicans who had killed the four 'B' Specials at Clones!

My colleague was still at the other end of the line.

"This place doesn't seem healthy," I said to him. "If I can, I will try and cross country to-night."

We said good-bye and cut off.

I went into the hall and spoke to the porter.

"One moment," he said; "five gentlemen want to see you."

"Five?"

The five, dressed in mackintoshes and leather leggings, advanced slowly. They formed a sort of ring round me, and the one at the back stuck his revolver into my side.

"All right," I said. "I'll put them up, but you hardly need five to search me."

"That's all right," said one of them; "we're only going to ask you to step across to the Court House."

"Can I ask why?"

"You know why, but the Colonel isn't back from Clones yet. You must have beat him to it in the train."

"What was he doing at Clones?"

"He was in charge of the boys at the station. You'll know all about that later."

We made a solemn entrance past the sentries and up the steps into the Court House—I leading, and the five with their revolvers pointed at me behind.

Our steps echoed through the dimly lit hall. We went into a large room with a bright fire burning. "We treat our prisoners well," said one of my captors; "we're waiting for the message you sent from the telegraph office and then, when the Colonel's back, you'll be judged. If we can stop your wire from reaching London, you may get away with your life."

We waited in this room till eleven o'clock. Possibly the Colonel had remained at Clones, but my trial was postponed and I was taken back to the hotel and told to stay there.

Dr. Warde, the liaison officer of the district, came in to see me. He told me that the 'B' Specials had been missed further up the line and that an armed man who stopped the engine from coupling on at Clones had done so to ensure the capture of the constabulary.

I was the only guest at the hotel that night except for the local district inspector whom I met at breakfast the next morning. He was a tall, good-looking fellow who careered round the town in a battered Ford car, and he had an appetite that was strangely in contrast with mine. The church bells tolled for Mass, and from the dining-room window I saw crowds of people suddenly file out into the streets, but by midday, when the worshippers returned home, the town was deserted save for a few Republican soldiers wandering in pairs with their rifles slung over their shoulders.

The district inspector came in to see me from time to time. He claimed to be negotiating, but I think he wanted to play cat-and-mouse. I did not know that my colleague in Belfast had cabled to London the night before and given them all the facts.

The Colonial Office was advised and a telegram sent to Michael Collins. Only six months later he was to be shot and killed in a rebel ambush in County Cork.

By the Sunday night I was free to leave. I had been thoroughly frightened—mostly from brooding all Sunday alone beside a smoky fire in the hotel lounge, and I was glad to get back to Belfast, although it proved a more uncomfortable spot than Monaghan. There was continuous shooting in the streets and eighteen children had been skipping in the moonlight in Weaver Street when a bomb exploded in the middle of them.

I was told to file a story about my adventure at Monaghan and then return by the night mail. Incidentally our taxi was fired at half a dozen times on the way to the station, and I was not sorry the next morning to wake up in a sleeper outside Euston. I made a bee-line for the news-stall and found my name plastered over the front page. The only person who was really to be pitied in this affair was my mother, who, towards midnight on Saturday, had been brought down to the front door of our home at Brentford by a wild knocking. She hurried down with a light in her hand and an anxious expression.

A young man with a Canadian accent looked at her and said:

"Your son's certainly lucky! He's been condemned to death in Ireland."

The poor fellow was trying to get a photograph to enliven the news of my capture, but my mother gave him a cup of coffee instead and sent him back into our deserted High Street empty-handed!

Less than a month after this one of the pioneer air companies offered to get our papers to Paris each morning in time for breakfast. I made frequent trips across the Channel at the break of dawn and as commercial flying was then in its infancy, we were continually having trouble. Once, with Major Foot, a young wartime pilot, we lost ourselves over Calais, landed in a field and ran over a cow! The accident was not serious and we landed safely upside-down in a ditch, but the trouble started when Foot tried to extricate me from the cabin where I had been sealed in by the post-office authorities with the newspapers and mail. The mayor of the village where we had made our forced landing arrived with the tricolour ribbon round his waist, and looking at me, declared:

"No, Monsieur he is sealed in. He must stay in."

"But he can't stay there all the morning," said Foot.

"Then he must get out without breaking the official seals on the door," said the Mayor.

"That's easy," said Foot: "I'll cut the canvas with my penknife."

The Mayor was reassured but he added: "Now I must sign something. Where is your log-book? I will sign your log-book."

He signed the log-book and his face was a picture of delight. He marched us to the village and found two small motor cars— one for Foot and one for me, in which we were driven like the wind to the neighbouring airport of St. Inglevert.

I not only arrived safely in Paris but was eventually sent there to work under a senior correspondent. Our office overlooked the Boulevard des Italiens and was a small bright room in a modern building. I took the same pleasure in learning my way about Paris as I had taken in making myself acquainted with London during my holidays from school. No language difficulty arose, for, thanks to Mallalal's teaching, I found myself thoroughly at home. Paris was then the gayest city in the world, crowded with people of all nations, but, curiously enough, I was not yet attracted by its bright lights. I lived next to the Comédie-Française, where I went so often that I began to know their repertory by heart, and made many friends in the law courts, where Maître Henri-Robert, then France's most golden-voiced criminal barrister, drew huge crowds to hear him speak.

We were, of course, much closer to the changes that were going on in Europe than were most people in London. By July the

German currency was starting its headlong flight to obscurity. Austria was again on the brink of a revolution and in Vienna a two-pound loaf of bread cost £108 at the nominal rate of exchange. Mussolini was working up towards his October march on Rome and King Constantine of Greece was anxiously watching events in Asia Minor.

King Constantine had been forced off his throne by the Allies in 1917 because of his pro-German manœuvres, but had returned to Athens during the closing days of 1920. He then dreamt of making his country the Empress of the Near East and as a prelude to this imperialistic campaign had been able, early the following year, to seize Smyrna. For a short time his troops advanced with rapidity, but by the spring Mustapha Kemal struck back and all that autumn and winter the opposing armies faced one another without movement.

It was at the end of August that the Near East campaign flared up once more. We had been busy telephoning French politics that seldom got into the paper because of the fundamental difference between the British and French viewpoints. It now became obvious that interest at home was centred on the war. Mustapha Kemal hurled ten divisions against the centre of the Greek line and cut it in two. Each successive day brought news of fresh Turkish victories. The Greeks not only evacuated Anatolia but Smyrna, now crammed with refugees and wounded, was preparing to surrender.

By the end of September the Greek disaster was complete. Smyrna was turned into a brazier with five miles of flames sweeping across the city and King Constantine was made to abdicate in favour of his youngest son, Prince George.

After several weeks, during which Great Britain was within an ace of going to war to keep the victorious Turks out of Europe, a conference was called to take place at Lausanne in order to decide whether peace could be made between the Allies and Turkey.

Then one morning I got a cable from London saying:
"Accompany Poincaré and Curzon to Lausanne."

I took this to be a simple assignment merely covering the events of the journey to Switzerland and accordingly carried no luggage at all—only what was necessary for my return by sleeper the same night. When the special train reached Lausanne, however, M. Poincaré was told that everything was ready at Ouchy, including dinner, but that Mussolini, the recent hero of the March on Rome, had not arrived. While the train remained at the station, it was discovered that Mussolini was waiting at Territet thirty minutes away. M. Poincaré then went back with Lord Curzon to their compartment and the engine-driver was told to continue the journey.

When the allied train reached Territet there was not a soul on the platform to bid the foreign diplomats an official welcome. Mussolini, however, stepped forward and introduced himself, saying: "Gentlemen, you are my guests. I invite you to dinner at my hotel."

This little drama immediately put the limelight on the Italian Fascist Premier, who, only twelve years before, had been a wandering exile on the shores of this Swiss lake.

Remembering those days of vagabondage, he undoubtedly preferred to play the rôle of host at Territet rather than become a mere guest of two such experienced statesmen at Lausanne.

With the passing of Mr. Lloyd George from power, the conference had to seek elsewhere for a star performer. Lord Curzon and M. Poincaré were famous actors whose faces and mannerisms were well known, but it was the Italian newcomer who stole the real thunder of the Lausanne circus. His presence in an hotel foyer caused intense excitement. People watched for his frown and jerky raising of the bowler hat, and women queued up to catch a fleeting glimpse of his corrugated forehead.

We were already in the third week in November and thick snow lay on the ground, but the sky was deep blue and the sun shone warmly over the lake-side. The air was dry and exhilarating, and official cars sped along the snow-covered roads in an atmosphere of pent-up excitement. The huge, well-ordered hotels were crammed to overflowing, the flags of eighteen nations fluttered in the wind, from the Lausanne Palace with its French tricolour and Turkish crescent to the Beau Rivage at Ouchy where the red, white and green flag of Italy waved proudly beside the Union Jack.

Each evening three miles of lake-front glittered with electric signs, while the foreign correspondents of a dozen nations, many of them as famous in their way as the star diplomats, broke up into small parties in search of restaurants where the food was good. The Swiss road to peace in the Near East was strewn with champagne bottles.

At the Lausanne Palace we were treated as royally as Poincaré's own staff. The cable and telephone facilities were luxurious, and the Swiss proved themselves perfect and courteous organisers. I had daily tried to make up for my lack of luggage. I first bought a collar and shirt and then another and a pair of socks, and finally a suitcase to put them in.

One evening I stood with the manager of the hotel. He was trying to get me interested in a small Persian carpet stained with ink. The French Premier had been signing letters that morning when he upset the inkwell, so that the dark fluid trickled all over the precious carpet. He rang for the manager and apologised personally. "I will see that it's replaced," said M. Poincaré.

"No," answered the frock-coated Swiss: "I'll replace it, for the ink-stained carpet is now valuable. You've made it historic."

The telegraph clerk called out my name and handed me a telegram. It was from London and read: "Prepare to go to Athens."

I was crazy with excitement. I did not sleep all night, fearing that I should get another cable countermanding the first. But early the next day I took a train to Basle in order to get a visa for Greece.

The papers were full of the news that had prompted the sending of this telegram.

A revolutionary tribunal in Athens, exasperated by the crushing defeat of its army in Anatolia, passed sentence of death on General Hadjianestis, ex-Commander-in-Chief of the Greek forces in Asia Minor, and upon five ex-Ministers accused of treason. They had been arrested in September when the Greek army, risen in revolt, drove King Constantine from his throne.

Only a few hours after the trial these men were driven to a lonely spot outside the city and shot at dawn. M. Gounaris, an ex-Premier, was dragged from a sick bed to the field of execution. World opinion was shocked by these murders and feeling had been aggravated by the fact that they took place in defiance of an energetic protest on the part of Great Britain.

A few hours later my orders were confirmed. I set out for Greece, as my great-grandfather set out in 1838, but in different circumstances.

CHAPTER THIRTY-FOUR

I boarded the Simplon-Orient at Lausanne before dawn the next morning and went off to sleep again as the heavy train rumbled along the shores of Lake Geneva. I got up late. We were approaching Stresa, and the sun gleamed on the blue waters of Lago Maggiore.

We were supposed to reach Venice before tea, but we were late and it was dark before we came in sight of the city. I had in mind a letter that Robert Browning had sent to my grandmother long years before, in the late 'seventies, I think, in which he was thanking her for some songs she had written and sent to him. My mother had given it to me and I had slipped it into my own copy of the poet's works.

"Shelley," wrote Browning, "wishes in one of his poems for 'some world far from ours where Music and moonlight and feeling are one': he must have forgotten that there was such a place as Venice, or rather as Venice might be. I found there moonlight and feeling in abundance—but music was altogether to seek—and now your goodness supplies the want most pleasantly. I shall associate your songs with the gliding on the Canale Grande and pacing up and down the Piazza, and forget the violin's purgatorial screech from the lower regions. Thank you exceedingly. As for your proposal to throw a little Venice colour on something of my own—all I can say is, you will probably enable me to hear, for the first time, that harmony and my verses do not altogether disagree, and I may even apply to the case some old lines that occur to me:

'Lorsque de tes lèvres de rose
Mes vers échappent embellis—
Ô prodige, ô métamorphose!
Je les trouve presque jolis.' "

278

Strange that it should have been Browning, through this delicate piece of letter-writing, who first made me want to set eyes on Venice. I looked at my watch, but it was already past five. The country-side was impenetrably dark and there was not a ray of moonlight to be seen.

But I saw it—or rather imagined it—from a girdle of sparkling lights. As the train pulled out and we started on our way to Trieste and the long ramble (because of the bad track) across Yugoslavia, I pictured the glorious city through my grand-mother's eyes—the Lido with a still lagoon on one side and a northern-looking sea on the other where the waves splash up the sandy banks.

How many times, in the days of Ruskin and Browning, had she lunched here under the shade of a Venetian garden ragged with the careless luxuriance of the South, where scarlet pomegranate flowers peeped through the lemon branches and myrtle bushes, and where some old priest in black garb and with sombre face would come out and smile a serene welcome!

All next morning we made a tortuous way to Belgrade and by evening reached Skopje, which was then in bad renown for its lice-ridden hotels. The next morning I woke up at Larissa. We were in Greece and never shall I forget my first sight of those olive-trees and violet hills. Since then I have travelled round the world, but never have I seen such country as this—so desolate and invocative of the past.

Lianokladi . . . Delphi . . . Thebes. As I deciphered the names of these places on the primitive platforms, I could have cried with joy. Thebes! This was the same place where FitzRoy had changed mules one morning to ride into Athens. I would have gladly changed my train for a mule. Strange coincidence, he arrived on December 3. On the same date I, also, was making my first entry into the city of Pericles.

We reached Athens in early evening and I drove to the Hôtel de la Grande-Bretagne in an open horse-carriage. I had left Switzerland three days earlier with thick snow on the ground. Here the air was sweet and warm and spring-like.

At the hotel I was met by our local correspondent—a thick-set, dark-haired Greek with a fund of good humour. He told me all about the executions, and as he talked he waved a bundle of local newspapers in which every other column was a blank, the news having been deleted by a strict censorship. We went for a quick dinner in a restaurant where small boys armed with feather brushes made determined attempts to wipe off the dust from our shoes. We ate black, oily olives and pilau, and drank to each other's health in ouzo, an aromatic drink that turns to the colour of milk when water is added.

The court martial, I learnt, had not ended until midnight, owing to interminable speeches by counsel. The accused men, with the exception of M. Gounaris, who was ill in a clinic, were then taken off in a van to the Averoff prison and the Court retired to confer. The judges, looking pale, haggard, and grave, did not return until six in the morning. After sentences of death had been passed, Colonel Plastiras, head of the Revolutionary Committee, signed the warrants and the prisoners took Holy Communion and were then driven to an open space outside Athens called Goudi for the executions. Gounaris was so ill that he could hardly drag himself to the death-spot. Stratos handed a cigarette case to the officer in charge, requesting him to give it to his son with the advice never to enter politics. The will of Protopapadakis was found all ready in his pocket. General Hadjianestis, alone, was in uniform. Slight of figure and bearded, he stood at attention while the ribbons were torn from his tunic.

It would have been useless to send a cable. The censors were carefully spiking every message. My Greek was pleased to have company and said: "Shall we go to the cinema?"

"Certainly, if you wish," I answered. "I would be delighted."

I bought the most expensive seats because I did not think he went often and we settled in fair comfort, though it was in-tolerably stuffy. Suddenly he bent towards me confidentially and whispered in broken French:

"You can't think how lucky we are to be here!"

"Really," I answered. "How's that?"

"This theatre will be closed to-morrow. It will be a hospital."

"Is that so?"

"It's waste, don't you think?" he went on. "As soon as they get it they die."

"As soon as they get what?" I asked.

"It depends," he answered. "Mostly typhus."

"What do you mean?"

"Oh," he said. "You mustn't get alarmed. The city's filled with refugees. Sometimes one or other of them collapses. Then it's too late."

"Does that often happen?"

He shrugged his shoulders. "To-day I saw quite a number in the street, but at other times one doesn't notice them."

"I understand."

"How do you like this picture?" he went on.

"I'd like it a lot better," I answered, "if you didn't talk so much."

Brilliant sunshine woke me the next morning, and I had breakfast on the balcony overlooking the square, beyond which the oranges in the Palace gardens were turning a yellowish gold. An Evzone, with his pointed shoes and white skirt, kept guard outside the home of the military dictator, Colonel Plastiras. At the corner of the main street an old man sat with his legs tucked underneath him, holding a newspaper in one hand and with the other stirring his Turkish coffee that warmed in a copper pot.

I dressed quickly and went out. The whiteness of the houses was almost blinding. Every few yards little urchins stood on the curb offering salted crescents of bread strung on a stick and the market was crowded with country people selling eggs and chickens, and Jews who displayed yards and yards of coloured silk.

I thought it my duty to give some sign of life and sent to London a short cable about an exhausted Greek soldier who had crossed the Ægean in a cockle-boat to die within sight of his home on the mainland. Unfortunately, the censor let it pass, because a couple of days later I received a wire from my office reproving me for wasting the firm's money.

After this I decided to take my time and look around. The new King was virtually a prisoner in his Palace. Royalists kept well below the surface, meeting only behind closed doors. Although at Lausanne Venizelos repeatedly declared that he refused to interfere in Greek politics, it was generally supposed that he was the brain behind Colonel Plastiras. At home the members of the Revolutionary Committee were considered common murderers. Popular feeling against the men who had shot the ex-Ministers grew rather than diminished with time.

Just before Christmas I had a feeling that Colonel Plastiras was running into trouble. General Pangalos, the War Minister, was a man of equally strong character and sooner or later there was bound to be a battle of wits between the two. One afternoon I wrote a long cable and took a taxi to Piræus. The drive is a real enchantment past the Parthenon to the sweeping bay of Phaleron where the water is a sapphire blue. I had one or two friends who lived along the beach here—ex-Ministers like Gounaris, but who had escaped the firing party, and when they thought it safe they would occasionally give me an inside, though probably biassed, account of what was taking place. From Phaleron Bay the road to Piræus is along a corniche as lovely in its way as that between Mentone and Monte Carlo. The harbour was a busy multi-coloured place where small native sailing-boats bobbed up and down beside the big liners that took the mail to Constantinople and Trieste.

I made friends with the captain of a large cargo-boat. A few days before I had climbed up the side of his ship and barged straight into his cabin where he was lying in bed with his boots on smoking a Manila cigar. I told him who I was and said that I thought he might help me to get a cable out. He looked at me with interest, clambered out of his bunk and said:

"Why not? You don't suppose I'm afraid of a few Greeks!

During the war this ship sunk two German submarines."

"How long are you going to be in port?" I asked.

"A week at least," he answered.

"All right—I'll bring it to you."

This was my return visit.

I found my captain sunning himself on the forecastle.

"Listen to me," he said as I came up with him. "If you ever become the skipper of a tramp steamer, always have yellow men for your crew."

"Why so?" I asked.

"Well," he drawled, "a skipper stays by himself all the time, so it doesn't make any difference that way whether his crew be yellow or white. But those fellows work better, make less noise and . . . anyway," he went on as he spat with determination over the side: "that's my experience."

He took me by the shoulder and led me to the wireless room.

"My operator!" he announced, introducing me to a young man who was reading a novel. "He'll be glad to help you."

I gave him my story and he checked it over. Then we settled up in hard cash and the captain and I sat until evening smoking on the deck while the sun set over the violet sea.

Presently the operator made his appearance.

"Your message has gone . . . or nearly all of it," he said. "As I was finishing the Athens station got wise and began to jam."

The captain puffed reflectively at his cigar.

"You see," he said with a slight twinkle in his eye, "a ship has no right to send a wireless message out of port."

"Then I shall get you into trouble?" I asked.

"Trouble!" he gave a short laugh.

I took him back to dinner in Athens that evening. We had a really grand time. It was the first and only message we got out that way, but it was well worth it, and the captain of this tramp was one of the finest men I ever met. He sailed out of Piræus three days later.

"So long!" I cried. "Maybe we'll meet again someday."

Two years later these words were to come true—in Norfolk, Virginia!

On Christmas Day I joined two young Englishmen who were in Athens with a naval mission and we drove out to Kephisia, where we ate black olives and the tenderest chicken I have ever tasted on a wooden table of a farmyard. I fell desperately in love with this country, where the only person one ever met was a patriarchal shepherd who might have stepped out of Homer.

A fortnight later the Greek 11th Division occupied Karagatch, opposite Adrianople. Under the provisional settlement reached at Lausanne this was within the neutral zone that ran alongside the Maritza river dividing Greek and Turkish Thrace.

I received instructions to investigate. My recent cables had not improved my relations with Colonel Plastiras, who must have been handed a copy of the telegram from London, for the same afternoon he sent for me, and received me surrounded by several members of the Revolutionary Committee.

I found a small, lithe, good-looking man of military bearing with proud moustaches and a face of bronze. I could hardly blame him for feeling this way about it, but he told me that I would definitely not be allowed to reach the front, and that he had given strict orders to arrest me if I attempted to make the journey by road.

I thanked him, saying that I would have to decide for myself. That night I took the Simplon-Orient as far as Salonika, but instead of showing myself in an hotel sought out an agent for whom I had been given a word of introduction.

He made arrangements to put me on a Greek steamer bound for Dedeagatch, a small town on the Ægean that was within a few miles of the neutral zone. It poured with rain and I sat writing all day in a café, feeling damp and intolerably bored.

Towards evening I walked down to the harbour and boarded my ship. It was a tiny coasting vessel, and we dined that night under a spluttering oil lamp in the only public room—four of us altogether, with the captain at the head of the table. We carried olives and dates and a couple of dozen refugees, who were huddled up in the hold. Most of them were shivering and obviously ill. Nevertheless, this journey remains one of the most beautiful things I have ever done. It got me nearer to the Odyssey than I could have dreamt it was possible, and the sight of that violet coast-line with its sparkling white villages built in tiers was unforgettable. We called at Cavalla, where we took a load of tobacco, the cranes and pulleys screeching all night, and one morning towards eight o'clock we steamed slowly into the bay of enchantment that is Dedeagatch.

I bade farewell to my companions and started in search of an hotel. The town had been fought over so often that the streets were churned-up mud and the houses half wrecked. There was a low, one-storeyed café but no sleeping accommodation. Soldiers with torn tunics and frayed caps tramped wearily along the street that, a hundred yards from the café, became nothing more than an uneven field. Sad women with drawn faces, from whom I attempted to learn the name of an hotel, put up their hands in a hopeless gesture and passed on. I went back to the café and demanded information.

"There is one," said the woman.

"Where is it?"

"At the corner there—the tall house."

"Is that the only one?"

"Oh yes. That's the only one."

I walked across to the building. It did not look like an hotel. There was a narrow passage at the end of which was a rickety wooden stair. The smell was past belief.

After a few minutes a bent old man shuffled down and asked me what I wanted.

"Room for the night," I said.

"Yes," he said, "I have one more left. Come upstairs."

He led me into a room in which there was not a stick of furniture. But radiating from a circle in the centre a dozen worn rugs had been laid out on the wooden floor. The inn-keeper took the stick he was leaning against and pushed one of these aside.

"There," he said: "one drachma."

"Does one sleep with one's head at the circle or away from it?" I asked.

The old man shrugged his shoulders.

"Who cares?" he asked.

I bent over to see just what the hole in the centre consisted of. There were a few pieces of stained newspaper lying above it. The inn-keeper grabbed my arm as I leaned forward.

He shook his head.

"No," he said, "you don't want to touch that."

"If I sleep here," I said, laughing, "I'll lay my head the other side!"

I paid him the money and disappeared. I had spent rather less than a penny.

Outside the rain was falling fast, and my shoes sank into the mud. I decided to shelter at the café, but time never passed so slowly.

As soon as the weather cleared I took my coat from the coke fire where I had hoped to dry it and decided to walk out of the town. About a mile away a regiment of infantry was quartered round a wrecked wireless station. The men were badly clothed, and looked demoralised, and it struck me that the Greek attempt to invade the neutral zone must be doomed to failure. There were just the remnants of a beaten army. I hired a car and went as near the zone as I could, arriving back in the town towards nine o'clock.

It seemed a waste of time to remain any longer at Dedeagatch, and I wondered if I could return to Salonika by train, for I was anxious to get an idea of the country that lay between the army's headquarters and their front line. I discovered that there was a train at midnight that would bring me into Salonika the following afternoon.

For sixteen hours we crawled through this mountainous country, stopping every few hundred yards. I arrived at Salonika fairly tired, and decided that there was no longer any use in playing hide-and-seek with the military authorities. I therefore went to the best hotel in the town and registered under my own name and occupation.

Within a quarter of an hour an orderly came to enquire for me. He asked me if I would accompany him to headquarters.

"I should be delighted," I said.

General Pangalos received me personally, surrounded by his staff. He struck me as a much bigger, broader man than Plastiras, with features that were less harsh. I had expected to be put under immediate arrest, but I found him puzzled rather than angry.

"Where do you come from?" he asked.

"Dedeagatch."

"But how?" he asked. "I have had several cars on the look-out for you during the last three days."

"I took a boat," I answered: "it was quite simple."

The big fellow looked at me and burst out laughing.

"Would you believe it?" he exclaimed. "I never thought of that."

We parted the best of friends. This meeting told me a great deal more than I had learnt at Dedeagatch. I received a strong impression that the General was only waiting for the time when he could take the reins of government from Colonel Plastiras. I sent another cable from Athens, when I got back, repeating this view, but it took longer than I had thought. General Pangalos did not become dictator of Greece until two years later.

I was convinced that the Greek thrust into Turkish Thrace was bluff, and I thought that the rising epidemics were becoming much more important news. I therefore asked Colonel Plastiras if he would see me, and I said to him:

"I am sorry if I've offended you politically. That is neither your fault nor mine. But every day cholera and typhus are claiming more victims. It must be to your advantage that the outside world should know about this. Will you co-operate with me and let me use the cables without fear of the censor?"

The Colonel agreed.

There was an American staying at the 'Grande-Bretagne' attached to the Hoover Relief Fund, and I went down with him to a bay on the coast some twenty miles outside Athens. For some days a large ship filled with refugees from the Black Sea had been cruising in Greek waters trying to get entry into a harbour. The tragedy was that nobody would receive the death-ship.

I saw it first through a group of olive-trees riding gently at anchor on a blue stretch of sheltered water. The yellow flag hung limply from the top of the mast.

A young New York doctor was in charge of this vessel. He had set forth from Samsun on the Black Sea with 2,000 refugees. Cholera, typhus and smallpox broke out in turn. There remained only four hundred passengers who were not stricken with disease. We rowed out to speak to him and he told us that, owing to the danger of infection, the bodies of the victims were burnt in the ship's furnace. Chutes were arranged from the decks to the stoke-hole down which the bodies were thrown.

In Athens the supply of vaccines was coming to an end, and it was said that 1,000 refugees were dying a day. Crowds flocked to the cathedrals of Holy Trinity and Spiridion on the last day of January to pray for deliverance from the plague, but in each place of worship a member of the congregation suddenly sank to the floor and the people flocked out in a panic, leaving only the priests at the altar.

After the first few cables, interest in London lessened. France had marched into the Ruhr, and Essen had been occupied. The Near East shrank into the background. Even we who stayed in Greece no longer thought seriously of the epidemic. The diplomatic world danced each evening in a night club where the faces never changed. I spent many happy hours there, for the foreign colony was amusing and resourceful. There was a little, dapper diplomat from Central Europe who owned a richly furnished house overlooking the Palace gardens. We would often dine there and afterwards go on to our night club, where he would entertain us until the small hours. I remember him chiefly for having brought a drunkard back to his senses by making the brawling fellow smoke an ordinary cigarette into one end of which he had inserted a microscopic amount of cocaine. The effect was instantaneous.

One evening in the bar of the 'Grande-Bretagne' I came across a stranger. He was a tremendously tall, blond Frenchman—a clean-shaven Hercules with a frank, easy smile. He told me he was a Parisian, and had been in Salonika buying American army lorries from old war stock. I took him round the town and introduced him to the foreign colony, and that night we opened champagne in his honour and ended up in a night club in Phaleron, whence we saw dawn break over the Parthenon.

He told us all the latest news from Paris until I thought that the Polish Minister who was with us was going to burst into tears. I also felt an urge to get back and the next day I cabled London asking if there was any point in my remaining longer in Greece. Ten days later I was ordered home, and this time chose the sea route by way of Corinth, the Straits of Messina and Marseilles.

CHAPTER THIRTY-FIVE

I ALSO came back to London on a cold February morning and, like FitzRoy, exchanged the violet mountains of Greece for winter mist and the roar of traffic.

Interest had shifted to the Ruhr, where nearly a month before the first trainload of French troops, with their tanks and machine-guns, passed through Cologne on their way to Düsseldorf. Germany's richest industrial area was now occupied by General Degoutte, who controlled all communications between the Ruhr and the rest of Germany.

At home, news came down to its true perspective. Football and a resounding case in the law courts were responsible for half the excitement in the office. Men with whom I had worked nine months ago barely looked up from their typewriters to acknowledge my greeting. I doubt whether they had noticed my absence.

I was not to remain in London for long. Almost immediately I was drafted to Düsseldorf to relieve one of our men who was to return home. I changed my money at 180,000 paper marks to the pound, and found the great German town filled with French soldiers in their sky-blue uniforms. General Weygand had been sent from Paris to give his advice. "Seventy-fives" rumbled through the streets on heavy motor lorries, while day and night cavalry patrols rode up and down.

I took over the apartment that my predecessor was vacating. It was in a luxurious hotel, and the rooms were a rich contrast to my humble four walls at the 'Grande-Bretagne.' We spent the morning together visiting the telegraph and telephone exchanges, then occupied by French signallers, and we looked over the railroad bridge opposite our hotel, where an occasional locomotive rumbled past under an escort of blue-capped engineers.

German railwaymen had everywhere tampered with the signals,

removed lengths of line and blocked points at important junctions. A bridge not far away had been mysteriously blown up during the night.

It was probable that my first duty would be to cover a conference then taking place between General Weygand, who had been Chief of Staff to Marshal Foch, General Degoutte and M. Le Trocquer, French Minister of Public Works. They were meeting to discuss fresh penalties for German resistance all through the Ruhr valley.

We returned to the hotel just after midday, and found that a number of foreign correspondents had arranged to give a farewell luncheon to my colleague. We were served Rhine wine and Bismarck herrings, and the meal was not far advanced when somebody noticed that we were thirteen at table.

For a moment there was a slight chill. Then my predecessor, to ease the stuation, rose to his feet and said:

"I believe ill luck is supposed to fall on the first of thirteen who gets up from his place at table. So that you shouldn't feel embarrassed, I rise to drink to your good health."

It was a delicate thing to do, and we responded warmly. A few minutes later everybody forgot the incident.

I went over with an American that afternoon to French headquarters and together we saw the Commander-in-Chief. He told us that over four thousand French railwaymen were then on their way to the Ruhr, and that this would bring the total number of allied railway employees both here and in the Rhineland to just over ten thousand. These men would run the essential transport services by which France hoped within a month to obtain a million and a half tons of coal and coke.

The French experiment was even then proving successful. Nevertheless, opinion at home was strongly divided, and a large section of the British press was accusing France of militarism. Poincaré was not influenced by this. He claimed only to be carrying out the Treaty of Versailles, and pointed out that Germany, far from being impoverished, was then building up a gigantic air force with the money that she should legally be paying to the Allies.

We walked back to the hotel and, as usual, I went into a shop to purchase a much-needed shirt and collar, for I had left London at accustomed short notice. I was now accumulating quite a wardrobe of wearing apparel from different parts of Europe. The people appeared courteous and keen to help and I found no open antagonism.

The next morning it was clear that General Weygand was tightening up his organisation. German railwaymen who interfered with the normal working of trains were henceforth to be expelled into unoccupied territory. These scattered railway strikes harmed the German population more than the invaders. They were unable to find means of transport.

At my hotel I found some excitement. It appeared that my colleague, bound for England, hired a car to drive himself and several friends to the railroad station at Cologne. The car crashed against a tree and was now a tangled mass of ruins. The driver was killed outright and my unfortunate predecessor scalped. The news cast a gloom over us and many said that he should not have defied fate.

*　　*　　*　　*　　*

That spring I returned to Paris, where I remained all the summer. I was now well acquainted with the routine, and these six months passed quickly.

I was anxious to meet again my tall giant from Athens, but I forgot both his name and address. I hunted for him systematically. It seemed incredible that I should not come across him. One fine Sunday afternoon I was sent to cover the races at Longchamps and climbed, for the sake of the view, to the topmost tribune. As I watched the huge crowds slowly passing along the gravel paths, my Frenchman suddenly appeared like a pygmy below. I darted down three flights of stairs into a seething mass of people and it was not until the end of the day that I traced him again.

He told me that his Salonika deal had fallen through because his partner had withheld the cash, but that he had changed his business. He was making wireless apparatus. He owned an old open-seater American car and we sped back to Paris. He reigned supreme over a gang of about a dozen other young Parisians who gathered at bodegas each evening at cocktail time, afterwards all, or as many of them as were free, dining together. We changed our restaurants often and made a habit of seeking out some cheap café where the owner had a talent for cooking. During the first evenings our companions would be taxi-drivers and crossing-sweepers, but as the place became famous the clientele would change until finally the prices were put up and we would go.

Our office had a fixed time-call every evening with London at nine o'clock, and my chief generally left it to me to call over our day's copy. He wrote each afternoon at least a column of politics rehashed from the *Temps*. That, I often felt inclined to abridge when the wire was bad, for his copy seldom made more than three lines in the paper the next morning.

In principle I was free after nine-thirty p.m., and would then make a dash for our rendezvous. I learnt my way about Paris as I never would have done otherwise, and there was no lack of transport. At one time we careered around town in a big F.W.D. lorry purchased by one of us from American army stocks.

By now Montmartre was at the height of its glory. As darkness fell a thousand night clubs would hurl their lights across the pavement, and the noise of jazz bands would blare into the crowded streets. People from all over the world came to empty their pockets in Paris, and with coal now pouring into France from the Ruhr, prosperity rose towards its crest.

This life went on until early August when, one morning, I received a cable to go immediately to Doorn, in Holland, to interview the ex-Kaiser.

I feared this assignment from the start, for the exiled monarch was impossible of approach. When, two days later, I reached the little dolls'-house village that is Doorn, I found the position even worse than I had expected. Sitting quietly on the balcony of the little blue and white hotel, smoking his pipe, was Sir Percival Phillips.

The tranquillity on his face told its own story. He had already been there three days and had written a brilliant account of the ex-Kaiser supervising the making of a bonfire on his estate which he had mailed to London. I was no match against Sir Percival Phillips at the best. In this case I could do nothing but wait and be recalled.

We dined together and he told me how he had seen the old man dressed in tweed trousers and leggings gazing grimly at a bonfire outside his château, while the ex-Crown Prince and the Marshal of the Court humbly did as they were told. The next day I also saw him, this aged ex-monarch with his snow-white hair and withered left arm pushed into his waistcoat pocket.

For a couple of days I just stayed around. The six-foot barrier topped by three strands of barbed wire that surrounded the estate was symbolic. I found it impossible to cross the threshold.

I hired a bicycle and for an hour or so each afternoon would get some exercise peddling round the village. The Crown Prince, in golf stockings and field-grey suit, would roar past me in his powerful sports car at a good sixty miles an hour. The day of my departure I came across him at the end of a long avenue of trees. He was standing dejectedly in front of his machine and, having hailed me, asked that I should help him change a tyre.

We worked for a quarter of an hour and as he was ready to start, I told him that I had been chasing his father for the last three days. He laughed, and sitting on the running board talked for a few minutes about life inside the barbed-wire netting. I cabled the story that evening, but the trip to Doorn was not a success.

*   *   *   *   *

I was back in London during the middle of the month, and by autumn I was planning to cross the Atlantic.

One October evening my mother and I sat over the fire in our dining-room at Brentford watching the little flames curling round the logs from our garden.

"Have you saved any money?" she asked.

"Just the fare," I said: "twenty pounds."

I felt that there was reproof in the look she gave me. "We're putting one hundred pounds to your name at the Bank of Montreal," she said quietly. And then she took my hand.

A moment later she got up and walked to the sideboard.

"There's a box here that your aunt gave you," she said. "What am I to do with it?"

It was a square wooden box covered in leather, not unlike despatch boxes used by Cabinet ministers.

"It belonged to Arthur," she said. "He always kept it by him and it's just as he left it."

As the key turned and the lid sprang back, there were his books, his papers, his letters. . . .

"Thanks," I answered: "I'll look at it when I come back."

CHAPTER THIRTY-SIX

I DO not remember from what station I left London that autumn, and I have only a vague recollection of my journey to Liverpool. But I know that it was raining, and I have a clear picture of the few moments that my mother spent with me in the ill-lit compartment of the train before my departure.

My journey promised just the experience I needed. I was leaving a comparatively well-ordered life to court adventure. I was curious how far I could travel round the world by the exercise of my own craft, using newspapers as stepping-stones. My mother commended me into the care of God, and bade me good-bye.

My passage was booked on the *Andania*—a slow but comfortable cabin ship, bound for Quebec and Montreal. It was my first trip across the Atlantic.

I still consider the St. Lawrence route the loveliest approach to the North American continent. It is gentle, romantic and infinitely exhilarating. The biting cold and the smell of incense that suddenly fills the air after passing Belle Isle, the glimpses of fishing smacks through the mist of the Newfoundland coast and then those green, undulating banks of the mighty St. Lawrence river give a strictly personal welcome to Canada. I remember leaning over the liner's bulwarks to pierce the violet haze off Gaspé. Jacques Cartier sailed here three hundred years ago in a vessel of sixty tons on behalf of the King of France. I knew that French was spoken in the Province of Quebec and I imagined that, being bi-lingual, my chance to obtain work was slightly enhanced, but I was still excited and nervous.

I lost my heart to Canada the moment I inhaled its glorious perfume. Nowhere in the world is the air so clear and yet so agreeably scented with sea spray and pine. There are times when, tired of the city, I would give a great deal to stand buffeted by the sharp wind on the top-deck of a liner in the Gulf of St. Lawrence and draw one deep, glorious breath.

The *Andania* glided with a majestic indifference past Tadoussac and the mouth of the river Sanguenay, cradle of the European commerce with Canada, and towards evening Quebec burst into view with the tips of the Laurentian mountains bathed in blue mist.

That evening as the lights of Three Rivers came into view I took a fresh-water bath and packed my cabin trunk in readiness for debarkation the next morning.

I booked a room at the Mount Royal in order to have the benefit of its address. Although I had not yet worked on an evening paper, it struck me that the best idea was to storm the office of the first publication that I bought at the news-stand. This proved to be the *Star* and I sent up my card.

My reception was not exactly warm but it proved successful. I was accepted on a linage basis and told to report the following morning. This was just what I wanted, for it gave me a chance of making good first and talking money later. The great thing was to get a quick idea of the city's lay-out. There was the St. Lawrence waterway by which I had come, and the mountain in the shadow of which nestled my hotel. The lovely city stretched between river and mountain, the grain elevators and business houses nearest the river, and the residential quarter on the flank and at the foot of the Mount Royal. One great shopping artery, St. Catherine's Street, appeared to run from east to west, and along this I took a trolley car into the heart of the French-speaking part of the city. I left the car at the corner of the Boulevard St. Denis, walked some fifty yards along the road and knocked at the first house where the notice: "Room to Let" hung from the parlour window.

This house was owned by a Lyonnais and his wife by the name of Emery. The man was a carpenter, and his wife worked beaded dresses then much in vogue. They received me with open arms, being delighted, I think, to find somebody freshly arrived from Europe, and after offering me an airy bedroom for twenty dollars a month, insisted that I should join them for dinner. I ended by staying with those people for rather more than six months and was treated the whole time as one of the family. The old lady actually wept when we finally parted.

The first snow fell that night, and although it was not yet to last, the city wore a mantle of white in the morning. By my first assignment I was to learn that news stories are the same (or nearly so) the world over. I was told to enquire into the prospects for Christmas turkeys.

There were several big open-air markets in Montreal, but for some reason I chose that of Bonsecours. I found it in St. Paul Street East, a stone's throw from the quayside and in a district that is strangely similar to London's Thames Street. It is in the shadow of the grain elevators and of Bonsecours Church, on the summit of which is a figure of the Virgin with her hand outstretched as a sign of welcome to sailors who enter the port.

There are only two ways in which the turkey story can turn out. The headline for the first is: "Your Turkey will cost you more this Christmas," and the second is: "Your Turkey will cost you less." I do not remember the result of this enquiry, but I know that it was an easy story to write, and that it hit the front page with one of those double-decker headlines that are peculiar to American newspapers. Meanwhile I dawdled at the market and looked with interest at the stacks of dried tobacco leaves that the farmers brought in half green from the country.

For a week I remained at the *Star*, but although I produced over a column a day my pay envelope was not encouraging, and I walked across to the *Gazette*, where I was offered a salary of twenty dollars a week. This was considerably less than even a beginner can earn in London, but I was glad to get it, and as my rent only represented a quarter of my monthly wages, I had sufficient to live tolerably well.

By the end of the month winter had come to stay and the St. Lawrence was ice-locked. The city began to look different. It assumed character. Icicles clung from the roofs, and the red window-frames took on a new brightness against the eternal, blinding snow. The mountain disappeared under a blanket of white, and the young people brought out their skis, while all along the pine-girt paths echoed the pleasant jingle of sleigh bells. Office buildings were intolerably hot, and outside the temperature registered thirty below zero and numbed the tips of my ears. I rushed with enthusiasm round this city where modern finance prospers on the fringe of mediævalism. A few rather stunted skyscrapers housed the banks, but the priest in his pulpit represented real power. Richly endowed convents and monasteries dotted the country-side, while monks and nuns of every order trod silently along the city's snow-bound streets.

For the first six weeks I spent most of the time in the law courts, where I worked with a Dane who showed me the ropes. It took me some time to get attuned to the French Canadian's accent and his weird mixture of American slang and sixteenth-century French. But this was nothing compared to the close atmosphere of those heated rooms where judge and witness frequently used the same spittoon.

Experience here gave me a solid background. It was a good opportunity to learn the French–Canadian mind with its religion and folk-lore. I had not been in the courts a week before a peasant, brought up on some petty charge, described how on a dark night in the Valley of the Two Mountains he had seen what he supposed was a birch-bark canoe piloted by the devil flying rapidly over the tops of the spruce under a full moon.

I remained in Montreal longer than I had at first intended. Christmas, with dense crowds thronging to midnight mass through a blinding snowstorm, was more picturesque than I imagined possible.

The following spring I was sent to a village near Megantic, not far from the United States border-line. It was at the height of prohibition, and there were wild stories of bootlegging. As the heavy train rumbled over the country-side the white carpet of snow was already pierced, here and there, with tufts of brown withered grass, the rivers were beginning to rid themselves of ice and the green, churning waters flooded over their banks. The air was crystal pure. It was shortly after four p.m. when I arrived at my destination, and on the platform stood a Roman Catholic priest and an Anglican minister, each waiting to observe the passengers who stepped off the train.

On the whole the Anglican minister appeared the better entrenched. Maples bordered the road that ran up a steep incline from the railroad track while two churches, one Catholic and the other Protestant, dominated the main street. More people in this township appeared to talk English than French-Canadian.

I left my bag at the hotel and walked back across the track to the river, where freshly cut pine and hemlock were being sorted. The perfume of the sap as the saw sped round with a grinding whirl was overpowering. It was a fine sight to watch the logs being brought in from the woods by sled, while a couple of sturdy men stood ready with canthooks to unload them and roll them towards the sawyer.

With the monotonous drone of the mill engine in my ears, I walked across the snow and began to explore. Beyond the bridge that spanned the river, thick woods stretched far into Maine. The young silver birches caught the last of the sun's rays and reflected the light as if they had been mirrors.

I went back to the hotel, where I found a dozen woodmen grouped together on the verandah. Federal agents had been busy five miles up the road. Two apparently law-abiding nuns who were driving a sled filled with logs across the border had been challenged and somebody was wounded. I arrived just in time to see the doctor drive up. He was off to the accident and agreed to take me along with him.

This doctor was a small wizened man with an ashen complexion, and I think he was not sorry to have a companion.

The road was half-bare in parts and the hills proved hard going. The fields, however, were still covered, and the snow was tinged with a delicate rose in the setting sun. Green firs and spruce lined the woods, and in the distance was a low range of violet hills.

"Who's been wounded?" I asked.

"I don't know," answered the doctor. "They told me by telephone it was a young man."

"Strange!" I said. "Surely the nuns didn't shoot!"

The doctor grunted: "I make it no business of mine," he said. "This farm where we are going marks the border. It's half in and half out, if you get my meaning."

Some time later he pointed with his whip to the wood on our left. A track in the snow was just visible in the failing light.

"Whom does the farm belong to?" I asked the doctor.

"The man who sold me this buggy," he answered: "they call him Jock. I think you'll like him."

Jock's house, with its white verandah standing out like a ghost in the moonlight, slept under the shade of six large cedars. It looked peaceful enough. A light logging sled beside an old wooden shack, a manure heap with a fork sticking into the dung and a pile of firewood . . . these were about the only other things that caught my eye as I jumped out of the buggy.

The door was opened to us by a small man with a red jersey who held a frying-pan in his hand.

"Come in, doctor," he said: "I was making them a bit of supper."

Two Federal officers sat beside the stove, while a youth lay stretched out on a camp bed in a corner of the room.

"It's a leg wound," said one of the officers, rising.

The doctor bent over the sick man while 'Jock' went on quietly making preparations for supper.

When the wound was tended and the leg bandaged the doctor looked round and said:

"What was this I heard about two nuns crossing the border?"

The officer who had spoken first answered:

"That was one of them you have just been bandaging. His disguise is outside in the sled."

"And the other?"

"He escaped. We shall have time to round him up in the morning."

The sled I had seen outside was the one used by these youngsters. They were carrying a load of logs of which the insides were scooped out to conceal light metal cylinders filled with liquor. Disguised as 'nuns' they might have crossed the border if only they had kept their heads, but as soon as they were challenged both sprang from their sled and started running into the wood.

The doctor went back after dinner, but I asked to stay. I wanted to see the place in the daylight and have a look at the pine logs.

This story only made a dozen lines on an inside page, but it was to give me my first sight of a maple camp.

Sunshine streamed into my room when I awoke the next day. The Federal agents and their prisoner had disappeared, but I found some hot coffee on the stove in the kitchen, and as I stepped out of the house I found myself in a thick maple wood where the trees stood out majestically from the carpet of snow, while in the far distance the balsam and hemlock and spruce made a deep green border. Half a dozen 'roads' branched out from the house, while the vivid red pails fastened to the tree-trunks to collect the precious sap sparkled in the sun.

There was no other sound but the plop, plop, plop of the liquid as it dropped into the tins, and the occasional cawing of rooks that had returned with the advent of spring, but overhead the sun continued to burn and the sky was deep blue. I made my way along one of the 'roads,' trying not to sink into the snow. Old Jock, a clay pipe in his mouth and wearing long blue overalls that completely covered his body, was just visible in the distance as he stood in front of a hut where the sap was to be boiled. This hut, like the pails on the trees, was painted a bright, flaring red.

The roof was black, although the shaded side was still covered with a thick layer of snow.

A pile of birch logs stood beside the door, while above, some dead leaves, still clinging fast to a couple of beech-trees, waved in the breeze and dabbed the landscape with a touch of gold.

"Sunny days and cold nights," said Jock as I came up with him. "That's what I need now. Only half my buckets are set."

"I'd like to give you a hand," I said.

The old man took his clay pipe from his mouth and looked up at me with surprise.

"Well," he drawled, "I won't refuse."

I helped him harness his team and we drove through the woods while the bells of the horses made music. Some of the trees were a hundred yards from where our sleigh stood and we had to fight our way through thick undergrowth. Nothing but a rare skunk or a woodchuck disturbed the still, even surface of the snow. The rooks cawed incessantly and a few English sparrows slipped out of their winter retreats, more dead than alive, and began chirruping in the sunlight. All that morning I floundered in the snow collecting sap from the trees, wading back to the sleigh with my pail to pour the contents into the tank it carried.

That afternoon smoke rose from the camp chimney, while from the skylight and the two windows could be seen clouds of white steam. The furnace was already red hot and the first sap of the season was being turned into thick, sweet syrup.

The doctor who had been visiting in the neighbourhood called in to give me a lift back to the town. It was too bad! I bade farewell to old Jock and his maple camp and jumped into the buggy.

There is an old joke about the Canadian Pacific owning everything in Canada, including the time. There was a long coloured map of their railroad system in the *Gazette* office over which I spent hours when I was on late duty. I would have liked to stay longer in Montreal, but when I looked at the map of Canada I wanted to move on. I had worked myself into a pleasant, easy-going job and there was no reason why it should not have gone on indefinitely. I needed the thrill of attacking another newspaper office.

I decided to collect my savings and make Toronto my next stepping-stone. That evening I resigned from the *Gazette* and went to see John Murray Gibbon, of the C.P.R., who gave me a pass on the railroad. I had originally received a letter of introduction to Murray Gibbon from Sir William Beach Thomas, whom I had met in Cologne. The C.P.R. has in its chief publicity officer one of the most erudite men in the Dominion.

I travelled on the night train and reached Toronto first thing in the morning. I made another bid for an evening paper and tried the *Toronto Star*. I got my job and a salary of thirty dollars a week within four hours of my arrival, and that little triumph still gives me a flush of pleasure.

I was luckier than I realised. The *Toronto Star* had a first-rate staff, and its city editor was a man of considerable charm.

My bag had remained at the King Edward Hotel, then the largest in Toronto, and the first person I met on my return was the massive Sir Henry Thornton, at that time at the height of his power. He stood surrounded by a dozen reporters, who looked pygmies at his side. A benevolent smile spread over his features, and he could little have dreamed how events during the next years were to shatter his hopes.

There are some newspaper offices that radiate energy. The *Star* proved to be one of these. My first assignment was unexpected. I have a fancy that nobody else in the office cared to undertake it. Although Ontario was a 'dry' province, publicans had the right to sell a weak and sickly beer. It was rumoured that this law was being totally disregarded, and the *Star* was apparently eager to prove that the beer sold in the majority of bars was not far off the real stuff.

I went to Woolworth's and bought a small syringe and a number of medicine bottles. I concealed these in my overcoat pocket and for the next two days I pub-crawled, taking from each glass of beer a sample that was later analysed.

The story covered most of the front page and made a sensation, but for some days I was in fear of reprisals from angry publicans.

We worked hard on the *Star*, and from my point of view this was an advantage. Unlike Montreal, Toronto is a city where work comes easier than play. My beer adventure gave me a good start and for the next month I flew over forest fires, raced up to the gold-mining district of Timmins and even carried on a campaign against the city's dog-catchers. Then I fell ill.

That is to say, before leaving London I had been warned that an operation on my tonsils was more or less urgent. I preferred to wait and for nine months I gave up smoking rather than have the tonsils out. Then they became poisoned.

I went to a Scot, who sent me to a nursing home and carried out the operation. After a week I left, but on my way home I fainted outside the General Hospital! That evening I looked in at the office and the big, heavy-shouldered city editor must have been impressed by the whiteness of my normally healthy features. He told me to go away for a week's holiday and that he would foot the bill.

He even told me where to go. I was packed off to a fairyland on the fruit belt, and between mountain and blue lake lazed myself back to health.

This Ontario fruit belt is one of the most glorious spots in the world. It is a comparatively narrow stretch of rich, fertile soil running between Hamilton and the Niagara Falls, where apples, peaches, cherries, plums and grapes grow in abundance. The railroad runs parallel to the lake, and in the evening the farmers return to the sleepy villages to play bowls, while the heavy trains stop to take up the loads of fruit waiting at the stations. Many of the people in this part of the world are English-born. They welcome the Londoner with open arms and speak of the mother country with an affection that is touching.

Although prohibition with its various sidelights was always the big story at this period, there was another form of bootlegging the news of which happened to break at the end of my short holiday and I was sent to Niagara to investigate.

An organisation had been formed for passing aliens into the United States by a sort of underground railway. The 'passengers' were collected in Toronto or Hamilton, taken by car to the Canadian bank of the Niagara river a couple of miles below the Falls and a crossing would then be attempted by night.

Lewiston, with its cheery orchards and white sleepy-looking houses, was a favoured spot. The immigrants were packed in a small boat and the agent would then signal to the other side with a flash-lamp. The opposite bank is low and sandy, so that a landing could generally be made with safety, although the tangle of branches and undergrowth proved a good hiding-place for United States immigration officers, who were always on the watch. I saw a real battle here with sub-machine-guns and rifles, while in the distance came the muffled roar of the Falls.

I returned to Toronto in perfect health, but one of my tonsils was carelessly cut. The surgeon who did the operation had left for England and I went to another—a Canadian who had studied medicine in Germany. It was a long and ticklish job, because what remained of the infected tonsil had to be cauterised.

We struck up a certain friendship, and when the time came to settle the bill, he answered, smiling: "Don't worry about that. You haven't enough to pay what I ought to ask you."

This was probably true. Most of my savings had gone into my operation. Nevertheless; I looked around for some method of showing my gratitude.

I found a present that no money could have bought. The owner of a brewery told me casually one day that if I wanted a case of real beer he would see that I was not disappointed. I accepted the offer gratefully, borrowed a car and took my precious cargo round to the doctor.

I stayed in Toronto until the end of the summer and was able to radiate on a fairly wide scale. It became clear, however, that my original intention of working my way to the Pacific would take too long if I remained for six months on each newspaper. I was conscious that I must not stay away from London too long or I would run the risk of returning as a stranger. Quite suddenly, also, I felt an inexplicable desire to visit South America. One morning my city editor sent for me. He told me to work for a month in the library. I made no objection, but at heart I took the order as an insult and walked out of the building for good.

I bought a third-class passage for Rio de Janeiro, and that same night took the mail train for New York. It was early September.

My first look at New York was from the Grand Central Station. I admit that it took my breath away. I did not know a soul in the city, and as I was in no mood to stay at the Ritz I did not even take a taxicab on my arrival. I would not have known where to direct him. For about half an hour I walked the streets trying to get my bearings, and finally landed up at an hotel that I have not been able to trace since. It was probably in the neighbourhood of Times Square.

I suddenly decided that it would be foolish to leave New York without at least trying to get a job. Technically I had no business to do so, because I was an alien without permission to work, but secretly I thought my old luck might last. It did, but without success.

Most of the big newspapers turned me down flat. I heard the story about there being more Italians in New York City than in Rome. I could not claim to know my way about and there was nobody to give me a hand. For a moment I thought I had made headway with one of the evening papers, but it was no good. The city editor flung this jibe at me: "You wouldn't get a story in a month."

"If," I said, playing my last card, "I can hit the front page with a story of my own during the next two days, will you give me a job?"

"Sure," he answered. But the smile with which he said it riled me.

I was due to sail on the *Vauban*, a sister ship of the ill-fated *Vestris*. The liner was not leaving New York for three days, and I had therefore ample time to look round.

In Toronto I had struck up a strange friendship with the chef of the King Edward Hotel. He was a Frenchman, and I liked to meet him in the evening in the cubby hole of his kitchen and talk about France. He had given me a letter to a friend of his who was then chef at the Bankers' Club in New York and I thought it would be an excellent idea to look this man up.

I took a taxi and drove there. The elevator was half-way up the building when two shots rang out as we passed one of the floors. The lift-boy stopped and I jumped out. Facing us was the half-open door of a diamond merchant. I remember seeing the firm's Polish-Jewish name written on the glass panel.

A couple of men rushed past as the elevator came level with the office. I walked across to the door and looked inside. A man was lying with his face to the floor and he had obviously ceased to breathe. He had a nasty gash and blood trickled down from the back of his head.

I did not stop to think of the risk. There was a sort of reception desk within easy reach and a telephone. I took up the receiver and asked for the paper that had just refused to give me a job. Then I dictated the story.

Luckily the elevator boy had remained an interested spectator. He made me a sign and we sped back to the lift. When we reached street level, the main doors were closed and there was a police officer on guard.

"Nobody is allowed to go out," he said.

I stayed there for half an hour while excited people came down from the various offices. I have no idea how I got in and out of that office unnoticed. When finally we were released I heard the newsboys in the street yelling out the story—and it was my story!

I rushed back to the office. I never was able to see the man with whom I had made the bet. I was paid six dollars for information and left white with rage.

Later in the evening I took the subway and came across a man I knew. His name was Popkin, and he had come to Toronto some months before to act as publicity manager for a convention. He owned a flat about half an hour's journey away and invited me to supper. Much later I was able to repay his hospitality. When Henry Segrave needed a publicity man for his speed record at Daytona Beach, I put him in touch with Popkin and he did the job extremely well.

I stayed one more night in New York, and like the buyer from Cactus City, walked up Broadway blinking at the lights. For dinner I had an orangeade and a "hot-dog." The next day I decided to take my liner to South America. New York had turned me down.

The steerage accommodation in the *Vauban* was not luxurious. Indeed, I looked despairingly at my quarters. A steward came down with a message from the captain. He had received a letter from a mutual friend in Toronto and, as I was apparently the only passenger in the steerage, would I do him the honour of moving up into the second class? Would I? There were no difficulties I knew of.

That evening we passed the Statue of Liberty and steered south into sunshine. Almost immediately the heat became intense. Off Bermuda I came away from the swimming pool before lunch-time with a slight tingling round my shoulders. I could not understand it because I had gone straight into the water without exposing myself to the sun. All the same I was badly caught and by tea-time the flesh was raw. The ship's doctor fixed me up with a piece of wood upon which to rest the back of my head that night, but for several days I suffered agony.

We steamed into Rio shortly before eleven p.m. one clear warm night while the Brazilian fleet, brilliantly illuminated, lay at anchor in the shadow of the Sugar Loaf mountain. That spectacle was irresistible. Many of the streets of the city were still crowded despite the lateness of the hour, and I did not return to the ship until close on five a.m.

During the next four days of my journey I had ample time to think seriously about my situation. I did not speak more than a few words of Spanish, and with the exception of a rather vague letter of introduction to the English owner of an *estancia* near Rosario, I had no contacts whatever in the Argentine. My short stay in New York and the passage on board the liner had more or less cleaned up my spare cash. I was definitely not going to be in a position to laze round Buenos Aires for long. With great care I could perhaps last out ten days.

Such thoughts returned to me more forcibly when I bade farewell to the *Vauban* at the end of my journey. My second-class quarters had proved a good home for three weeks and I was almost sorry to leave. I put myself and my cabin trunk into a cab and told the driver the name of an hotel.

As we drove up Rivadavia, I looked at the midday crowds thronging the pavements and suddenly thought: "Can I be less able to live in this city than the humblest of these?"

It was, of course, the language problem that frightened me. I never felt discouraged in Canada, and, if I had wanted to, I could certainly have settled down in New York. This was mainly because there were other things besides newspaper work that could have brought me a livelihood. I could have served in a store or worked on a railroad. These things were ruled out in Buenos Aires until such time as I spoke the language fluently.

The sight of the people in the streets gave me new hope. Yes, surely, there must be greater fools than I in the crowds. I repeated this sentiment several times and felt better.

I discovered within a short time of my arrival that there were three newspapers that held out reasonable prospects. Two of these were printed in English and the third in French. As an extra string to my bow I booked a ticket for Rosario the following Saturday. I would therefore spend the week-end with the people for whom I had a letter of introduction.

After lunch I went in quest of my first job. I got it from the owner of the paper, with a reservation—that I should gain the confidence of the man who more or less ran the office single-handed. In this I was not successful. We took a violent dislike to each other from the first and as there was not room for both of us I left for Rosario determined to explore the possibilities of life on a ranch.

I misjudged the distance between Rosario and the *estancia* and landed up at the house after most of the occupants had gone to bed. I walked the last part of the way in the darkness through thick mud and was greeted at the door by a young man who held a loaded pistol at my head, while all the dogs on the estate barked.

My letter produced the right effect and by the next morning we had become good friends. I returned to Buenos Aires delighted with my reception.

Nevertheless, when I came to think things over carefully, I determined to make a last bid to remain in newspaper work. That afternoon I called upon the owner of the *Herald*, and this effort met with more success. I was put on the salary list and my immediate worries were at an end. When, a few days later, I received a letter from Rosario asking me to come out and work on the *estancia*, I refused.

I took lodgings with a family whose house was built round a patio where each morning a woman's voice could be heard singing plaintive Spanish songs with a rare purity. I never sought to discover who she was, but I took to expecting her matutinal song. There were many nights, especially at the beginning of my stay, when sleep would not come. The atmosphere was hot and damp, and I would dress and wander towards the docks and those picturesque streets where rowdy but colourful cabarets, filled with sailors of all nations, kept open until dawn.

Then one morning, just as I was carving out a place for myself on the *Herald*, I felt an urge to return home.

I went to the office where, against his usual practice, I found the owner. He made me a pretty compliment and put me on an enquiry of his own. I listened to him in silence, walked slowly down the Calle Florida and suddenly realised that I was heading for a shipping office. The *Almanzora* was due to sail that afternoon. I booked a passage and hurried back to my lodgings, where I collected my cabin trunk, never daring to return to the *Herald* for fear of changing my mind.

In the train that took me to La Plata I was conscious of having done something wrong and I looked with regret at the fleeting country-side. Even when I stepped on board the liner, the decks of which were covered an inch deep with thousands of locusts, I nearly turned back.

The truth is, that I realised how near I had been to remaining for ever in the Argentine.

CHAPTER THIRTY-SEVEN

IT was not until 1930 that I again met Prince Leopold of the Belgians. I was going to Rome for the wedding of his sister, Marie-José with Crown Prince Humbert of Italy. I had asked permission to travel by way of Brussels, and it was there, on a bitter January morning, that I sent a request to see him.

Within a few hours I found the answer at my hotel. He asked me to come out to the Villa Rose, where he and Princess Astrid were resting before the official train journey south. I took a car and went there immediately. It was a small country house with rose-coloured walls and bright green shutters standing in the wooded grounds of Laeken.

Leopold seemed fortunate among Royal heirs. He had a personality just as striking as that of Edward, our own Prince of Wales, and though the Empire he was destined to rule over was smaller, he appeared radiantly happy in his marriage with a niece of the King of Sweden. Strange indeed had been the union between these two Royal houses. Both were dynasties dating from the days of Nathan's more active participation in the affairs of Europe. It was a hundred years since France and England, having placed the names of three men in a bag, drew out that of Leopold of Saxe-Coburg to become first King of the Belgians. Twenty years earlier a native of Pau called Bernadotte, a superlatively intelligent soldier of Napoleon I, much more intelligent than most of the Emperor's generals, had travelled to Sweden to form a modest and democratic new line of northern kings. This Béarnais was a realist who contented himself with what they gave him. That is why there was still a Bernadotte on the Swedish throne a century later. Princess Astrid, whose very name was looked upon with suspicion by the Belgian people, had come from a country known to them chiefly for its snow, its pine-forests, its universities and grand memories of vikings and sagas, and over which Lutheran pastors and Socialist Cabinet ministers held an almost evenly divided sway. There was nothing particularly pleasing to the crowds in the idea of a Protestant wife for their future king, but when in the port of Antwerp (where in 1830 a revolution was paving the way for a monarchy) Prince Leopold kissed his bride from across the sea, the country, as if by enchantment, fell in love with her and remained so. A baby girl had blessed the union. Joséphine was little more than two years old, but her presence in the Villa Rose was immediately discernible. The room in which the Prince met me was comfortable, airy and modern, with big French windows looking over the garden, and everything in it told of the woman's hand. Below a large sprig of mistletoe hanging from the ceiling stood a cot with the doll that Queen Elizabeth had given to her grand-daughter for Christmas. One felt instinctively that there was happiness in and around the house. A teddy bear lay on the cushions of a chesterfield, a grandfather clock chimed the hour in a corner, and the books that were about the room appeared to have been well read.

The young Etonian with whom I recited Racine eleven years before, with his gawky arms and shy manner, had turned into a tall and handsome man. He said little things with enthusiasm and big things with simplicity. The throne he was so soon to occupy, though one of the youngest in Europe, had yet weathered the storm of the great war and its aftermath. He had returned from a colonial trip with pride and confidence.

We walked together across the lawns in his garden, past the strawberry beds to the greenhouses. One of these he arranged as a sort of zoo for the benefit of his little daughter. There was a parakeet he had, I think, brought back from the Congo, a multitude of parrots in gay colourings and a rabbit, white as snow and of enormous proportions, that he bought when Joséphine was only a few months old. Each day the little girl came out with her mother to feed it with lettuce and green leaves.

314

The trees had suffered from the high winds. Some were to be cut down. There was a lake to be dug and flowers to be planted.

Eton years had left their imprint on Prince Leopold. An English school had smoothed away the last traces of accent when he spoke our tongue, and it did not finish there. His study was lined with English books as well as French ones, while London newspapers were strewn on the carpet by his desk. In many ways his upbringing had followed the same lines as that of our own heir to the throne. Each had a father to whom the world gave unstinted admiration. Each had seen the war from reasonably close quarters, and toured lands across the sea. Not yet could any foretell the tragedy that was to enter into each life.

We walked slowly back to the house and looked into the garage. The Prince asked me to climb into his sports car with him and we drove out through the gates of the estate, where a guard on duty sprang to the salute. He drove quickly, impetuously, in strange contrast with the careful modulation of his voice. If I was frightened at the time I did not give it serious thought until five years later. There came to meet us, as we drove back to the Villa Rose, the tall, stately, laughing woman who had so greatly blessed him and brought such joy into his life. Though she spoke neither French nor Flemish, the whole nation was already under her spell.

That night I took a train for Rome—the Eternal City being more lovely than I have ever seen it and heavy with the scent of bay-leaves. The wedding was a rich, never-to-be-forgotten pageant, with peasant women in their native costumes thronging the streets and elbowing the Roman soldiery. It was like a page out of an old scrap-book that was sufficiently colourful and romantic to make harassed men and women forget the rumblings of war and the oppression of tyrants. But these things were always so. One winter's night, a century before, France's ambassador Talleyrand (whom young Hannah had seen kneading his bread into salt cellars when he came to dine at the Rothschild house) had sat before his candles in Portland Place to write with a quill pen:

"Europe, at this moment, is certainly passing through a moment of crisis. Well, England is the only power that, like ourselves, really wishes for peace; the other nations recognise some sort of Divine right. They uphold their Divine right with the cannon. England and ourselves uphold public opinion with principles; principles are recognised everywhere but the cannon has only a power the range of which is known."

CHAPTER THIRTY-EIGHT

ON the night of May 10th, 1937, some thirty-six hours before the Coronation of King George VI, Captain the Rt. Hon. Edward Algernon FitzRoy, Speaker of the House of Commons, stood receiving his guests in the historic library overlooking the darkened Thames. The sombre passages were thronged with a colourful assembly of people many of whom had just arrived from the first State Banquet of the new reign at Buckingham Palace. It was a dry, warm night and there was something of a carnival spirit in Parliament Square with its massive stands decked in blue and gold cloth and its seething crowds of people drawn there by the floodlit buildings, impeding by their numbers the long lines of shining limousines converging on the Palace of Westminster. This was possibly the most notable gathering that these famous walls had ever seen. The Archbishop of Canterbury, a cloaked figure, trod slowly up the steps leading from Speaker's Court to the library. In a few hours he was to place the Crown on the head of the King—symbol of Britain's Majesty. The staircase was filled with a great number of people. There were Indian Maharajahs in multi-coloured turbans, black-faced crinkly-haired potentates from sunburnt African lands whose swarthy arms glittered with gold bracelets, the Alake of Abeokuta, Nigerian ruler, who walked through the streets with his crown and ceremonial umbrella, short and stocky Nepalese with bird of paradise feathers sweeping back from shining helmets, Field-Marshals in scarlet tunics, European generals and Commanders-in-Chief from half a dozen South American republics whose uniforms were weighed down by clinking medals. All these people fought a polite battle on the narrow staircase and formed queues along the Commons Library Corridor waiting to pass into the great room with its sombre bookcases and tall lilac blooms where the Speaker was shaking hands. There were foreign admirals here whose flag-ships lay at anchor in English waters, Bishops and Privy Councillors and Peeresses with pearl-tipped diamond tiaras and white dresses sparkling with precious stones. In the House of Commons the guests admired the Speaker's canopied chair and sat laughingly down on the Opposition benches where so many dramas have been played.

Captain FitzRoy left the library to await his Royal guests. They came almost together—the Duke and Duchess of Gloucester, the Duke and Duchess of Kent, the Princess Royal with the Earl of Harewood and the Earl of Athlone in scarlet tunic. From across the sea came Princess Juliana of the Netherlands, the Crown Princes and Princesses of Norway, Denmark and Sweden, Prince and Princess Paul of Yugoslavia and Prince and Princess Chichibu of Japan. As the orchestra played an air from Puccini, I stood aside to let these Royal people pass and I thought how much and how little had changed since another FitzRoy aspired to the Speakership. It was a hundred years since Henry FitzRoy left for his trip round Europe, eighty years since this office slipped through his fingers and Brand, Secretary to the Treasury, wrote to him: "If we cannot have you in the highest place, do not let us be deprived of your services altogether." Time had avenged him. The FitzRoys had their Speaker after all. He was there in front of me—son of Henry FitzRoy's brother, the 3rd Baron Southampton. Tall as the other had been with iron-grey hair, pronounced cheek-bones and piercing eyes. Elected nine years before, a fellow member said of him: "He comes of one of those families that for generations in various capacities have performed useful service to the State. It is only seventy years ago that a near relative of my right hon. friend held the position of Chairman of Ways and Means in this House and it may be interesting to the House to know that he was the first Chairman of Ways and Means who was allowed to take the Chair as Deputy for the Speaker."

Thus the name of FitzRoy was carved on the list of Speakers

in the Library. I looked up at it during the hand-shaking and idly considered the names of his predecessors until one stood out and seemed familiar: "1857. E. Denison." As I let my mind wander the name faded out and I read in imagination: "1857. Henry FitzRoy."

The Royal guests passed along the corridor and once more the crush began. It is doubtful whether the Victorian era could have outshone the brilliance of these uniforms, these turbans, these diamonds and pearls. True enough they would have had the representative of the Czar of all the Russias in gorgeous apparel. I saw his counterpart or rather the Soviet Ambassador to the Court of St. James walking up and down the floor of the Chamber. The face of Europe was changed and its frontiers were altered by the Great War, but the pageantry remained and the millions of people who were about to line the route of the Coronation procession would witness a sight that no upheaval was yet able to modify and in which there was no place for mechanism—only gorgeously uniformed troops, men on horseback, swaying carriages and a golden coach!

On a table in the Speaker's house as I passed by stood the painting of a man with dark hair, bright blue eyes and curly side-whiskers, looking out of his frame at the distinguished guests with a slightly amused expression. It did me good to find him there where he would so much have liked to live, for the picture was that of Henry FitzRoy.

THE END

SOURCES AND OBLIGATIONS

I SHOULD like to express my sense of obligation to my aunt, Mrs. George Ramsay (Helen Lindsay) for giving me access to the manuscripts and letters in her possession. This book owes its existence to her kindly help. I am indebted to Lord and Lady Southampton for permission to quote from a letter written in 1819 describing Laura FitzRoy's operation and I would like to thank both my mother and my aunt for allowing me to reproduce many of the illustrations in this book. All the photographic work was done by John Chilcott.

R. H.

INDEX

INDEX

INDEX

INDEX